CONSCIENCE OF A
CONSPIRACY THEORIST

CONSCIENCE OF A
CONSPIRACY THEORIST

ROBERT LOCKWOOD MILLS

Algora Publishing
New York

Library of Congress Cataloging-in-Publication Data —

Mills, Robert Lockwood.
  Conscience of a conspiracy theorist / Robert Lockwood Mills.
      p. cm.
  Includes bibliographical references and index.
      ISBN 978-0-87586-825-7 (soft: alk. paper) — ISBN 978-0-87586-826-4 (hard: alk.
paper) — ISBN 978-0-87586-827-1 (ebook) 1. Conspiracies. I. Title.
      HV6275.M55 2011
      001.9—dc22
                                        2010050440

Front cover: © Mehau Kulyk/Science Photo Library/Corbis

Printed in the United States

Acknowledgments

The author wishes to thank the following friends and acquaintances who have contributed to this book. They are listed alphabetically to avoid any suggestion that one was more helpful than another.

- Rosemary Strouse Clifton, fellow author and partner for life, whose technical skills and promotional zeal are exceeded only by her belief in the author.
- Ronelle Delmont, for starting and maintaining the Lindbergh Kidnapping Hoax Forum.
- Brad Friedman, for his doggedness in behalf of election integrity and governmental accountability through Bradblog.
- Dr. Nancy McCagney, scholar and lifelong friend, for bringing the teachings of Sir Karl Popper to the author's attention.
- Dr. David Oliver, for introducing to the author a scientist's perspective on the nature of conspiracy theories.

TABLE OF CONTENTS

ACKNOWLEDGMENTS   xi

PREFACE   1

INTRODUCTION   7

CHAPTER 1. IT'S DANGEROUS TO SHAVE WITH OCCAM'S RAZOR   11

William of Ockham, a monk living in the 14th century, devises principle suggesting that among competing theories, the simplest is best. Latter-day conspiracy debunkers use Occam's Razor in their arguments. The principle works in some cases, not in others.

CHAPTER 2. OF MERGERS, ACQUISITIONS, AND NEWS BLACKOUTS   17

Beginning in 1733, the press assumes a watchdog role over governmental lies and misconduct. But in the late 20th century, media mergers reduce number of newspapers and broadcast networks. Survivors adopt the corporate culture, avoiding controversy. They fail to investigate stolen elections and ignore possible conspiracy angles regarding 9/11/01.

CHAPTER 3. THE INTERNET BECOMES THE FIFTH ESTATE   27

Mainstream media belittle clear evidence of fraud in 2000 and 2004 presidential elections. Internet sites fill the void and establish themselves as the new watchdog over government.

CHAPTER 4. ACADEMIC CONSPIRACY THEORISTS AND MINDLESS DEBUNKERS   37

Mainstream media ignore 9/11 truth movement, which is comprised of physicists, architects, engineers, firefighters, intelligence officers, lawyers, clergymen, and government officials. Official account of 9/11 is called into question. Evidence contradicts government's version.

CHAPTER 5. THE PRESS MAINTAINS ITS OWN PATRIOT ACT   45

Possible conspiracy angle in Lincoln assassination ignored by press and historians. False sense of patriotism disallows investigation of government involvement in wake

of Civil War. Similarly, objections to conspiracy theories in re 9/11 are phrased in pseudo-patriotic language.

CHAPTER 6. FALSE FLAGS HAVE FLOWN FOREVER 53

Corrupt government leaders and tyrants have falsely used scapegoats to escape blame for criminal misconduct since the time of Emperor Nero. Operation Northwoods (1962) included plans to kill Fidel Castro and included certain false-flag stratagems that were not revealed until 2000. Project for New American Century (PNAC) suggests multiple foreign wars are necessary to fulfill American responsibilities, lacking only a "new Pearl Harbor" (such as 9/11) to justify unilateral action.

CHAPTER 7. DEBUNKERS AND DEBUNKERS OF DEBUNKERS 61

Commonly offered objections to conspiracy theories, e.g., "Too many people would have had to keep the secret..." are examined for their applicability to JFK assassination and 9/11. Fate of whistleblowers shows that those in a position to reveal secrets can become victims of the system.

CHAPTER 8. DEATHS OF THE RICH AND FAMOUS 77

Conspiracy theories surrounding possible foul play tend to flourish when the victim is rich, famous, or powerful. Assassinations of Lincoln and Kennedy remain controversial, but reasonable conspiracy angles in the murders of Garfield and McKinley, lower-profile presidents, were never pursued. Deaths of Marilyn Monroe and Princess Grace of Monaco demonstrate the effect of celebrity on post-mortem analysis.

CHAPTER 9. THE PECULIAR LEXICON OF CONSPIRACY THEORISTS AND DEBUNKERS 81

An imaginary conversation between two friends illustrates how unique language patterns inform the debate over possible conspiracies. One is a conspiracy theorist, the other a debunker, but both use a reflexive verbal approach in their arguments.

CHAPTER 10. GRAND CONSPIRACY THEORIES WITH QUESTIONABLE MOTIVES 85

Large-scale, enduring conspiracy theories involve the Illuminati, Elders of Zion, Rothschild dynasty, and Catholic Church. How anti-Semitism and anti-Catholicism influence the theories, and how the grand conspirators supposedly interact together.

CHAPTER 11. SOMETIMES COPS ARE THE CONSPIRACY THEORISTS 93

The 20-month-old son of aviation icon Charles A. Lindbergh is kidnapped in 1932. New Jersey and New York police suspect a gang is responsible, as do agents of the Bureau of Investigation. Bruno Richard Hauptmann is arrested in 1934, indicted as a lone conspirator, and executed. The case is closed.

CHAPTER 12. WHEN A RULING AUTHORITY BECOMES THE CONSPIRACY THEORIST 107

Examination of anti-Communist hysteria and Domino Theory. Nixon, HUAC, and Alger Hiss. Joseph R. McCarthy exposed by Edward R. Murrow. Vice President Cheney's incoherent "Muslim Caliphate Theory," and how it influenced Bush administration policy in the Middle East.

CHAPTER 13. REINVESTIGATING 9/11 115

Argument for new investigation, based on many unanswered questions. How patriotic fervor and Realpolitik have acted against full disclosure, beginning with Lincoln assassination and extending to 9/11. Chapter speculates on what future circumstances could bring the truth about 9/11 out, in spite of media indifference and governmental obstinacy.

CHAPTER 14. DAN FOOL AND TREY COOL MEET AGAIN 121

An instant replay of Chapter 10. This time the argument is focused on governmental conspiracy theories.

CHAPTER 15. OF COVERT ACTIVITIES AND PARAMILITARY OPERATIONS 125

Discussion of CIA conduct and misconduct since 1947. In 1963 Former President Harry S Truman, who had signed the agency into law, laments CIA's "cloak and dagger" operations. Mossad is Israel's equivalent organization. Chapter shows how highly motivated secret organizations like the CIA and Mossad could have been involved in 9/11.

CHAPTER 16. WHAT DID IAN FLEMING KNOW, AND WHEN DID HE KNOW IT?   131

Creator of James Bond worked for British Naval Intelligence during World War II. There he created quixotic schemes involving deliberate plane crashes and switched identities. Chapter examines similar tactics as studied by CIA and contemplated for Operation Northwoods, and observes that John F. Kennedy, who had praised Ian Fleming's books publicly, pulled the plug on CIA activities and fired its leader, Allen Dulles.

CHAPTER 17. WOULD PEOPLE IN OUR GOVERNMENT DO SOMETHING LIKE THAT?   135

Applies the detective's trinity, Means/Opportunity/Motive, to historical controversies, and uses the question, "Does the end justify the means?" and the rationale, "A greater good for a greater number" to intuit the likelihood of insider treachery in 9/11.

CHAPTER 18. OPPORTUNITY, MEANS, AND A HUGE DILEMMA   141

The official account of 9/11 is impossible to believe for a variety of reasons. But theories that purport to answer the difficult questions are also incomprehensible. Only a new investigation, unencumbered by political considerations, can resolve the conundrum.

CHAPTER 19. DID THEY REALLY SAY THAT?   145

Owner of World Trade Center admitted on television that Building 7 was "pulled" (deliberately demolished by explosives). His spokesperson explains away his admission with ludicrous word play. Other comments about 9/11 from Bush, Cheney, and Rumsfeld suggest that contrary to popular belief, Osama bin Laden did not mastermind the terrorist attack.

CHAPTER 20. THE GOSPEL ACCORDING TO THE HISTORY CHANNEL   151

Examination of History Channel's account of Kennedy assassination. Network used same formula as the Warren Commission, i.e., it started with the assumption that Lee Harvey Oswald was a lone assassin, built a case around that mind-set, and ignored or dismissed contrary evidence.

CHAPTER 21. CONSPIRACY THEORISTS, DEBUNKERS, AND ANONYMOUS TROLLS   157

How Internet bloggers, who face none of the corporatist inhibitions or editorial filters that restrain the mainstream media, approach controversial cases. Tactics used to win arguments are highlighted, including ad hominem attacks by trolls on conspiracy theorists. Focus is on the Lindbergh Kidnapping Case and the 2004 presidential election.

CHAPTER 22. GRESHAM'S LAW OF CONSPIRACY THEORIES   161

Gresham's Law (1558) posited that bad money drives good money out of circulation. Gresham's Law (Revisited) argues that bad conspiracy theories compromise good theories. Thoughtful conspiracy theorists are penalized for the sins of careless theorists, and outlandish theories that emerge immediately after a horrific event tend to nullify logical theories that develop later.

CHAPTER 23. CONSPIRACIES AND ONE-PARTY SYSTEMS   171

American political system fails to allow for action against misconduct in either party. Corporate-controlled mainstream media refuse to investigate governmental wrongdoing, so as not to displease stockholders and advertisers. A one-party system has developed, not unlike those in banana republics and totalitarian states. President Obama, who brushed off 2004 election fraud allegations while a senator, was elect-

ed in 2008 on a platform of "change we can believe in," but has proved to be even more obsessed with secrecy than the Bush administration was, especially regarding whistleblowers.

CHAPTER 24. KARL POPPER AND CONSPIRACY THEORIES, SCIENTIFIC AND OTHERWISE   177

Philosopher of science Sir Karl Popper posited that theories that cannot be disproved are unscientific. But whenever government officials offer an implausible explanation for a controversial event (in particular, 9/11), said explanation becomes a conspiracy theory in and of itself.

CHAPTER 25. MRS. FOOL MEETS MRS. COOL   181

The wives of Dan Fool and Trey Cool, who are old friends, meet for lunch. The discussion turns to conspiracy theories, as argued by their husbands. During the meal a surprising role reversal takes place.

CHAPTER 26. WHAT MAKES A GOOD CONSPIRACY THEORIST?   185

Qualities of persistence, a thick skin, and integrity separate the conscientious conspiracy theorist from the polemicist. Examples are given of men and women in public life who best exemplify those criteria.

CHAPTER 27. WHAT ARE THE MAINSTREAM MEDIA AFRAID OF?   197

Since 1982 technology and hybrid investment products (derivatives) have increased volatility in financial markets, exaggerating the effect of bad news. Corporate media avoid controversies like 9/11 and the 2004 presidential election for obvious and obscure reasons.

CHAPTER 28. THE INVISIBLE SMOKING GUN   205

Bush administration Solicitor General Theodore Olson, whose wife Barbara was listed as a victim aboard Flight 77, appears twice on national television, three days after 9/11. Olson invents a story about two phone conversations he supposedly had with his wife while Flight 77 was airborne. FBI deposition at Moussaoui trial in 2006 exposes Olson's lie, but it remains an unknown circumstance to most Americans because of a media blackout.

CHAPTER 29. A PRESIDENTIAL REPORT CARD   219

Presidents who served during author's lifetime are graded for their skill in balancing the need for governmental secrecy against the public's right to know.

POSTSCRIPT   225

BIBLIOGRAPHY   227

Cass Sunstein, a former Harvard University law professor, is head of the Office of Information and Regulatory Affairs in Washington, having been appointed to the position by President Obama. Before leaving Harvard Mr. Sunstein co-authored an academic article titled "Conspiracy Theories: Causes and Cures," which suggested that "government agents (and their allies) might enter chat rooms, online social networks, or even real-space groups and attempt to undermine conspiracy theories by raising doubts about their factual premises, causal logic or implications for political action."

Clearly, Mr. Sunstein is more concerned about the motivations of conspiracy theorists than about the governmental lies and obfuscations that so often give rise to their ideas. He's concerned enough to threaten the civil liberties of anyone who doesn't accept the government's version of a controversial event. In this context the phrase "conspiracy theorist" becomes a political weapon that converts a skeptic into a threat to the country.

Cass Sunstein isn't alone. In his book *American Conspiracies* (Skyhorse Publishing, 2010), former Minnesota Governor Jesse Ventura describes his own experience at Harvard, where after leaving office the previous year he taught in 2004 at the Kennedy School of Government. Ventura invited a college professor and ex-Marine, David Fetzer, to lecture to his class on the assassination of President Kennedy. Fetzer wasn't a conspiracy theorist, and he was hardly a disloyal American. Fetzer was there as an acknowledged expert on ballistics, and his analysis of the evidence from Dallas had led him to conclude that Lee Harvey Oswald could not have been a lone assassin.

Ventura noticed an increase in attendance at Professor Fetzer's lecture, versus his previous classes, but the new "students" were all older men, clearly not Harvard undergraduates. As Fetzer outlined his scientific case for multiple gunmen on November 22, 1963, one or another of the new attendees would interrupt him with suggestions that it was unpatriotic to delve into history and undermine the work of the Warren Commission, which had decided in 1964 that Oswald was a lone assassin. The challenge from the new attendees wasn't to Fetzer's qualifications or the merits of his arguments, rather to his patriotism. Within the most prestigious halls of academia, an ex-Marine with impeccable credentials in his field of study found himself subject to accusations of disloyalty, merely because his conclusions had contradicted the conventional wisdom. The phrase "conventional wisdom," in practical terms, means "the government's official story," though it might itself be a conspiracy theory. Only a government may theorize without being called a conspiracy theorist.

Many conspiracy theories are in fact outlandish, so it's easy for an academic like Cass Sunstein to maintain an air of condescension toward those who claim the terrorist attacks on New York and Washington on 9/11/2001 constituted an "inside job," or at least that the Bush administration had foreknowledge of them. At Harvard, this just isn't done these days, and if Ralph Waldo Emerson and Henry David Thoreau would recoil at such mind control efforts, they'd have to be reminded that we're in a "war on terrorism," and in a war one cannot accuse the commander in chief of venality.

In the lexicon of conspiracy theorists, Mr. Sunstein is a "debunker." Other debunkers have insisted that Oswald acted alone, that James Earl Ray murdered Martin Luther King Jr. without help, and that Sirhan Bishara Sirhan was the only assassin of Robert F. Kennedy. Debunkers also insist that the presidential elections of 2000 and 2004 were fairly decided.

The core problem for Sunstein, and for the visitors at Harvard who suggested Professor Fetzer was unpatriotic for having questioned the Warren Commission, is that since the onset of the Cold War era, the United States government has repeatedly failed to tell the truth. Nothing gives birth to conspiracy theories more surely than government deceit. It was a deep dark secret that the Shah of Iran had come to power following a CIA coup that overthrew Iran's elected leader, Mossadegh, or that the CIA conspired to oust Arbenz in Guatemala and Allende in Chile, both of whom had been elected according to a democratic process. In these cases and in others, leaders of government vehemently denied rumors of CIA involvement. Since then, the CIA has been identified with assassinations, drug trafficking, kidnapping, and the operation of secret prisons, all according to documented evidence and all in the face of official denials. The Gulf of Tonkin incident seemed legitimate, because Lyndon Johnson said it had really happened, so it became justification for ramping up our presence in Vietnam. Throughout that conflict the public was deliberately misled about its progress, and protestors were scorned for "cooperating with the enemy" simply because they accused the powers-that-be of lying. Citizens were assured that Watergate was an isolated event, and that the hoopla that followed the break-in at Democratic headquarters was a creation of the liberal media. Richard Nixon said that's all it was, and our leaders held our trust in those days. But conspiracy theorists now respect the adage, "Fool me once, shame on you. Fool me twice, shame on me."

The Reagan administration sold weapons to Iran in violation of an arms embargo, using Israel as a conduit, then illegally funneled the profits from the sale to "Contras" in Nicaragua, essentially because Ronald Reagan didn't like Ortega, the country's leader. This plot was hatched in the National Security Council to circumvent scrutiny under the Boland Amendment, which had barred the CIA from engaging in such conduct. When George H.W. Bush ran for president in 1988, he claimed he'd been "out of the loop" on Iran–Contra while serving as vice president. Enough believed him that he won the election, and the same people evidently took Bush's promise not to raise taxes under any circumstances at face value.

Governmental deceit isn't a partisan matter. Bill Clinton lied about Monica Lewinsky, which wasn't quite the same as lying about war and CIA misconduct, except he was under oath at the time. If a president can commit perjury without blinking, the public can't be blamed for asking, "How can we tell when someone's telling the truth?"

George W. Bush elevated lying to almost an art form. He said invading Iraq had never been discussed before 9/11, when in fact it had been discussed in policy meetings *even before his inauguration*. He told us Saddam Hussein had weapons of mass destruction in a State of the Union address, even while the most current intelligence available to him suggested the opposite. He said Saddam was allied with Osama bin Laden, when the truth was that they were mortal enemies. He said that Ken Lay, disgraced CEO of Enron Corporation, was "Ann Richards' friend," not his own (Richards being Bush's predecessor as Texas governor), even though Lay had stayed overnight at the White House at least twice, once after the scandal had broken. In point of fact the man Bush called "Kenny boy" had been, through Enron, the strongest financial backer of Bush's political career and a partner with him in oil deals. Bush falsely denied having spied on Americans, even emphasized the need for a warrant before doing so in a series of speeches throughout 2005, all the while doing the opposite...spying without a warrant in violation of the FISA law he professed to be abiding by. Bush repeatedly said, "We don't torture," when in fact he had approved the use of torture. He promised that anyone involved in the outing of Valerie Plame as a CIA operative would no longer serve in his administration.

Bush's entire presidency was conducted contrariwise to the expectations that derived from his 2000 campaign, where he offered himself up as a "compassionate conservative." Politics is politics, but no president is entitled to presume that little white lies uttered during a campaign justify a succession of whoppers about substantive matters while in office. The author confesses to not comprehending how any US citizen, regardless of political affiliation, could have taken at face value any pronouncement from Bush or a loyal member of his team. But throughout his incumbency the media acted as enablers by failing to subject administration statements to a test of truthfulness, instead portraying all its prevarications as one side of a political argument.

Debunkers are strange birds, more so than even the strangest conspiracy theorist. They tend to be politically conservative, which should mean they distrust government. Ronald Reagan, the avatar of the late-20th century conservative revolution, famously said, "Government is the problem, not the solution." One would expect modern conservatives to be the first to question official statements about assassinations, disputed elections, and terrorist attacks. They hate government, and no one denies that governmental lies give rise to conspiracy theories. Yet if someone suggests 9/11 was an inside job, or that JFK's murder was by a cabal, or that the 2000 and 2004 elections were rigged, conservatives rush to defend the status quo, no doubt because they know exposing unpleasant truths can lead to bear markets on Wall Street (Watergate is the best example of this, but hardly the only one). Whenever governmental misconduct threatens the status quo, Washington, DC is no longer the debunkers' enemy...it's those kooky conspiracy theorists, who "hate America."

Even more bizarre, the so-called "liberal media" that drive conservatives to distraction become establishmentarians where conspiracies are concerned. *The New York Times* poo-poohed documented evidence of election fraud in 2004, then several weeks later published front-page headlines about the fraudulent election in the Ukraine for two days running. No big-city newspaper and no television network bothered to investigate the hundreds of thousands of official complaints of computer fraud lodged in the immediate aftermath of the US election. The media ignored a statistically impossible divergence between exit poll results and tallied votes (6.5 percentage points), so uniformly as to suggest collusion among broadcast executives and executive editors to gainsay the laws of mathematics. Does that sound like a conspiracy theory? If so, it must be conceded that to the corporate-controlled mainstream media, governmental conspiracies that lead to stolen elections overseas are real. Ergo sum, conspiracy theories are only unacceptable within our own borders, and the Ukrainians who protested in the snow and cold in 2004 were heroes for confronting a corrupt process.

It's clear that neither a liberal/conservative nor a Democrat/Republican template will work in analyzing the tacit partnership of government and media in the year 2010. The proper distinction is between establishmentarians and dissidents. Proof lies in the fact that no mainstream media outlet, regardless of its political sympathies, has acknowledged the growing 9/11 truth movement, which despite disagreements among its own ranks has gained dozens of adherents every day. Nor have the media recognized the reality of overseas skepticism toward the "official" story. In Europe, where the public has dealt with villainy in high places for many centuries, nobody is ashamed of being called a conspiracy theorist.

This book might get me killed if it reaches critical mass. But I'm 69 years old, have lived a good life with many blessings, and I'm not afraid to die. The Vietnam conflict taught us that anti-establishment thinking and even civil disobedience are well worth the risk of censure. It also taught us that we can't be policemen for the world, but that's been said before and belongs in a different book. Here follows an analysis of the most controversial events in our history, from the perspective of one unapologetic conspiracy theorist.

Introduction

This book will discuss conspiracy theories from various perspectives, with particular emphasis on the assassination of President Kennedy on November 22, 1963, and the terrorist attacks in New York, Washington, and Pennsylvania on September 11, 2001. For younger readers and others unfamiliar with these domestic tragedies, here follow details that the author considers beyond cavil. Other points that remain in dispute and/or have given rise to conspiracy speculation appear throughout the text, but are omitted here.

11/22/63—President John F. Kennedy was riding through downtown Dallas, Texas in an open limousine that also carried First Lady Jacqueline Kennedy, Texas Governor John B. Connally, and Mrs. Nellie Connally. JFK had been on a public relations visit to an area of the country where anger against his administration had been rife. As the presidential limousine rounded a corner in Dealey Plaza, shots rang out. Witness accounts and ballistic evidence showed that at least three had been fired, but some witnesses heard four and five. At least one projectile struck President Kennedy in the upper body, and the final one blew his head open. Governor Connally was also struck once. Kennedy and Connally were rushed to Parkland Hospital, where the president died. Connally survived his wound.

President Kennedy's body was flown back to Washington, accompanied by Jacqueline, the newly sworn-in president, Lyndon B. Johnson, Lady Bird Johnson, and others. An autopsy was performed in Maryland.

The Texas School Book Depository, a six-story building, is located adjacent to Dealey Plaza. An employee there, Lee Harvey Oswald, brought a rifle to work that morning, wrapped in paper, and told a traveling companion the package contained "curtain rods." Oswald fled the building immediately after the gunfire and returned to the rooming house where he lived (Oswald was separated from his wife at the time). A Dallas policeman, J.D. Tippit, was shot and killed on a residential street near Oswald's rooming house, shortly after Oswald left the Book Depository. Police found spent rifle shells and a Mannlicher-Carcano rifle next to a window on the sixth floor of the Book Depository. The rifle was later tied to Oswald, who evidently had bought it by mail using the alias "A. Hidell." Under questioning, Oswald denied killing anyone. He said he was "a patsy." Nonetheless, within hours of his apprehension Oswald was named as the sole murderer of Tippit and President Kennedy.

Two days later, as Oswald was being transferred from police headquarters to the city jail for arraignment, a local nightclub owner with longstanding organized crime connections, Jack Ruby, entered the basement area of the building through a driveway. He shot Oswald at close range in the stomach before a live television audience. Oswald died several hours later. Ruby, a familiar figure to Dallas policemen (a number of whom patronized his club regularly), claimed to have been acting out of sympathy for Jacqueline Kennedy and her two children.

Ruby was arraigned on murder charges, convicted in court, and sentenced to death in the electric chair. Before his sentence could be carried out, Ruby died in prison of cancer.

The evidence against Oswald as the solitary killer of both President Kennedy and Officer Tippit seemed immutable. But after Ruby shot Oswald, doubts were raised about possible organized crime connections to the assassination. Other speculation centered on the CIA, Fidel Castro, anti-Castro rebels, the FBI, the Russians, and even President Johnson and Texas oilmen. In response to this speculation LBJ convened a commission, chaired by Chief Justice Earl Warren and including future President Gerald R. Ford and former CIA chief Allen W. Dulles, to investigate. The Warren Commission returned a report to President Johnson in September 1964, concluding that Lee Harvey Oswald had murdered President Kennedy, and had acted alone.

9/11/01—American Airlines Flight 11, bound from Boston to Los Angeles, was hijacked after takeoff. Likewise American's Flight 77 was hijacked after leaving Dulles Airport in Virginia, headed for Los Angeles. United Air Lines Flight 175 (Boston to Los Angeles) was commandeered, as was United's Flight 93 (Newark to San Francisco). A short time later Flight 11 was observed crashing into the North Tower of the World Trade Center in New York. Subsequently Flight 175 was seen striking the South Tower. Everyone aboard both planes, and several thousand inside the buildings, died. Meanwhile Flight 77 was redirected toward Washington, where it apparently struck the Pentagon. No one aboard survived. Flight 93 was presumably heading for Washington when it crashed near Shanksville, Pennsylvania, also leaving no survivors. Reports followed that passengers on Flight 93 had overpowered the hijackers and forced the plane down; these were based on cell phone conversations that supposedly had originated from within the aircraft.

The Twin Towers collapsed vertically within two hours of contact by the planes. About seven hours later a neighboring building that hadn't been struck by a plane, known as WTC 7, collapsed vertically in an identical fashion. Authorities identified 19 Muslims as the hijackers of the four jetliners, and said they had used box cutters as weapons in taking over the controls. Several of the alleged perpetrators were said to have taken flying lessons in the United States, but apparently none of the 19 were experienced pilots.

On 9/11 President Bush was in Sarasota, Florida, reading a book to grammar school students. Vice President Cheney was in charge in the White House basement. It turned out that the United States was conducting anti-terrorist war games that morning, and our air defense system was therefore in a stand-down posture.

The investigation was shrouded in secrecy, officially so that information that could have proven helpful to future hijackers would be safeguarded. Doubts arose that untrained pilots could have managed the intricate flying maneuvers necessary, especially at the Pentagon. Six widows of men killed at Ground Zero (the "New Jersey widows") pressed the Bush administration to appoint a commission to investigate further. After initially resisting an inquiry, President Bush agreed to allow former Governor Thomas Kean (R-NJ) and former Representative Lee Hamilton (D-IN) to head a commission that would seek facts and offer recommendations for preventing future incidents. President Bush refused to offer testimony unless Vice President Cheney accompanied him.

The commission's findings were inconclusive. Its report never cited the collapse of WTC 7, and Chairman Kean claimed afterward that witnesses from the North American Air Defense System (NORAD) had lied to the commission repeatedly.

Chapter 1. It's Dangerous to Shave with Occam's Razor

A 14th-century Franciscan friar named William of Ockham has been credited with an exercise in logic, now known as Occam's Razor. In brief, William told scientists through his principle that "Entities should not be multiplied unnecessarily...when you have two competing theories that make exactly the same predictions, the simpler one is the better." Or, in Latin, "Pluralitas non est ponenda sine necessitate."

Physicists evidently appended the word "razor" to William's postulate while seeking to "shave away" metaphysical concepts that might interfere with pure physical science. It's doubtful whether the good monk shared that concern; his most provocative utterance, that "God's existence cannot be deduced by reason alone..." sounds more metaphysical than physical. Regardless, William of Ockham was speaking only to the scientific community of his day. He never could have imagined that seven centuries later, Occam's Razor would become a cudgel, wielded by debunkers of conspiracy theories that contravene a government's official account of a controversial event.

The establishmentarian's thinking goes as follows: "Conspiracy theorists must be wrong. Occam's Razor tells us to seek the simplest and best answer...." Ipso facto, the best and simplest solution to a controversy necessarily excludes a conspiracy angle.

The Warren Commission never cited Occam's Razor in its 1964 report to President Lyndon B. Johnson about John F. Kennedy's murder. But the commission followed its guiding principle to the letter. The easiest and simplest conclusion it could draw (and the one LBJ wanted so badly for it to draw) was that an enigmatic loner named Lee Harvey Oswald entered his workplace, the Texas School Book Depository in Dallas, with a rifle on the morning of November 22, 1963, and used it to fire three shots at JFK's motorcade. The last two of those shots struck the president, the final one killing him instantly, after the first had missed.

At first blush Oswald's solitary guilt seemed to be a no-brainer. He had a rifle, he worked at the building, he fled from the scene, and he was later identified as the killer of Dallas Patrolman J.D. Tippit, who was shot with a pistol during Oswald's escape. Oswald was also found to have allied himself with a radical group known as The Fair Play for Cuba Committee, which might or might not have been an actual organization.

Oswald-as-lone-assassin was the simplest conclusion, and it certainly suited President Johnson's political priorities. LBJ had importuned the commission to complete its work in time for the 1964 presidential election, and without embarrassment cited dangerous rumors that he himself had been involved in the assassination plot. But it was hardly the best conclusion, as things turned out.

The assassination of President Kennedy was exceptional, in that a movie camera operated by an onlooker named Abraham Zapruder recorded it for posterity. The Zapruder film was released to the media only after the Warren Commission report had been issued; thus many who had already accepted the report ignored the film. By the time it was first seen on television in 1965, a number of assassination skeptics, including Mark Lane, Harold Weisburg, and Edward Jay Epstein had published books in vehement opposition to the Warren Commission's conclusions on separate grounds, without considering the film. These books, which hinted at CIA involvement, Mafia connections, anti-Castro rebel anger (because Kennedy had aborted the Bay of Pigs invasion), and even the evil doings of Texas oilmen allied with President Johnson, in turn engendered a backlash from LBJ, his supporters, and virtually the entire mainstream media community.

"How dare anyone question the hard-working and conscientious men of the Warren Commission?" became Johnson's theme. People were asked to believe that hard-working and conscientious men couldn't have been in error, a possibility William of Ockham would certainly have countenanced.

The Zapruder film, though it clearly showed that the fatal shot could not have come from Oswald's location, never reached critical mass with the public, because the Warren Commission's report had already been filed and President Johnson had been reelected. For many (including most media), the question of Oswald's solitary guilt had been settled. But in and of itself, the film makes a mockery of the Warren Commission's finding.

If a physicist were to apply the Occam's Razor principle to the Zapruder film, his conclusion would be as follows: "The final and fatal shot drove President Kennedy's brain matter backward and to his left...that is, from a 2 o'clock position (viewed from behind the motorcade) to an 8 o'clock position. Parts of the president's scalp and brain tissue landed on Jacqueline Kennedy, who was seated to her husband's left and slightly to the rear of him. Thus, the fatal shot must have come from a 2 o'clock position." That wasn't merely the simplest and best conclusion to draw from the filmed evidence. It was the only one.

Oswald couldn't have fired the final shot from the Book Depository unless the projectile had reversed course in midair. According to Newtonian physics, it must have come from the grassy knoll area, close to where Zapruder himself had been standing with his camera. A body in motion stays in motion until an external force, viz. gravity, friction, an impediment, alters its course. Nothing changed the course of the projectile that ended John F. Kennedy's life. And we don't need Occam's Razor to know that a shot fired from directly behind someone first strikes that person in a rear portion of his body. Indeed, the Warren Commission postulated that the first shot that struck JFK (Oswald's second) entered through the back of JFK's neck. But could two shots from the same rifle, fired seconds apart from the same location, possibly have struck the president on opposite sides of his body?

Defenders of the Warren Commission, even when faced with the Zapruder film's contradictory evidence, engaged in their own theorizing (it's OK for debunkers to theorize, not OK for skeptics). Their response was, "President Kennedy's body jerked forward and backward from the fatal shot in a normal reflex." Sure...except Kennedy's bodily movements had nothing to do with the direction in which fragments of his scalp flew. Their path followed the flight of a projectile that had to have been fired from ahead and to the right of the motorcade. It's impossible to view the Zapruder film and conclude otherwise.

Perhaps strangely, the lasting controversy has dwelt less on ballistics than on other questions...Oswald's motives and associations, Jack Ruby's motive for killing Oswald, Oswald's life in Russia, and conflicts between

JFK 's autopsy report and the testimony of a nurse at Parkland Hospital who has always insisted the hole in Kennedy's throat was an entry wound. These are all interesting issues to study, but separately and even together they cannot refute the Warren Commission, because motive and conflicting testimony are matters of conjecture. The Zapruder film, on the other hand, is conclusive. The Warren Commission blew it.

Remember, people who advocate the government's official account are allowed to theorize. No theory advanced by any skeptic was as purely conjectural as the single-bullet theory (or "magic-bullet theory"), a brainchild of Arlen Specter, then a legal adviser to the commission (later US Senator from Pennsylvania). Faced with a difficult timeline factor to support the commission's conclusion that Oswald had acted alone (he couldn't have gotten off four shots in the time allotted), Specter postulated that a second shot from the Book Depository had struck Kennedy in the back of the neck, continued through his body, passed through the torso and wrist of Governor John Connally, and eventually lodged in Connally's thigh. This magic projectile, having transited the flesh, bone, muscle tissue and clothing of two husky men, was later found on Connally's stretcher at Parkland Hospital, barely scarred.

Specter's theory must work for the Warren Commission's finding to be credible. If we apply Occam's Razor to that theory, it doesn't hold an ounce of water, because it wasn't the simplest and best answer to a dilemma. Mrs. Nellie Connally, who was seated next to her husband in the limousine, went to her death insisting that her husband and the president had been struck separately. She identified a time interval that the single-bullet theory didn't allow for. Obviously, Mrs. Connally was closer to the scene than Specter was, so her testimony (and that of people on the scene who heard at least four shots being fired) must carry more weight than the speculation of a lawyer who wasn't a witness and was trying to fit a farfetched theory into a predetermined conclusion. The simplest and best answer was that more than three shots had been fired, and because Oswald could only have fired three at most, someone else had to have fired the other(s).

Applied to the terrorist attack on 9/11/01, Occam's Razor works for the destruction of the Twin Towers, but fails for the fate of WTC 7, which wasn't struck by any airplane. WTC 7 imploded into its own footprint seven hours later, supposedly from debris that had deflected from Ground Zero.

The simplest and best explanation for the collapse of the towers (when considered independently from WTC 7) is the official version, i.e., a domino effect from white-hot jet fuel, combined with the impact damage from two huge jetliners, caused the buildings to implode from within. Many scientists have argued to the contrary; they insist steel reinforced skyscrapers can withstand far greater heat than jet fuel generates, and can resist the impact of any airplane. But without historical evidence to support it, that is a theoretical argument. When had such an attack occurred previously? How would we know for sure whether a building could withstand the impact of a jetliner going 500 mph until it happened?

Alternate theories are reasonable. But the official version of the destruction of the Twin Towers is the simplest and best. Whether right or wrong, it does conform to Occam's Razor.

The case of WTC 7 is a Trojan horse of a very different color. Its demise (supposedly from white-hot particles that had deflected from Ground Zero) was never mentioned once in the Kean–Hamilton Commission's report, no doubt because no deaths had resulted there. It was only anguished protests from Ground Zero widows that had coaxed the Bush administration into reluctantly accepting the commission's creation to begin with. WTC 7 had been evacuated before it imploded, so there was no political pressure to investigate it. Clearly politics and Occam's Razor don't mix.

What is the simplest and best explanation for a tall office building's collapse into its own footprint? It's an absurdity to assume that particles carried through the air from 300 feet away brought down such a structure. No pedestrians in the immediate area were affected by debris or reflected heat. Four other buildings in the WTC complex suffered only minor fires, and skyscrapers made of steel have caught fire thousands of times without ever collapsing, let alone from external heat. Indeed, WTC 7 fell vertically, in what respected scientists have described as a classic demolition mode. Its demise was a carbon copy of the implosion of the Twin Towers. Applying Occam's Razor and using common sense, we conclude that WTC 7 was deliberately demolished by explosives that had been earlier placed within and/or beneath the structure.

Herein lies the fallacy of Occam's Razor in re 9/11. Would anyone, conspiracy theorist or debunker, aver that the identical collapses of three skyscrapers in close proximity on the same day constituted separate and unrelated events? If Occam's Razor fails to explain the collapse of WTC 7, assuming the collapses are somehow linked, Occam's Razor fails altogether as a defense of the official version.

If the Twin Towers and WTC 7 aren't linked as to motive, and anger at the United States on the part of al Qaeda doomed the Twin Towers, then who destroyed WTC 7, and why? "Reflected particles" doesn't work as an excuse, so we have to theorize.

Insurance motives have been suggested (the building was for sale at the time, and might have been "worth more dead than alive"). WTC 7 was known to have housed records of investigations into Wall Street wrong-doing; absent the destruction, rich and powerful folk might have gone to prison. Other sinister possibilities exist, but they fall under the rubric of "classified government secrets."

We digress. Occam's Razor seeks the simplest and best answer from among many. Thus, it suffices to tell us that the official version of 9/11 is impossible to believe.

CHAPTER 2. OF MERGERS, ACQUISITIONS, AND NEWS BLACKOUTS

The print and broadcast media once recognized their presumptive roles as watchdogs for the public against governmental misconduct. American freedom to speak truth to entrenched power evolved from the bravery of a German immigrant, John Peter Zenger, who in 1733 took an editorial stance against the tyranny of William Cosby, a territorial governor in New York and appointee of King George II. Cosby, using severe British libel law as a predicate, had Zenger brought up on sedition charges.

The case pivoted on the question of truth. Did it matter where libel was concerned? Cosby said even truthful criticism was libelous, but the jury disagreed and acquitted Zenger, thus setting a precedent. The right of the press to act as a balance wheel against abuse of power in high places was established. It was later embedded into public policy as part of the Constitution.

From 1733 until approximately 1980 newspapers, radio and television acted in Zenger's spirit for the most part. When the Sedition Act threatened individual freedoms during John Adams' administration, newspapers served as a conduit for public anger. The press spoke truth to power in the 19th century, even during wartime. It labeled the War of 1812 "Mr. Madison's War," consigning blame for the burning of the White House to President James Madison. A hero of that war, Andrew Jackson, later stood accused in the Northern press of creating an un-American spoils system as president. During the War Between the States Abraham Lincoln was derided in print as an inept commander in chief. He was reviled for suspending the right of habeas corpus, for allowing the executions of pitiable teenage deserters, and for sending soldiers to shut down newspapers critical of the war effort. William McKinley hesitated before declaring war on Spain following the sinking of the battleship Maine in 1898, unsure if it had been an act of war or a mere accident; when the Hearst and Pulitzer newspaper chains demanded a declaration of war in banner headlines and their readers cheered, McKinley capitulated. William Randolph Hearst later boasted that he had started the war. The press reigned supreme in the 19th century, when it held a monopoly on public information.

When radio and television came in, they inherited the watchdog mantle, even to a fault. Journalist H.L. Mencken went on radio in 1925 at the so-called Monkey Trial to belittle the court system in Tennessee, sarcastically calling the prosecution of John Scopes (for teaching evolution), "...the greatest story since the Resurrection." Will Rogers and Fred Allen used radio as a platform to mock politicians and business executives with humor and sarcasm. Walter Winchell spared no sacred cows as a muckraker in nightly broadcasts. A Catholic priest, Charles Edward Coughlin, and aviation hero Charles Lindbergh railed against Franklin Delano Roosevelt on air for leading the country into war.

After Pearl Harbor the media were united in support of the Allied cause, but their passivity was short-lived. Television, the technological wunderkind that had been first introduced at the 1939 World's Fair but whose wider influence had been postponed in the wartime economy, now focused on House Un-American Committee investigations, the Alger Hiss case, and the Army–McCarthy hearings. The Cold War had begun, and the media spared no one in their zeal to advance the anti-Communist hysteria that swept the nation. Eventually Edward R. Murrow, a journalist from the bygone era of media responsibility, indicted Senator Joseph R. McCarthy on air on CBS for his tactics. Largely thanks to Murrow, the word "McCarthyism" is now eponymic for demagoguery.

In the 1960s TV dutifully covered civil rights marches in the South, exposing the brutal response of local law enforcement officials; the Civil Rights Act of 1964 followed. In 1968 TV was in the streets of Chicago during the Democratic Convention riots, and throughout the Vietnam era it fully dramatized antiwar protests and draft-card burning, notwithstanding Richard M. Nixon's "silent majority." Television brought the brutality of the Kent State Massacre in 1970 into living rooms without editorializing, giving citizens an opportunity to judge the circumstances from a non-authoritarian perspective.

Within the editorial offices of US newspapers, the watchdog imperative remained in effect in the early 70s. The *New York Times*, in the face of intense pressure from the Nixon administration, published the Pentagon Papers, exposing Vietnam as a misadventure. Needless to say, the *Washington Post* scored a coup and ended a presidency by exposing Watergate as a full-blown scandal. For its part, television walked the public through the entire process, not concerned that the stock market might go down from the negative exposure (it did) or that advertisers might take offense at seeing the US political system hung out to dry for viewers. The movie "All the President's Men," starring Robert Redford and Dustin Hoffman, made heroes out of Robert Woodward and Carl Bernstein, the reporters who had broken the scandal. When Nixon at last resigned and the new president, Gerald R. Ford, pardoned him, the media didn't hesitate to reflect public anger, indeed appended it with editorial calumnies against Ford.

Nixon's career-long contretemps with the media had culminated in a victory for the fourth estate. Unknown to the public then was that certain officials in the Ford White House deplored the forfeiture of executive power and prestige that came out of Watergate and its aftermath. These men resolved to someday rectify the perceived imbalance, and they've largely succeeded. More about that will follow in future chapters.

During the 1980s and beyond, things went askew. Almost overnight and for reasons that weren't apparent at first, the media abandoned their historical role. They subordinated press freedom and their watchdog mandate to a higher priority...pleasing corporate sponsors, stockholders and advertisers. Ironically, the transition from openness to quietude began during the presidency of "The Great Communicator," Ronald Reagan. But it wasn't Reagan's fault. The Law of Unintended Consequences prevailed.

A history lesson is called for. In 1890 Congress had passed the Sherman Antitrust Act. Named for Senator John Sherman (brother of Civil War General William Tecumseh Sherman) and signed into law by Benjamin Harrison, arguably the most business-friendly president in history, the law recognized a public interest in protecting small and emerging companies from the monopolistic practices of big conglomerates. Sometimes called "gorilla capitalism," the domination of markets by Rockefeller, Carnegie, Vanderbilt, and their ilk had driven competitors into bankruptcy or forced them to submit to acquisition on extortionate terms. Limited competition meant pricing power (and the country's economic well being) remained in the hands of self-interested capitalists whose lust for greater riches was limitless. After becoming president, Theodore Roosevelt, himself a child of privilege who had grown up a short trolley ride from Wall Street, decried these "malefactors of great wealth."

For 90 years the Sherman Antitrust Act (and the Clayton Antitrust Act, passed in 1914) were honored by business and industry as necessary adjuncts to laissez-faire capitalism. The government enforced the laws by litigation in extreme cases, and used mild threats and compromise in others. John D. Rockefeller's Standard Oil Company was split. Northern Securities was broken up. American Tobacco spun off R.J. Reynolds, Liggett & Myers, and P. Lorillard. By the 1940s the National Broadcasting Company had grown into something of a radio gorilla, with a Blue and a Red Network. Recognizing the need for competitive balance in news outflow, the government forced NBC to jettison the Red. It became the American Broadcasting Company.

This was no victory for socialism. In the vast majority of cases companies were allowed to make acquisitions without interference and without undue harm to free enterprise. Often a merger would be allowed if the combined companies agreed to spin off a single division as a compromise. Whenever sanctions were called for, the Justice Department and Securities and Exchange Commission shared responsibility. Companies developed strategies to conform their expansion plans to antitrust law so that they could pass muster, and sometimes abandoned them if warned they faced sanctions. The public trusted the system to work, and it did.

By the 1980s the United States' free enterprise system had lost its autonomy. A global economy, supported by a free-trade bias in Washington and liquid international currency markets, meant worldwide competition would now inform corporate planning. Executives pleaded that rigid antitrust enforcement would disadvantage their companies versus foreign competitors that weren't so hampered. The Reagan administration was fiercely anti-regulation to begin with, and Alan Greenspan, Federal Reserve Bank Chairman beginning in 1987, helped the cause by railing against the Sherman Act publicly. Wall Street was on a bullish roll, corporate America was winning the debate, and one searched in vain for a dissenting voice in the print and broadcast media. An unacknowledged reason for media silence was that media companies themselves were becoming incestuously corporate because of consolidation.

On Wall Street a brave new world had opened up to the investment banking community. Mergers and acquisitions ("M & A" in street parlance) proliferated, often without regard to the economic merit of a particular transaction. American Tobacco, a victim of antitrust enforcement seven decades earlier, was merged into American Brands (1986), just after R.J. Reynolds, which had broken off from American Tobacco back in the day, had merged with Nabisco (1985) in a deal so bizarre it gave rise to a best-selling book, *Barbarians at the Gate*. RCA/NBC, which had once given birth to ABC, became part of General Electric when GE bought RCA (1986). For its part ABC became part of Capital Cities Communications (1986), which was merged into Walt Disney (1996). American Telephone & Telegraph (Ma Bell) broke up voluntarily in 1984, but gradually put itself back together again as its regional companies merged with one another. Wall Street firms earned syndicate fees for both the original break-up and the subsequent reconciliation.

By the 1990s mega-mergers had become the rule. Bigger was better, even when it wasn't. The banking conglomerate Citicorp emerged from a series of Rube Goldberg-like transactions masterminded by Sanford I. Weill, an erstwhile stockbroker who acquired Travelers Insurance and merged it into Citibank (1998), using Primerica Corp. (which itself had derived from American Can Company) as a conduit. To this day Weill pats himself on the back for having built a financial Goliath, but recent headlines have shown that his financial prestidigitations didn't play out so well for taxpayers.

Chase Manhattan and Chemical, two giants on a scale with Citibank, joined forces in 1996, and later merged with J.P. Morgan & Co. (2000). The auto giant Chrysler merged with Germany's Daimler-Benz in 1998. Chevron (once Standard Oil of California) acquired Gulf Oil in 1984 (the biggest energy company merger in history at the time), then absorbed Texaco in 2001. But the granddaddy of all corporate mergers was the 1999 combination of two elephantine fully integrated oil companies, Exxon (once Standard Oil of New Jersey) and Mobil (once Standard Oil of New York). The Rockefeller Trust had long since been compelled to divide its empire into pieces via antitrust enforcement; now, as had been the case with the AT&T peregrinations, a Humpty-Dumpty pattern of reconciling those companies had gone into effect. The Sherman Act was being honored in the breach.

When banks, insurers, car manufacturers and oil companies merge, negative implications for the economy are limited to the capacity of the combined entity to control pricing and monopolize the marketplace. That's bad. But when *media* companies join forces, an even more sinister threat looms. Since John Peter Zenger's acquittal in 1733 the public's right to know has depended upon the willingness of newspapers and opinion magazines, radio, movie newsreels, and television to speak truth to power on public issues. They are the public's immediate line of defense against governmental misconduct and the stonewalling that follows in its wake, bridging the gap until the next election and at once informing voters about their choices. For the media to do their jobs well, healthy competition is obligatory. Media consolidation inevitably becomes the public's adversary, a truism that was forfeited to Wall Street greed in the last quarter century.

When the New York Times Company acquires the *Boston Globe*, when Walt Disney takes over American Broadcasting, or when Time Warner and America On-Line join forces (three prominent examples among hundreds of media conglomerations since 1980), the public suffers three degrees of separation from full disclosure, as follows:

1. The fact of fewer companies in the news business, along with the demise of family-owned newspapers, make a breakthrough like the *Washington Post's* exposure of Watergate less likely. Confronting the established order entails more risk because a single misstep can alienate the incumbent administration.

2. The line between news and entertainment blurs, and celebrity gossip and "news fluff" take priority over substantive issues, especially on television. The time required to investigate a scandal like Watergate is costly (time is money); meanwhile "infotainment" requires nothing more than a gorgeous blonde, a teleprompter, a TV camera, and the latest rumor from Hollywood.

3. Worst of all, media giants by definition are steeped in the corporate culture. The larger the company, the more concerned it is with the sensitivities of stockholders and advertisers (Wall Street and Madison Avenue favor stability over controversy, and their preferences will always be reflected in stock prices), and the less concerned it will be with the public's right to know. In the not-so-brave new world, corporate media moguls have a clear disincentive to investigate controversy. They have sound financial reasons to avoid it, to substitute opinion for facts, and

to hire only newscasters biased in favor of the status quo or one political viewpoint.

By the end of the 20th century the mainstream media had come full circle. Muckraking in the style of Hearst and Pulitzer was a lost art, except on the Internet, which became the medium of choice for those who won't take the government's word at face value.

The Bush–Cheney administration was arguably the most secretive in history. It had the benefit of the corporate media's aversion to controversy as described above, but it further insulated itself from the truth by threatening a loss of access to reporters who dared to challenge its version of certain events. This process was implemented by Bush adviser Karl Rove, one of a new breed of media "consultants" (managers of news, in practice) who somehow had wangled his way back into the family's good graces after being fired by President Bush 41 and ridiculed with the nickname "Turd Blossom" by Bush 43. Rove was a staff employee at the White House, thus US taxpayers were paying his salary. But his duties were limited to helping George W. Bush and the Republican Party.

Vice President Cheney held a top-secret summit meeting on energy policy in 2001. In attendance were the heads of all the major oil companies (Cheney himself had been CEO of Halliburton in the 1990s), but Cheney insisted that the press be kept out. This represented a glaring double standard, because Republicans had (justifiably) cried bloody murder when First Lady Hillary Clinton sought to escape scrutiny of her plans for national health insurance in 1993–94. To this day we don't know what was discussed at Cheney's energy conference, but we do know that even before the United States invaded Iraq in March 2003, Halliburton and other energy companies friendly to Cheney and Bush had been awarded no-bid contracts to help rebuild Iraq's energy infrastructure. Meanwhile Cheney retained stock options in Halliburton, which soared in value as the underlying stock rose throughout the decade. Cheney became a very wealthy man as a direct result of the war he promoted.

When had the decision been made to invade Iraq, a sovereign nation that posed no threat to the United States? Without saying so overtly, President Bush allowed the public to assume the terrorist attacks of 9/11/01 had been the trigger, together with weapons of mass destruction that proved nonexistent. But diplomat Richard Clarke and (then) Treasury Secretary Paul O'Neill both said an Iraq invasion had been discussed in cabinet meetings before 9/11; their averments jibe with the secrecy surrounding the Cheney energy conference and with the many false excuses offered after the fact for the invasion.

What was going on here, from the press' standpoint? In another era reporters from the *Washington Post, New York Times*, and Associated Press would have competed to glean the truth about Cheney's mysterious parley on energy policy, and to the victor would have gone the spoils. If Edward R. Murrow had been reporting for CBS News, the prelude to our invasion of Iraq and its link to a secretive energy conference would have been his Topic A. But in 2001 the silence from the mainstream media was deafening. The nation's energy policy was made in secret, and the link between war and oil was reduced to speculation on Wall Street and Main Street.

What about 9/11? The press and television provided full coverage of the destruction at Ground Zero. America was under attack. New York was the primary war theater and at once the nation's media capital. Relatively less was published and shown from the Pentagon crash site and from Shanksville, Pennsylvania, but the shock to the senses was such that few if any complaints were heard. In the days afterward President Bush and New York Mayor Rudy Giuliani earned high marks from the public for quick and empathic verbal responses. The stock market crashed, then recovered. Funerals and prayer vigils continued for weeks. A primary election in New York was postponed, but the World Series went on a month later. Things began to return to normal.

But already questions were being raised about inconsistencies in the government's story about 9/11, and demands for a full investigation were being voiced. How could 19 obscure Muslims have evaded security at four separate airport locations simultaneously, and with box cutters alone somehow seized control of four jetliners and maneuvered them expertly, even though none of the 19 was an experienced pilot? Who were they, and why had at least six of the names released afterward corresponded to living men, so identified by British Broadcasting? The Bush administration resisted an inquiry at first, preferring secrecy to openness in its fashion, but pressure from a small group of 9/11 widows forced its hand. The Kean–Hamilton Commission, headed by former Governor Thomas Kean and former Representative Lee Hamilton, was convened to investigate.

Beginning only seven days after 9/11, an anthrax scare spread like a discordant echo of the terrorist attacks. Senators Tom Daschle and Patrick

Leahy received infected envelopes. Poisoned letters were sent to the news headquarters of ABC, CBS, NBC, and to the *New York Post*. The public was warned about certain kinds of mail it shouldn't open. Citizens were given a toll-free number to call to give and receive information. Five people died, 17 others were infected, and millions were scared out of their wits.

Then, as quickly as it had loomed, the scare abated and news coverage stopped. Had bio-terrorism been Step Two of a grand conspiracy against the United States, or was it just a remarkable coincidence? What was the truth about anthrax? Mail had crossed state lines, so the FBI assumed jurisdiction over the investigation, at which point the story vanished from the media's radar screen...either to safeguard the FBI's detective work, or at the behest of the White House, or both. The public was left in the dark about the extent of "Amerithrax," and most importantly about whether the whole business was connected to the events of 9/11.

Fully seven years later the FBI identified one Bruce Edwards Ivins, a bio-defense scientist based at Fort Detrick, MD, as the sole culprit. Before he could be tried for his crime, Ivins committed suicide by overdosing on Tylenol, and the case was closed. Neither his pending prosecution nor his death was prominently mentioned in the newspapers or on television, which were then consumed with the 2008 election campaign, Sarah Palin's daughter's pregnancy, and a looming debacle in the financial markets. Even on the Internet, which was now filling the vacuum created by the mainstream media's silence, Amerithrax remained a historical footnote.

On February 19, 2010 the FBI closed the case, reiterating the evidence against Ivins and adding a theory of its own about a supposed coded message Ivins had included in the mailings. It referenced two unnamed female colleagues with whom Ivins supposedly had been obsessed (remember, only those in authority are allowed to theorize in controversial cases). Rep. Rush Holt of New Jersey, a physicist by profession, criticized the bureau for closing the case and said its report had laid out "...barely a circumstantial case (that) would not, I think, stand up in court." But Amerithrax is now history. Because the media allowed the matter to disappear from its radar screen, people will probably never know if the scare was connected to 9/11.

Progressives recognized the deleterious effect of media mergers upon the public's right to know from the outset. In June 2003, following a Federal Communications Commission vote (3–2) in favor of removing all barriers to corporate media conglomeration, liberal foes of the ruling were joined by an odd bedfellow, conservative columnist William Safire, who had once been Richard Nixon's speechwriter.

Safire wrote, "[While] political paranoids accuse each other of vast conspiracies, the truth is that media mergers have narrowed the range of information and entertainment available to people of all ideologies." He continued, "Does [opposing the FCC's vote] make me [gasp!] pro-regulation?... my conservative economic religion is founded on the rock of competition, which—since Teddy Roosevelt's day—has protected small business and consumers against predatory pricing leading to market monopolization." Safire meant that the availability of information, not merely the pricing of consumer goods, must suffer from lax regulation of monopolies.

Thanks in part to Safire, the FCC reversed its decision. But this simply meant that *further media consolidation would face problems.* The control of public opinion had already fallen into the hands of five mega-corporations, and nothing could change that. On Wall Street, a deal is a deal.

Paul Craig Roberts is an economist, award-winning journalist, and a former Assistant Treasury Secretary under Ronald Reagan. In 2006 Roberts wrote that "...during the 1990s the US government permitted an unconscionable concentration of print and broadcast media that terminated the independence of the media...more importantly, the values of the conglomerates reside in the broadcast licenses, which are granted by the government, and the corporations are run by corporate executives—not journalists—whose eyes are on advertising revenues and the avoidance of controversy..."

Roberts was focused on 9/11, and he decried the fact that every major media outlet had chosen to ignore obvious flaws in the government's story about how 19 Muslims had somehow violated airport security four separate times, had commandeered four jetliners using box cutters as weapons, and had crashed the planes while the North American Defense System (NORAD) did nothing in response. He was right, but Roberts could just as easily have been writing about the 2004 presidential election, when a major political party commandeered election machinery and crashed the expressed will of the American people. As we will observe, Roberts' was a voice crying in the wilderness.

CHAPTER 3. THE INTERNET BECOMES THE FIFTH ESTATE

America has a bleak history when it comes to the process of electing its presidents. In 1800 Thomas Jefferson ran against incumbent Federalist John Adams, who had defeated Jefferson four years earlier. The Electoral College allowed electors to vote for two candidates back then, and anti-Federalist forces, including Jefferson and Aaron Burr, swung enough electors away from Adams to bring about a tie between Jefferson and Burr. The election went to the House of Representatives, which after an interval of backroom negotiating elected Jefferson president. Burr, as the second-place finisher, became vice president, as had Jefferson after the closely contested 1796 election.

Burr was livid. He blamed Federalist leader Alexander Hamilton for using improper influence in the matter. Hamilton did consider Jefferson the lesser of two evils, but the extent of his involvement in the final decision remains a matter of dispute among historians. Burr wasn't in doubt, though, and in 1804 he challenged Hamilton to a duel. Hamilton fired his pistol in the air, Burr aimed straight ahead. Hamilton died.

In 1824 the Adams family got even for 1800. Democrat Andrew Jackson defeated National Republican (Whig) candidate John Quincy Adams and two other candidates, one of which was Henry Clay, in the popular vote. Jackson also had a plurality in the Electoral College, but lacked the required majority of pledged electors. Again the House of Representatives had to decide. Adams won, largely thanks to the behind-the-scenes efforts of Clay, who had finished fourth in the popular vote. Jackson's supporters cried foul, but the result stood.

The public was angry, too, and four years later swept Jackson into office by an indisputable margin. The problems created in 1824 by the four-way race gave rise to a two-party system that remains in effect almost two centuries later and has been taken for granted as necessary for the government to function. Until 1856, it was Democrats vs. Whigs; since then it has been Democrats and Republicans. Having only two parties does eliminate the possibility that a candidate earning a plurality of electoral votes (but short of a majority) could lose the election in the House of Representatives, as Jackson did. But it also allows for the homogenization of two parties into one for all practical purposes, a possibility that George Washington, who hated all political parties, no doubt foresaw.

The 1876 presidential election is seldom used to teach civics to schoolchildren. Democrat Samuel Tilden defeated Republican Rutherford B. Hayes by a wide popular vote margin, and led in the Electoral College 184–165, with 20 votes in dispute. Three states had submitted two sets of results, one favoring Tilden and the other Hayes in each case, local election officials being unable to adjudicate the matter. Tilden stood a single electoral vote from the presidential chair, but would never occupy it.

It hadn't happened before. Congress appointed an electoral commission to decide how to apportion the disputed votes. Because the Republicans were in control, the commission included eight of their number and seven Democrats. After lengthy arguments and legal threats, a vote was taken. Everyone voted on party lines. By an 8–7 count, Hayes was awarded every disputed vote and was elected president. Rumors circulated that Hayes had promised to remove federal troops from the South if Democrats would accept the result, and also promised not to stand for reelection in 1880. Whether the rumors were true or not, Hayes did remove the troops, thus ending Reconstruction, and he didn't run for reelection in 1880.

By 1876 big-city newspapers had become deeply involved in the political process. In the 19th century it wasn't considered unseemly for a journalist to openly accuse a politician of wrongdoing. Horace Greeley of the *New York Tribune*, a Whig–Republican loyalist who once had been Henry Clay's editorial mouthpiece and later became a devoted if erratic supporter of Abraham Lincoln, went further. Greeley became so disgusted with his Republican friends and the Ulysses S. Grant administration that he switched parties and ran against Grant in 1872 as a reform Democrat, promising to clean things up in Washington. He lost, but the mere fact of a journalist being nominated for president by a major party showed the influence of the press. Ironically, Greeley never would have taken office had he won, because he died several weeks after the election.

Most papers favored Republicans in the Reconstruction Era, but the Hayes–Tilden election outcome was too much even for them. The press derided "Rutherfraud B. Hayes" and called him "His Fraudulency." Hayes was in fact a decent man and an honest public servant, a one-time Civil War hero who had remained in Ohio throughout the electoral contretemps and had little or nothing to do with whatever shenanigans had gone on in his behalf. Later the press mocked First Lady Lucy Webb Hayes as "Lemonade Lucy" because she refused to serve alcohol in the White House. It was a freewheeling era for newspapers and opinion magazines, all of which were family owned. Editorial writers did sometimes go too far by 20th-century standards, but at least in 1876 the public wasn't shielded from the truth about dishonest elections. By the year 2000, this had changed drastically.

In 1884 Democrat Grover Cleveland edged out Republican James G. Blaine in a bitter race that came down to a handful of votes in New York. The press wrote freely of how Cleveland had fathered a child out of wedlock, and it impartially questioned Blaine's involvement in Credit Mobilier, a scandal involving watered railroad stock, and other questionable acts that had tarnished his reputation. Nothing was sacred. Cleveland's supporters took advantage of a gaffe by Rev. Samuel Burchard, a prominent Republican loyalist who referred to Democrats as the party of "Rum [read alcohol], Romanism [read Catholic], and Rebellion [read Civil War and secession] in a speech just before the election. Irate editorial writers in New York, few of whom attended Burchard's church, stirred their readership to action. Democrats passed out their papers for free in Irish neighborhoods, newly registered Catholic voters flocked to the polls, and Cleveland carried New York by a whisker and won the election.

The GOP got even four years later, without help from the press. Cleveland ran well ahead of Republican Benjamin Harrison in the popular vote, but the Electoral College outcome again depended on New York's vote, which was threadbare close. In the end Harrison came out ahead by barely over 2,000 votes. The dour Indianan was quoted as saying, "Providence has granted us the victory," to which Matthew Quay, a Republican operative in New York who had worked for Harrison's election behind the scenes but didn't care for him personally, was quoted saying in reply, "Tell that SOB that providence didn't have a damn thing to do with it." Quay didn't elaborate, but he didn't need to. The press had already conditioned the public to distrust political power brokers, in contrast to the current era, when stolen elections are ignored and when a Karl Rove threatens retaliation against uncooperative journalists and earns five-figure fees for lecturing on college campuses.

Chicago's Mayor Richard Daley, a Democrat who ruled over a political machine without apology, was another big-city boss who served his party at election time. In 1960 John F. Kennedy carried Illinois by a whisker over Richard M. Nixon and won the presidency. Although Kennedy would have won in the Electoral College even without Illinois' votes, Republicans were bitter, certain that Daley's forces had rigged the outcome and denied Nixon a possible popular vote win nationally. JFK himself added fuel to the fire in an after-dinner speech by "joking" that his father, Joseph P. Kennedy, had asked Daley not to steal even one more vote than was necessary. The audience roared.

There's something harsh about big-city politics that makes pragmatists out of idealists. When asked to comment about the disputed 2004 election, which saw widespread claims of fraud and a challenge from Senator Barbara Boxer to the certification of George W. Bush's victory, newly elected Senator Barack Obama, who had built his reputation as a community organizer in Chicago and knew the ropes, replied, "Get real! There was fraud on both sides." In other words, if both sides are cheating, it's OK to cheat, and if you're convinced the other guy is stuffing the ballot box, the only recourse is to stuff it yourself.

This kind of cynicism is the inevitable byproduct of a two-party system. "What do you mean we cheated in Ohio? You guys were doing the same thing in Wisconsin! And what about New Mexico?" The truth is, election fraud has become a test of skill, and the fraudsters know the media won't be paying any closer attention than Congress. In 2000 and again in 2004, Republicans were simply better at cooking the books than Democrats were. No third party had the clout to buck the system, largely because the mainstream media ignore third parties. Greens and Libertarians, who did challenge the 2004 election in court, are, to the corporate media, like conspiracy theorists...too far outside the mainstream to be worth their time.

George W. Bush is the only president in US history to have been elected twice under controversial circumstances. In 2000 television had a field day with butterfly ballots and hanging chads in Florida. It made for high drama, like an O.J. Simpson murder case without the blood. But TV was motivated by the drama, not by any sense of duty to the public.

The election was eventually settled by the US Supreme Court, which overruled the Florida Supreme Court's decision to order a second recount. The Supremes thereby flouted the Electoral College, which under the Constitution assigns to states the responsibility for conducting all elections, including national ones. What went unreported, because it wasn't entertaining enough to attract an audience and sell shampoo and deodorant, was the flagrant disenfranchisement of minority voters (most of whom would have voted for Al Gore) by Florida election officials, led by Secretary of State Katherine Harris, a Jeb Bush appointee and Republican party loyalist.

By the time the 2004 election came around, what had happened in 2000 was common knowledge. The Internet had filled the news vacuum, and the public knew that Gore had really won (although few understood the complex Constitutional questions surrounding the Electoral College vis-à-vis the Supreme Court). Determined not to allow fraud to decide two elections in a row, citizens' groups organized teams of poll watchers, who gathered in battleground states (populous states where the vote was projected to be close) to oversee the balloting. One could have expected the mainstream media to be alert to election fraud in 2004, based on 2000.

It didn't happen. In Ohio alone, in the first 48 hours after the election, 147,000 calls came in to a toll-free number that had been installed to handle claims of problems. The claims came in a rainbow of colors. As with 2000, minorities claimed disenfranchisement in one form or another. A shortage of voting machines in Democratic precincts created long lines, which meant many working-class voters had to choose between voting and returning to work on time to save their jobs. In Republican districts, plenty of machines were on hand. In Cleveland, where Democrats always did well, irrational totals for third-party candidates were recorded. Throughout the state (and elsewhere in battleground states) widespread allegations about computerized "vote flipping" were received, wherein a vote for Kerry somehow was recorded as a Bush vote. Were these computer accidents? It didn't seem so, because with a handful of exceptions all the flipped votes favored Bush.

The present author witnessed vote flipping first-hand in Bealsville, Florida, where I traveled at my own expense from Connecticut to serve as a poll watcher with the Election Protection Coalition. From inside the voting area a woman's voice cried out, "I voted for Kerry, but the machine said I voted for Bush!" I assumed it was a simple machine malfunction, a blip. But when it came out that hundreds of thousands of similar incidents were being reported in Ohio and other battleground states, it became clear how Kerry could have finished 3.5 points ahead in the exit polls nationwide, with Bush ahead by 3 points in the tabulated vote (a mathematically prohibitive discrepancy). One could understand how President Bush prepared a concession speech late that afternoon (based on leaked exit poll results), only to be reassured by Karl Rove, "Don't worry. You're going to win." As Josef Stalin once said, "It isn't who votes that counts, it's who counts the votes."

In Bealsville, a district with a large minority population, the "Ohio" problem of selective allocation of voting machines was also evident. Local poll officials lamented the fact that only five machines had been provided by the state of Florida to their precinct, whereas in the same district, ten machines had been used in an earlier primary. Given the expectation of a high turnout on Election Day and absent deliberate neglect by election officials, more machines, not half as many, should have been allocated. The Ohio pattern prevailed throughout Florida...long lines in minority areas, normal lines elsewhere. It was clear that selective distribution of voting machines had been part of a carefully orchestrated nationwide plan of rigging the vote in favor of Bush and Cheney. This was possible because Republican loyalists managed the electoral process in key states, and thus had direct control over the allocation of election machinery.

As I rode home on the plane two days later, I thought to myself, *When the media get hold of this, there'll be hell to pay.* Uh...hell, no. The only people who caught hell were the complainers, whom the liberal-minded (?) *New York Times* dismissed as conspiracy theorists in a front-page article a week later. Tom Zeller Jr. wrote that "as fast as the conspiracy theories came in, they were being debunked," as if to pretend that the laws of mathematics had been suspended on Election Day. Zeller evidently hadn't heard that a 6.5-point disparity between exit poll results and tabulated votes was impossible. His article had nothing to say about voter disenfranchisement or voting-machine allocations, either. Zeller's piece clearly had been written for the purpose of turning allegations of election fraud into conspiracy theories.

In the face of clear fraud, Senator Kerry conceded the election without even asking for a recount. "There aren't enough missing votes [in Ohio] to make the difference," Kerry said mournfully, oblivious of how easy it is for a voting machine or central tabulator to be hacked. Kerry bowed to the political custom of accepting defeat graciously, putting his own political future before the public's vested interest in honest elections. With a two-party system, the loser can remain viable as a future candidate, but not if he protests too loudly about fraud, in which event he'll earn a "sore loser" label.

Kerry surely knew the situation in Ohio had been a bottom-line disgrace, given that Secretary of State Kenneth Blackwell, who controlled the allocation of election machinery, was also chairman of the Bush–Cheney reelection campaign in the state. Blackwell had earlier fought vainly in court to deny registration to qualified minority voters, for which effort he had been rebuked by a judge. Walden "Wally" O'Dell, CEO of Ohio-based voting machine manufacturer Diebold Systems and a major fundraiser for the Republican ticket, had said he'd do anything in his power to reelect Bush and Cheney. Neither O'Dell nor Blackwell seemed the least concerned about his conflict of interest, and the mainstream press didn't mention it, either. The atmosphere in Ohio was poisonous, but to learn about it one had to visit Internet websites. To *The New York Times, Washington Post,* Fox Network, and CNN, election fraud was only a legitimate story when it happened in places like Ukraine.

The influence of the Internet had grown since 2000, fortunately for the cause of election integrity. With the mainstream media turning a deaf ear to the issue, on-line groups such as Beverly Harris' Black Box Voting, Brad Friedman's Bradblog, and OpEd News (Joan Brunwasser, Election Integrity Editor) assumed responsibility for educating the public about how a voting machine could be hacked to control the outcome of any election.

Bradblog cited a computer programmer in Florida, Clint Curtis, who had an interesting story to tell. Curtis, a registered Republican, had once worked for Yang Enterprises, a software technology firm that contracted with the state of Florida and also with NASA. Curtis told Brad Friedman (and later swore an affidavit under oath and testified before Congress) that shortly before the 2000 election he was asked by his employer to design a software program that could "rig the vote" in South Florida. Present when the request was made, according to Curtis' affidavit, was Tom Feeney, then Republican leader in the Florida legislature and a one-time running mate of Governor Jeb Bush. Feeney was Yang Enterprises' attorney and lobbyist. His law office and Yang's headquarters were located in the same building in Oviedo, Florida.

As related by Curtis, Yang Enterprises requested that he design the vote-rigging software because they (and Feeney) feared that Democrats in South Florida would be trying to steal the state for Gore; therefore Republicans needed a fail-safe program that could neutralize potential electronic vote fraud. Curtis designed the program in good faith. He admitted to Friedman and to Congress that he didn't know if it had been put to use or not.

Feeney, questioned by one of the few Florida newspapers that covered the story, denied Curtis' allegations. He called Curtis a nut and a crackpot. Curtis responded that he had sworn an affidavit under penalty of perjury, and asked Feeney to do likewise. Feeney refused.

By the time Curtis' allegations appeared in Bradblog, Feeney had been elected to Congress (in 2002). Feeney claimed that he had severed all contact with Yang Enterprises at that point. Bradblog reported that Yang had over-billed Florida for contract work with Feeney's encouragement ("Charge them whatever you want") and had also over-billed NASA. It learned that Yang had thrown a party for Feeney in 2003, the year after Feeney claimed to have broken off all contact with the company. Bradblog also revealed that a Yang employee, one Henry Nee, had pleaded guilty to spying on the United States in behalf of China, and had received a token fine and suspended sentence for espionage, the same crime that had once sent Julius and Ethel Rosenberg to the electric chair.

Bradblog had a de facto exclusive on the Curtis/Yang/Feeney story because no major newspaper or TV network would go near it. The plot thickened. Curtis had left Yang Enterprises shortly after the alleged request for election-rigging software, and had taken a job with the Florida Department of Transportation. There he met Raymond Lemme, a DOT auditor assigned to oversee state contracts for possible fraud. Curtis, of course, already had first-hand knowledge of Yang's over-billing of Florida and NASA, so what Lemme was about to tell him came as no surprise.

According to Curtis, sometime in June 2003 Lemme told him that he, Lemme, had uncovered fraud that went "all the way to the top" in Tallahassee. That could only have meant the office of Jeb Bush. Several weeks after his conversation with Curtis, Lemme's body was found in a motel in Valdosta, Georgia, some 80 miles northeast of Tallahassee. Lemme had bled to death in a bathtub. An investigation by local police ended with a ruling of suicide. No autopsy was performed (unlike Florida, Georgia law didn't require autopsies in the case of a suspicious death), even though the evidence surrounding Lemme's demise was eerily evocative of an earlier case whereby a "suicide" victim's body from out of state had been transported to Valdosta to be discovered.

Bradblog undertook its own investigation. Lemme had no known personal or business reason to have traveled to Valdosta. The motel's records clearly had been falsified, because they showed Lemme checking in at a time when (it has been proven) that he'd been home in Tallahassee with his wife. Lemme's only daughter was being married that September, and he had told friends how eagerly he looked forward to the wedding. Lemme seemed like a highly unlikely suicide candidate, so Bradblog appealed to the Valdosta Police Department to reopen the case.

It did reopen the case in December 2003, but quickly shut it down again after receiving an urgent request from the Florida Department of Transportation. The police chief offered no specifics about the request, which he said he had honored, and he thereafter declined to comment.

The present author wrote the Georgia Attorney General's office, spelling out the facts and urging that the case be reopened. I asked, "Could any Florida bureaucracy possibly have a legitimate interest in aborting the investigation of a suspicious death in the state of Georgia?" And, "Wouldn't the Florida Department of Transportation want to know the truth about the untimely death of one of its valued employees?" Georgia's Attorney General never replied, nor even acknowledged my letter. The case remains closed, because of a direct request from the very office the "suicide victim" had been investigating for fraud. What would William Randolph Hearst's newspaper chain have written about all this in 1900, given the same circumstances?

Neither Clint Curtis' account of his conversations with Lemme, nor Lemme's "suicide," were covered by a major newspaper or TV network. Another suspicious death the mainstream media ignored was that of computer whiz Michael Connell; it connects to the 2000 and 2004 elections. Connell, an experienced pilot, died in a plane crash on December 19, 2008, near his home in Akron, Ohio. In the two months prior to his fatal accident Connell had twice canceled flights because of unexplained mechanical problems with his airplane. But he wanted to get home for Christmas, so he went ahead.

Michael Connell was a Republican loyalist who worked for Karl Rove. As early as 2000, Connell, a computer whiz, had overseen the creation of something called a "Trojan Horse" software application, whereby input could be freely transferred from one computer to another. After midnight on Election Day, 2004, with John Kerry on the verge of winning Ohio and assuming the presidency, late Ohio returns were mysteriously routed to a "backup server" in Chattanooga, Tennessee. When the tabulated results came back to Ohio in the wee hours of the morning, a massive swing of votes had occurred. George W. Bush had miraculously been reelected, in the face of a 6-1/2 point discrepancy between exit polls and tabulated votes.

Attorney Cliff Arnebeck, who specialized in voting rights issues and had been following the murky goings-on in Ohio for a while, filed suit against Secretary of State Kenneth Blackwell and others, claiming "election fraud, vote dilution, vote suppression, recount fraud, and other violations" in connection with 2004. He ran into problems. A judge authorized that all records from the election be turned over to the newly-elected Secretary of State, Jennifer Brunner, but most of the records had been destroyed or lost.

Eventually Arnebeck agreed to accept a deposition from Rove's right-hand man, Connell, hoping to prove that Rove had been "...the principal perpetrator of a pattern of corrupt activity [under the Ohio Corrupt Practices Act] ... [and that] we have been confidentially informed by a source we believe to be credible that Karl Rove has threatened Michael Connell [that he'd better] 'take the fall for election fraud in Ohio,' [otherwise Connell's wife] Heather will be prosecuted for [unrelated] law lobby violations."

Connell was subpoenaed but never deposed. Days before his court appearance, his plane crashed a few miles short of the Akron–Canton Airport, killing him instantly. It came out later that Connell never had a chance to land safely, because his airplane was entirely computer-operated; it lacked the mechanical controls a pilot would fall back on if his plane went into a nosedive. As reported by Jesse Ventura and Dick Russell in *American Conspiracies*, Connell's friend Stephen Spoonamore, a computer expert who said he had finally persuaded Connell that his actions had compromised election integrity and said that Connell was remorseful, described how a faulty chip, installed under the hood, would have sufficed to make certain Connell could never tell the truth about the 2004 election.

Connell apparently didn't know that in the hands of the right person, switching computer chips in a small plane is about as difficult as changing a typewriter ribbon. It cost him his life.

CHAPTER 4. ACADEMIC CONSPIRACY THEORISTS AND MINDLESS DEBUNKERS

The 9/11 truth movement might have assembled the most eclectic admixture of scholarly men and women that most people have never heard of. Individually and collectively their academic credentials belie the false image of conspiracy theorists as outliers. This is a picture the mainstream media openly encourage through passive neglect of unpleasant facts and a refusal to differentiate between conspiracy theorists and thoughtful skeptics.

The website 911Truth.org was begun in June 2004, having earlier been a switchboard and events calendar called the "9/11 Truth Alliance," which compiled data for various activist groups. 911Truth.org currently operates autonomously, but in cooperation with Architects and Engineers for 9/11 Truth, Intelligence Officers for 9/11 Truth, Firefighters for 9/11 Truth, Lawyers for 9/11 Truth, Journalists and Other Media Professionals for 9/11 Truth, Patriots Question 9/11 Truth, Religious Leaders for 9/11 Truth, Scholars for 9/11 Truth & Justice, and Scientists-Journal of 9/11 Studies.

When one examines the academic qualifications of these patriotic citizens, it becomes hard to fathom what Cass Sunstein of the Obama administration's Office of Information and Regulatory Affairs had in mind by suggesting that government agents might..."attempt to undermine conspiracy theories by raising doubts about their factual premises, causal logic or implications for political action." Did Professor Sunstein really mean it's a good idea to undermine scientific research? Would he argue that professional architects, engineers, lawyers, and religious leaders think and act il-logically, or that their political agendas supersede their scholarship?

9/11Truth.org's Mission Statement is blunt. Absent the qualifications of its members it could easily (and perhaps fairly) be dismissed as a hysterical screed, delivered by chronic dissidents with a political agenda.

The statement says they seek to "expose the official lies and cover-up surrounding the events of September 11, 2001, in a way that inspires people to overcome denial and understand the truth; namely that elements within the US government and covert policy apparatus must have orchestrated or participated in the execution of the attacks for these to have happened in the way they did."

They intend to "promote, and in part to provide, the best in investiga-tive reporting, scholarly research and public education regarding the sup-pressed realities of September 11th, its aftermath and exploitation for politi-cal ends, the toxic air cover-up, and the anthrax attacks; mindful always of standards of fact and logic, the limits of what we know in the absence of official investigative powers, and the dangers of rumor and unconfirmed or false claims."

They aim to "organize and network grassroots communities promoting truth and reform; and to support their development with materials, coach-ing, conference calls, working retreats, and other tools to enhance the peo-ple's democratic powers; and to promote global grassroots cooperation to halt corporatist crimes, abuse, and dominion worldwide."

They seek "justice and redress from those wronged on September 11th, or as a result of the events, beginning with complete disclosure of all records and evidence; reversal of all domestic and foreign policies following from the false premises of the official story; and full accountability for any and all individuals inside and outside the US government involved in the attacks who engaged in crimes of commission, facilitation, complicity, gross negli-gence, cover-up or obstruction of justice after the fact."

And, they intend "[to] advance the insight that ending a world in which 9/11-type and other 'synthetic' events dictate the agenda requires the fall of the present US and global system of warfare and fraud, of secret govern-mental and hidden economics, of power concentrated in the hands of the vanishingly [sic] few; the rebirth of constitutional, open and accountable republican institutions with absolute protection for the natural rights and liberties of human beings; the rise of popular sovereignty over polity and economy; and commitment to the purposes of truth and justice, freedom and equality, peace and solidarity among human beings of all lands, and security and a sustainable living for all; cognizant that the tensions inherent among these purposes are to be addressed and resolved only in an open and peaceful fashion by a sovereign, educated and fully informed people who always hold truth first."

Finally, they hope to "end, by way of integrity and god-given creativity, the regime and illicit power structures responsible for 9/11 and to replace the system that made 9/11 necessary. We solicit collaboration with others who are committed to achieving these goals by way of peaceful transformation."

Since a few days after 9/11, architects and engineers of unquestioned competence and sincerity have argued about the fundamental scientific question surrounding the collapse of the Twin Towers, i.e., "Could the towers have come down in the manner that they did simply from the effect of burning jet fuel?" Dr. Steven Jones, a Brigham Young University physics professor, insists they could not have. Dr. Jones further described the fall of the Twin Towers as a classic demolition scenario.

An article in Popular Mechanics and a TV documentary contradicted Dr. Jones, conceding that the melting point of steel was higher than that produced by burning jet fuel, but arguing that the steel structural supports could have at least weakened at a lower temperature, and that the weight of a sagging interior finished the process. For many neutral observers this argument settled the matter in favor of the government's account. No office building had ever been struck by a Boeing 757 before, so any scientific argument was inchoate at best. But there was more to the debate, as the ongoing dialogue (almost exclusively on the Internet) proved.

Dr. Jones, in his earliest writings in 2001, noted that thermite, a rare and highly combustible substance used almost exclusively for demolitions, had been found in the rubble at Ground Zero. Thermite is used to create explosions. It is not a byproduct of an explosion resulting from other stimuli, thus there could have been no benign reason for its existence at the site.

A 2009 study authored by Professor Niels Harrit of the University of Copenhagen identified the substance found at Ground Zero more precisely as nanothermite, the most destructive form of thermite. Nanothermite is used for military purposes only.

Then there is the matter of WTC 7, which imploded in a matter of seconds about seven hours after the second tower had fallen, not having been struck by any plane. Dr. Jones compared WTC 7's implosion with those of the Twin Towers, noting that the three skyscrapers collapsed similarly, in free fall into their own footprints in a matter of seconds. This suggested acts of deliberate destruction, because if burning jet fuel had weakened the steel frames of the Twin Towers, as Popular Mechanics Magazine argued, how do we explain the demise of WTC 7, where no burning jet fuel was involved? Could reflected debris from Ground Zero, or heat from several individual fires observed within WTC 7 just before its collapse, have sufficed to bring the building down in seconds? The fact that tens of thousands of skyscrapers have caught fire without imploding (including four within the WTC complex), combined with the similarity between the collapses of the three buildings, contradicts that notion absolutely.

Twenty-six minutes before WTC 7 fell, a British television newscaster, seated in front of a photographic backdrop of lower Manhattan that included a still-vertical WTC 7, announced that it had become the third skyscraper to fall. A clock on the BBC studio wall proved the anomaly. Readers of this book are challenged to offer possible explanations for this without entering the realm of conspiracy theory.

The New York City Fire Department lost 343 brave souls on 9/11. If anyone should be offended by conspiracy theories, it's a firefighter whose colleague perished in the line of duty. On the contrary, Firefighters for 9/11 Truth, which describes itself as a "...nonpartisan association of firefighters and affiliates created to increase public awareness, provide public education, demand a real investigation that follows national standards, and provide support to our brothers and sisters in need," has said the investigation failed to adhere to accepted investigative standards. Firefighters for 9/11 Truth has set forth five demands, as follows:

1. A truly independent investigation with subpoena and contempt powers to uncover the complete truth of the events related to 9/11/2001, specifically the collapse of WTC 7 and the possibility of explosive demolition.

2. The investigation to follow the national standards so clearly outlined in the National Fire Protection Association guidelines, specifically, NFPA 921 to include thorough analysis of the steel for the presence of "exotic accelerants."

3. Congress to honor the promises made to the rescue workers of 9/11 by passing the James Zadroga 9/11 Health and Compensation Act of 2008.

4. Prosecution of all individuals willfully involved in the planning and execution of the murders committed on September 11, 2001.

5. Prosecution of all individuals willfully involved in the obstruction of justice and destruction of evidence surrounding the events of September 11, 2001.

NFPA 921 is the National Fire Protection Association's accepted standard for fire and explosion investigations. The very existence of such a standard proves that fires can and do coexist with explosions, and not merely those explosions imagined by conspiracy theorists. Implicit in these demands is an accusation that people in high places acted willfully to prevent a thorough investigation.

There can be no doubt that the 9/11 attacks served as a pretext for the invasion of Iraq, even though no credible evidence ever existed to connect Saddam Hussein with the attacks themselves or with Osama bin Laden, the alleged mastermind. 9/11 has also served as a predicate for the so-called war on terrorism. James Bamford's book *The Shadow Factory* (Anchor Books, 2008) laments the excesses of the war on terrorism even while accepting the government's account of 9/11 at face value. Gabriel Schoenfeld's book *Necessary Secrets* (W.W. Norton & Co., 2010) excuses these excesses as necessary for national security, and also accepts that Osama bin Laden directed the attacks according to the government's version. Their political differences aside, Bamford and Schoenfeld concur that a direct link exists between 9/11, the invasion of Iraq, and the enforced forfeiture of civil liberties that followed by way of the Patriot Act.

Religious leaders of all faiths, meanwhile, have expressed dismay at the process of guilt by association through religious stigmatizing. Religious Leaders for 9/11 Truth emphasizes the moral and ethical dimensions of 9/11. Their petition to President Obama reads as follows: "Whereas religious leaders seek to promote various universal values, including love, justice, and truth; and whereas religious leaders throughout history have spoken out on moral issues; and whereas the official account of 9/11 has been shown by scientists and professionals in relevant fields to be false beyond a reasonable doubt; and whereas the official account of 9/11 has been used as a pretext for wars that have killed and maimed millions of innocent people and caused enormous ecological damage to our planet; and whereas the official account of 9/11 has been used to increase military spending and thereby to withhold needed spending for health, education, welfare, infrastructure, and the environment; and whereas the official account of 9/11 has been used to indict Islam as an inherently violent religion and to justify discrimination against Muslims and attacks on Muslim countries; and whereas the official reports about 9/11 have been produced by individuals closely affiliated with, or even employed by, the Bush administration; therefore we, the undersigned members of Religious Leaders for 9/11 Truth, ask President Obama to authorize a new, truly independent investigation into the attacks of 9/11 immediately, because such an investigation is long overdue, being owed to the 9/11 families, the American people, and the peoples of the world—especially the peoples of Afghanistan and Iraq."

Patriots Question 9/11 Truth is the largest affiliation under the non-confining umbrella of 9/11Truth.org. It consists primarily of active and retired military officers, many of whom own advanced degrees in fields separate from the military but germane to 9/11. All were brave enough to declare openly that the official story of 9/11 is hogwash. There are too many to cite individually.

Some state unequivocally that a Boeing 757 did not, could not have struck the Pentagon. Others say that a similar aircraft could not have caused the crater found in Shanksville, Pennsylvania. These are men and women with no ax to grind...on the contrary, as military officers trained to accept higher authority even when disagreeing with it, they risk censure from their peer group. Whether or not they have countenanced censure is unknown; their averments have never been subjected to public scrutiny or reported by the mainstream media.

Journalists and Other Media Professionals for 9/11 Truth is the smallest segment of the movement, no doubt because the mainstream media have willfully ignored all versions except the official story. JOMP911T began as a collection of five concerned New Englanders who "...contend that there are still too many unanswered questions, factual anomalies and conveniences surrounding the horrific events of September 11, 2001 to accept at face value the official legend that foreign entities were solely responsible for confounding the world's premier military power." The group adheres to the modern dictum, "Be the media." Its website continues, "...our efforts, while effectual at the local level, must also be in concert with worldwide media professionals to more readily and quickly achieve our goal. We have a deep respect for media 'professionals' [quotation marks in the original] who toil daily to ferret out the truths most important to the world. We seek their help, fraternity, and guidance in our common goal."

Those within the 9/11 truth movement often differ about points of emphasis or specific facts. But all agree that a new investigation is needed to arrive at the truth. If rogue elements within the Bush administration orchestrated or acquiesced in the attacks, a new, unbiased investigation would be fiercely resisted by anyone in public life who might be implicated. The inquiry would become a political football, with Bush administration apologists asserting political motives and a lack of patriotism to those participating. Echoes of Vietnam would resound, with political animals crying that the investigation was giving "aid and comfort to the enemy."

So be it. Enough is enough. The fox has been guarding the chicken coop, the American people have been the chickens, and thus far the mainstream media have been too chicken to argue with the fox.

CHAPTER 5. THE PRESS MAINTAINS ITS OWN PATRIOT ACT

The attacks of 9/11/2001 gave rise to the USA Patriot Act, empowering the executive branch in ways not imagined by the founding fathers. Despite its negative implications for civil liberties, the act passed both houses of Congress easily. Libertarians objected, but reaction in the mainstream media, which are usually drawn to controversy like moths to a flame, ranged from muted to strongly approving.

This wasn't surprising to historians. Context is everything. Abraham Lincoln was murdered in April 1865 at Ford's Theater in Washington, less than a week after Robert E. Lee had surrendered to Ulysses S. Grant at Appomattox. There was no doubt that actor John Wilkes Booth had done the deed, but considerable doubt arose about how Booth had been able to carry out his plan so easily. Had the nation's newspapers been the least bit interested in the enigma, they would have investigated and possibly saved later historians a lot of trouble. They weren't, and they didn't.

Lincoln's evening bodyguard, John F. Parker, abandoned his assigned post at some point during the play, "Our American Cousin." Historians who have mused about Parker's whereabouts at the crucial moment, without exception, have ignored the overriding point, i.e., Booth carried out his murderous plot according to a presumption to which he was not entitled, that Lincoln would be unguarded at the moment Booth had decided to strike. That chosen moment was inflexible. Booth had linked the shooting of Lincoln to a specific line of dialogue from the stage below, one that would engender sufficient laughter to muffle the sound of the gunshot.

There was no margin for error. Booth needed those precious extra seconds to make good his escape through the rear of Ford's Theater. He succeeded by a whisker, and only precise timing allowed him to escape. Even a brief interruption by a guard would have resulted in his immediate arrest, yet Booth's plot allowed for no such interruption.

Booth carried a Derringer pistol that allowed for only one shot at a time. He entered the theater according to a prearranged timetable, waltzed past the empty chair previously occupied by Parker, passed through the vestibule, and entered Lincoln's theater box after blockading the vestibule door behind himself (he had prepared the blockade earlier that day, using a broken music stand from the orchestra). He shot Lincoln in the back of the head just as the audience roared at the comedic line from the stage, "...you sockdologizing old mantrap," at the exact moment Booth had pre-selected. Simultaneously, a few blocks away, Booth's fellow conspirator, Lewis Powell (AKA Lewis Paine), assaulted Secretary of State William H. Seward at Seward's home, seriously wounding him. Booth and Powell had coordinated their efforts according to an agreed timeline, because they planned to escape together. Of course, any time interval following one assassination attempt would have alerted police and soldiers to the possibility of a second, so they had to be coordinated.

Was this all part of an eleventh-hour plot to throw the government into chaos and somehow reverse the outcome of the War Between the States? Most people thought so, but regardless, who had arranged for Parker to leave his post? It was clear that Booth had planned it all with precise timing...his arrival at the theater, his entry into the vestibule, his blockading of the door behind him, his fatal shot to coincide with the play's dialogue, and Paine's simultaneous attack on Seward across town. Booth obviously hadn't worried about being interrupted by a guard. But may an assassin presume a president who employs bodyguards day and night will be unguarded at a convenient moment?

Washington City Police Chief A.C. Richards, Parker's boss, brought him up on charges of neglect. Historians believe some kind of trial or inquest was held at which Parker was absolved, but this can't be proven because all records of this proceeding were somehow "lost or destroyed," and because no contemporaneous account of Parker's trial exists. Not one newspaper or magazine covered it. Not one interviewed Parker after the fact to inquire about his negligence. Parker vanished into historical anonymity, and died in 1890.

It's almost unfathomable in hindsight. This was the first presidential assassination in American history. The president's guard had abandoned his post, allowing an assassin to execute a precisely timed multiple-murder plot against the president and a cabinet officer (and, most historians believe, against Vice President Andrew Johnson). The neglectful guard was brought up on departmental charges. Some kind of proceeding followed, but only the person who destroyed the trial records could tell us what happened. No journalist or historian in the past 145 years has called attention to, let alone criticized, this whitewash.

A parallel with 9/11/2001 is inescapable, with regard to patriotism and media silence. Booth was a zealous Confederate sympathizer, albeit he'd never fought in combat. To "loyal" Americans in 1865 Booth was a traitor as well as an assassin, just as Rebel soldiers were thought of as traitors for having taken up arms against their countrymen. This is a subtle distinction that partially explains media passivity toward Lincoln's murder and Parker's neglect.

Americans born in the 20th century are inclined think of the Civil War as a struggle between North and South (or on a football field, Blue vs. Gray), but during the war itself and for decades afterward most Northerners thought of the conflict in terms of *Loyal Unionists vs. Traitors*. The Union won the war, and the winners determine the political post-mortem. Thus, for anyone in the mainstream to opine that Booth had had help from within the government would have seemed insidious and unpatriotic a week after the war had ended. Clearly somebody had arranged for Parker to abandon his post, and it couldn't have been Jefferson Davis or Robert E. Lee. But no newspaper would "go there," because the only leitmotif the public would accept was that a dirty Rebel had cravenly murdered a saintly martyr.

The über-patriotism that followed the war might explain why no paper covered Parker's trial, given that it was held mere weeks after assassination. But it doesn't explain why historians in the years since have seen nothing amiss in the destruction of Parker's trial records, or in the failure of the press to pursue the story once the patriotic fervor had abated.

On 9/11/01, so we've been told, 19 Muslims breached security at four separate locations, then hijacked four jetliners without a response from an air defense system that was at that moment inactive because of anti-terror war games. Had these Muslims borrowed John Wilkes Booth's crystal ball? Had they simply guessed the coast would be clear? Their remarkable timing, and the noninterference from nearby Andrews Air Force Base once it was known the planes had been commandeered, should have been a giant red flag to any newspaper editor who considers the press a watchdog over government. But 9/11 was Lincoln/Booth/Parker redux, at least in terms of media coverage. Muslims in 2001 were assigned the villain's role that Confederates played in 1865.

In the interest of full disclosure, the present author recognizes that mainstream historians in the late 20th century have contrived a rationale for John F. Parker's neglect on April 14, 1865. As the modern theory goes (yes, it's only a theory), Parker was responsible for protecting Lincoln at the Executive Mansion, but only there. He wasn't responsible for Lincoln on trips to the theater, so say the revisionists. Therefore, there's no mystery about why Parker had left his post...it really wasn't his post at all.

Academic historians who seek a silver-bullet rationale for historical enigmas such as Parker's neglect and kid gloves treatment afterward tend to follow one another in a kind of Orwellian group think pattern. One recognized expert contrives a theory, and others use it as source material for their own books. So the popularity of the revisionist approach regarding Parker isn't a surprise. But with all respect due for the qualifications of the historians who developed it, the theory that Parker wasn't responsible for Lincoln at Ford's Theater is incoherent. It can be rejected out of hand for the reasons that follow:

1) The assassination danger was greater outside the Executive Mansion than within.

2) Lincoln was constantly warned about his safety by those closest to him. He maintained a file he marked "Assassination," with reports of more than 80 plots. Lincoln was a marked man in 1865. His murder was a shock to the nation, but no surprise to his confidantes.

3) If Parker hadn't been responsible for Lincoln's welfare at Ford's Theater, as today's revisionists claim, Police Chief Richards would have had no reason to bring him up on charges in the first place. Parker was a Washington cop. Richards was his direct boss, and he knew better than anyone else what Parker's exact duties entailed.

4) Mary Todd Lincoln, who had signed the order accepting Parker as a guard in Lincoln's absence, was heard cursing Parker for his neglect after the assassination. Would she have blamed Parker if he hadn't been responsible for Lincoln at the theater? Would Mary Lincoln, who authorized his hiring, have been in doubt about Parker's responsibilities?

5) Lincoln's daytime bodyguard and close confidant, William Crook, cited Parker for his neglect in his own memoirs (authored in 1905). Crook served five presidents and was highly respected for integrity and loyal service throughout his career. He was there in 1865, and he had no ulterior motive for blaming Parker.

6) It is undisputed that Parker was at Ford's Theater that night. If he had been only an Executive Mansion guard, with no responsibility for Lincoln's safety elsewhere, why would he have gone to the theater at all? Who was protecting Lincoln that night, if not Parker?

7) The present author introduced a copy of Parker's obituary (1890) at a Ford's Theater assassination symposium in 1998. Information in any obituary comes from public records and/or the decedent's family. It unambiguously states that Parker in fact had been Lincoln's guard on April 14, 1865, 25 years before. His own family conceded the point. It's clear that any question about Parker's duties was settled 120 years ago. For some reason, historians over a century later decided they knew better than Crook, and better than Parker's own family members, what his exact duties had been in 1865.

The background to America's entry into World War II also represents a parallel to 9/11. The Roosevelt administration had blockaded the South Pacific. This denied Japan, which had been terrorizing its neighbors for decades and had no oil of its own, access to Indonesia and its vast energy resources. A considerable body of evidence exists that FDR knew from intelligence reports of an imminent Japanese attack in the Pacific, if not necessarily at Pearl Harbor, in response to the US blockade. For its part the Bush administration acknowledged that it had been warned over a month before 9/11 that a terrorist attack was coming. Then National Security Adviser (later Secretary of State) Condoleezza Rice has insisted that no specifics had been included in the warning. The press accepted this explanation.

Everyone would applaud the media for not revealing intelligence data that could imperil the country's response to an act of war. Author Gabriel Schoenfeld is surely right that press freedom has limits; bona fide national security interests supersede the public's right to know. But censorship also has limits. Once the immediate danger has passed, and especially after a warning has been ignored with adverse consequences, the public deserves a complete explanation. Media silence begets more terrorism. The needs of the military–industrial complex, a lust for oil, or preemptive nation building must submit to the test of public opinion, but informed opinion can only follow from accurate information. In this regard the mainstream media have failed the American people.

Things were very different in America's editorial offices back in 1898, when the battleship Maine exploded in Havana harbor. Cuba was then a sleepy outpost of a fading Spanish empire, a backwater of no strategic importance. William Randolph Hearst of the *New York Journal*, an unapologetic muckraker with political ambitions of his own, had traveled to Cuba the year before in pursuit of a sexy story involving a Spanish colonial officer and a beautiful local girl named Evangelina Cosio y Cisneros. It was rumored that the Spaniard had violated the personal sovereignty of the young senorita.

If every rape committed by a soldier at a remote outpost justified a declaration of war, there wouldn't be enough people to fight them all. Never mind that the case of the girl Hearst nicknamed the "Cuban Joan of Arc" might have been entirely bogus. Hearst took it for granted the rumors were true. He brought Evangelina to New York, put her up at the Waldorf Hotel, and spread her story throughout his newspaper chain. He then enlisted the signatures of Clara Barton, Julia Ward Howe, and First Lady Ida McKinley, among others, on a petition to the Queen of Spain, demanding justice for the poor girl.

The stage had been set. Several months later, something or someone blew up the Maine. President McKinley, a deeply religious and cautious man by nature, commissioned a naval board of inquiry to investigate. This was a statesmanlike act, but it didn't satisfy Hearst or his rival Joseph Pulitzer at the *New York World*, who instituted a tit-for-tat headline campaign to "Remember the Maine!" and bring belated justice to the Cuban Joan of Arc. The public ate it up.

McKinley prayed for guidance from above, and went to war. It was a brief affair that liberated Cuba, brought the Philippines under American control, and advanced the career of future president Theodore Roosevelt, who had led a civilian militia known as the "Rough Riders" up San Juan Hill in Havana. Roosevelt reveled in his brief foray into combat, and returned home a conquering hero to a public that had been deluded by editorial jingoism into believing Spain had challenged American sovereignty. The Rough Rider was elected vice president on McKinley's ticket in 1900 (Vice President Garret Hobart having died in 1899), and TR acceded to the presidency when McKinley was assassinated in 1901. McKinley's friend and political mentor Marcus Hanna, no fan of Roosevelt, lamented, "Now that damn cowboy is president."

It might never have happened without Hearst, who was a creature of 19th-century journalism. Unshackled by present-day corporate fears of offending advertisers or stockholders, not worried about losing "access" to the White House and its media control apparatus that denies access anyway, Hearst's only concern was competition from other family-owned newspapers. He used the printing press to influence opinion, not merely to reflect it, and at once to elevate the ambitious William Randolph Hearst as a public figure. Many historians dispute his boast of having started the Spanish–American War, but there's no question that the newspaper war with Pulitzer was a watershed moment in American journalism. It led to a gradual reappraisal among journalists about the extent to which newspapers should involve themselves in the politics of peace and war. This change took a while to become manifest, since most newspapers remained in the hands of family dynasties with long-standing loyalties to one party or the other.

The Spanish–American War was declared by Congress. So were both world wars, according to a Constitutional requirement. But parallel to the decline of newspaper influence over politics, declarations of war became passé beginning at the mid-century. Hearst died in 1951. Other media had already adopted a relatively passive editorial stance in matters of overseas military intervention. The Cold War had begun. With compliant media and little or no backlash from Congress, administrations of both parties began to send soldiers into combat without asking for declarations of war. These forays were officially called "conflicts," which was a tacit acknowledgement that war hadn't been declared by Congress. Thus followed Korea, Vietnam, Cambodia, Lebanon, Grenada, Somalia, Kosovo, Kuwait, Afghanistan, and Iraq.

The playing field began to shift after Vietnam/Cambodia, if only on paper. Congress passed the War Powers Resolution over President Nixon's veto in 1973, but it didn't reverse the trend away from undeclared wars of aggression. Ronald Reagan sent troops to Grenada and Somalia, Bush 41 went into Iraq and Kuwait, and Bill Clinton invaded Somalia and Kosovo. As this is written Barack Obama is managing occupations of Iraq and Afghanistan, having inherited the mantle from Bush 43.

Undeclared but public wars ("conflicts") exist at one level of unilateralism. Whenever Congress allocates monies for overseas intervention, such funding serves as a quasi-declaration of war. But arbitrary acts of aggression, unknown to American citizens and not debated or funded by Congress, are at another level. We learned after the fact (and in the face of vehement denials) about CIA operations in Iran, Guatemala, Chile, and elsewhere since 1953. In the name of the undeclared but heavily propagandized war on terrorism, the CIA has raised the ante. It kidnaps suspected terrorists and those thought to have information about terrorists off the street in foreign capitals; it operates secret prisons; and it fires missiles at suspected terrorist nests. We know about these activities not because our own media revealed them first, but from foreign sources via the Internet.

The Bush administration operated under a cloak of unprecedented secrecy. They asked us to trust them to do whatever was needed to keep us safe. But Bush and Cheney left office with very low poll ratings, and voters chose Barack Obama as president over the more hawkish John McCain because of Obama's campaign promise to bring "change [we] could believe in." So far the change has been slow in coming, at least overseas. The US is still in Iraq, and troop commitments in Afghanistan have increased by 30,000. Meanwhile the corporate-controlled mainstream media, once America's watchdogs, resist change even more stubbornly than does the government they once watched over.

Chapter 6. False Flags Have Flown Forever

Wikipedia defines a false-flag operation as one "...designed to deceive the public in such a way that the operations appear as though they are being carried out by other entities." That isn't wrong, but it's an incomplete definition.

Often in military and naval warfare, flying another country's flag has been a tactic to confuse the enemy. In peacetime, a false-flag operation may be used to mislead a citizen population that would otherwise recoil at a planned act of aggression. It can also take the form of blaming an enemy for a serendipitous accident, thus justifying a belligerent response. The common thread between all false-flag operations is that they seek to change public perception toward a real or perceived adversary.

Roman Emperor Nero might have the first in history to implement a false-flag strategy. Rome burned for five days and nights in 64 AD. Nero was no Smokey the Bear, but he saw and seized an opportunity to achieve a political goal.

An early Christian movement had spread from Palestine, at the eastern end of the Roman Empire, through Asia Minor and Greece to Rome itself. A remote development had become a real and present danger to Roman authorities. Two leaders of the movement, the disciple Simon Peter and the Apostle Paul, had settled in Rome when the fire broke out. They had been preaching Christ's gospel of self-abnegation, obedience to God ahead of civilian authority, and proclaiming His imminent return and reign. Roman

Christians held secret meetings, giving them a cultic reputation among the locals. Although Nero's popularity was in decline at that stage of his reign, he sensed that Roman citizens would prefer the devil they could see to the devils behind the curtain.

Christianity was a threat, and Peter and Paul were convenient scapegoats. So Nero simply declared that Christians had set the fire. The frightened public bought the lie, Peter and Paul were executed, and Nero's purpose was served. He might or might not have set the fire himself (we'll never know), but it didn't matter. The Christian movement had lost its shining lights, and those brave enough to follow in the footsteps of Peter and Paul by proclaiming Christianity along the Via Veneto became luncheon food for lions. Relieved Romans cheered the lions on for decades thereafter.

The Spanish–American War has been discussed. Because President McKinley's board of inquiry never issued its report, it will always be a mystery if the battleship Maine was deliberately blown up, or if so, whether or not Spain was culpable. It could have been an accident, or an unauthorized act by a lone nut. Sometimes false-flag operations begin without prior planning, and the first people to wave the flag don't necessarily implement the strategy.

In recent history false-flag operations haven't depended upon random fires or mysterious explosions to be effective. Japan wanted to wrest Manchuria from China in 1931, so their own operatives exploded a section of a railway owned by Japanese interests in Mukden, Manchuria. In Nero-like fashion, the Japanese found convenient scapegoats to blame it on...Chinese dissidents. It was a lie. There were no Chinese dissidents in the neighborhood, but the accusation satisfied people on the home front. The weak Chinese military was too far removed from the scene to respond effectively, so Manchuria became Manchukuo. Japanese imperialism took a quantum leap forward.

Not satisfied, in 1937 Japan invaded Mainland China on the pretext that one of its soldiers had been kidnapped while guarding the Marco Polo Bridge, near present-day Peking. The lad might simply have overdosed on rice wine and was sleeping it off somewhere, but not every kidnapping is perfect (see Hopewell, New Jersey, 1932). The Chinese got blamed again, and again people back home bought the story. Can't question the emperor, you know. The dragon was on the march. We don't need Paul Harvey to know "the rest of the story."

Adolf Hitler might have been the master false-flag tactician of all time. In 1933 Nazis were hoping to gain enough seats in parliament to seize power and make Hitler Fuhrer. The vote was seen as close. So a few days before the elections Nazis set fire to the Reichstag, home of parliament. Hitler summoned up his unique brand of righteous indignation and claimed Communists had done the deed. Hermann Goring said he had proof of this, but wasn't yet ready to produce it. Meanwhile the aging president, Paul von Hindenberg, signed the Reichstag Decree, which Hitler, who came to power as planned, used to undermine every civil liberty guaranteed under the Weimar Constitution. Within weeks the Nazis passed the Enabling Act, giving Hitler all authority previously invested in parliament. Germany became a pure dictatorship.

Dictators tell lies with impunity, but like medieval kings they aren't answerable to anyone, so in a dictatorship there's no practical difference between a lie and the truth. But despots still like to have public opinion on their side. Hitler's grand plan of European conquest included annexing Czechoslovakia, so in 1938 he claimed ethnic Germans in the Sudetenland were being mistreated by Slovaks. Hitler's claim was window dressing, because Germany was going to invade Czechoslovakia in any event. The Anschluss had brought Germany and Austria together in 1937 to assure Hitler military control of the region. But the lie did cement public opinion on the home front.

A year and a half later Hitler needed to annex Poland, en route to an attack on Russia. That was a bit trickier, but doable. A radio station in Gleiwitz, Silesia (just across the Polish border from Germany) was playing recorded music on the night of August 31, 1939. All was peaceful. Suddenly German operatives invaded the studio, seized the microphones and broadcast the "news" that Polish forces were en route to Gleiwitz and were preparing to attack Germany. After an interval of silence, Germans, speaking fluent Polish, resumed broadcasting and urged their "Polish comrades" to join in the invasion. German police were already on hand to quell the faux disturbance, and the next day Hitler used the Gleiwitz incident as an excuse to invade Poland and begin World War II.

Good guys use false-flag operations, too...or at least they try to. Successful or not, false-flag strategies always make good guys seem like bad guys to whomever the good guys think of as bad guys. The story didn't come out until 2000, and only then thanks to a request under the Freedom of Information Act, but in 1962 the Joint Chiefs of Staff had unanimously approved Operation Northwoods, a bold effort to deceive the public and justify a military invasion of Cuba.

As described in the book *Body of Secrets*, authored by James Bamford and published by Doubleday, Operation Northwoods involved a series of planned provocations that cumulatively would inflame American public opinion against Fidel Castro. Our military base at Guantanamo was to be the focal point of these incidents, which included the following (not a complete list):

1. Using anti-Castro Cubans posing as Cuban soldiers in an "attack" on the American base (a putative act of war).
2. Starting fires within the base and blaming them on Castro's loyalists.
3. Sabotaging our own aircraft located inside the base, and blaming the Cubans.
4. Firing mortar shells into Guantanamo from outside, where presumably only Cubans could have fired them.
5. Sabotaging an empty US vessel in the harbor, blaming Cubans, and publishing the "casualty" lists.
6. Conducting mock funerals for the imaginary victims.

Operation Northwoods planning went a lot further. It included having a US drone aircraft destroyed by (supposedly Cuban) MIG planes, which would be piloted by Americans. And, friendly Cubans would fake attempted hijackings of aircraft and ships, and when caught would say they were acting for Castro.

Even that wasn't enough. Falling into the "You can't make this stuff up" category was a plan to fill a chartered plane with CIA agents posing as college students on vacation, and to pretend to fly it over Cuba. Except the actual plane would have returned to Eglin Air Force Base, where an exact replicate, converted into a drone, would take off along the identical flight plan to the chartered plane's. Once over Cuba, it would transmit a "May Day" message that Cuban MIGs were attacking it, meanwhile it would be shot down by American planes. The public would then be asked to mourn for all the "dead college students."

Supposedly the Joint Chiefs of Staff loved this idea. That's hard to fathom, because someone would have had to create false identities for a planeload of nonexistent kids. Would they all have been orphans, with no relatives, no home addresses, and no Social Security numbers?

The boldest part of Operation Northwoods was the *planned blowing up of buildings* in Washington and Miami. Following the destruction, undercover CIA agents posing as Cubans would be arrested and would confess to the crimes. Phony documents purporting to prove Fidel Castro's approval of the bombings would be released to the press.

President Kennedy vetoed Operation Northwoods. The documents remained classified. We now know what had been intended, but we don't know if the Russians might have gotten wind of the plans and used them as a pretext for their missile program in Cuba, the one that brought us to the brink of war in 1962. The Russians used spies, too.

That brings us to 9/11/2001. It's impossible to examine the history of false-flag operations and then dismiss out of hand the possibility that forces within our government organized or at least acquiesced in the attacks. Operation Northwoods targeted Fidel Castro; in 2001 Osama bin Laden's image would have been on the dartboard, with the overriding goal being to justify unilateral aggression in the Middle East, already contemplated but lacking a catalyst to arouse public opinion. That possibility appears stronger when one scrutinizes the goals of the Project for the New American Century (PNAC), a neoconservative think tank organized in 1997 by William Kristol, son of movement co-founder Irving Kristol, and by Robert Kagan.

PNAC's Statement of Principles, released on June 3, 1997, stressed a need to:

> • Increase defense spending...to carry out our global responsibilities today and modernize our armed forces for the future.

> • Strengthen our ties to domestic allies and to challenge regimes hostile to our interests and values.

> • Promote the cause of political and economic freedom abroad.

> • Accept responsibility for America's unique role in preserving and extending an international order friendly to our security, prosperity, and principles.

In other words, PNAC believed America needed to shape the world for its own benefit. We should practice diplomacy only with our friends, and fight our enemies in the name of freedom, with no mention being made of the potential costs in dollars and soldiers and without regard to what the word "freedom" means in a Middle Eastern country where Western ideals have never existed. In particular, PNAC demanded regime change in Iraq, and in January 1998 it drafted an open letter to President Clinton to that effect.

In September 2000 PNAC upped the ante. It prepared a document titled, "Rebuilding America's Defenses: Strategies, Forces and Resources for a New Century." This was to be kept secret, but it's a wide world out there, and in 2002 Scotland's *Sunday Herald* got hold of it. The paper's investigative editor Neil Mackay (European media still employ investigative reporters) wrote that the document had outlined four "core missions" for the US military, as follows:

- Defend the American homeland.
- Fight and decisively win multiple, simultaneous major theater wars.
- Perform the constabulatory (policing) duties associated with shaping the security environment in critical regions.
- Transform US forces to exploit the "revolution in military affairs."

PNAC wanted to defend the American homeland, even though nobody was threatening it in 2000. Defending the homeland has been a core mission for our military since the American Revolution, so it was curious for a think tank to introduce it as an issue in peacetime, and prescient to introduce it a year in advance of an actual terrorist attack. PNAC wanted to fight multiple wars at once, which necessarily meant preemptive invasions of sovereign nations (all unnamed), in the name of preserving someone's security. It wanted us to be policemen for the world, despite the lesson of Vietnam, i.e., we neither can nor should be. And it proclaimed a revolution in military affairs that sounded Napoleonic.

"Rebuilding America's Defenses" included a section titled "Creating Tomorrow's Dominant Force." It posited that, "...the process of transformation, even if it brings revolutionary change, is likely to be a long one, *absent some catastrophic and catalyzing event—like a new Pearl Harbor.*"

In sum, the PNAC document argued that we can only defend ourselves effectively by fighting multiple wars of choice outside our borders, and to rebuild our defenses expeditiously we needed someone to attack us without provocation. It's hardly surprising that PNAC wanted all these plans kept on the QT at the height of a presidential election campaign. Neoconservatives were closely allied with Bush and Cheney, so to reveal plans for unilateral war would have been disastrous for the Republicans in 2000.

Then again, if PNAC really believed its own propaganda, should it have hid it under a barrel?

There's no question that "shaping the security environment in critical regions" meant safeguarding Israel's security. There was no need for PNAC to couch its meaning in coy language. A guiding tenet of neoconservative philosophy has always been that Israel represents a model for neighboring countries like Iran, Iraq, Syria, Lebanon, Jordan, and Afghanistan, none of which has adopted Western-style democratic ideals, nor is likely to.

Most Americans would endorse this thinking, at least in the abstract, but would balk at preemptive war. Indeed, only a "new Pearl Harbor" could have hastened the neoconservatives' agenda. Few respected public figures (none in the United States) have connected the dots and openly concluded that 9/11 was an inside job, but one who has is the former president of Italy, Francesco Cossiga.

Cossiga was Italy's president from 1985 to 1992. He resigned after admitting his role in creating Operation Gladio, an undercover intelligence network specializing in false-flag operations, specifically bombings that could be blamed on the government's political opposition. Shortly after 9/11, even as the world was reeling from the news and overwhelmingly sympathetic toward the United States, Cossiga boldly asserted that 9/11 was an inside job, and that it was common knowledge among intelligence agencies worldwide. In April 2009 he told an Italian newspaper, "...the disastrous attack has been planned and realized from the Mossad [Israel's CIA]...[to blame] the Arabic countries and...to induce the western powers to take part in Iraq and Afghanistan." Those strong words, from the former head of state of a US ally, were too strong to appear in any American newspaper.

CHAPTER 7. DEBUNKERS AND DEBUNKERS OF DEBUNKERS

Objections to conspiracy theories fall into three distinct categories. On the one hand we find well-researched books and magazine articles that present thoughtful cases in behalf of the common wisdom. Two examples among many are Gerald Posner's book, *Case Closed*, which purports to rebut all conspiracy angles to the Kennedy assassination, and the Popular Mechanics article that contradicts claims of deliberate sabotage at Ground Zero on 9/11/2001. In accord with scholarly debunkers, but using a very different approach, we find anti-conspiracy Internet bloggers, who refuse to deal with the merits of a particular theory or argument. Instead they resort to ad hominem attacks on the dissenters themselves. They tell us that conspiracy theorists "hate America," or are "nut jobs," "Kool-Aid drinkers," or "Tin-foil hat wearers." The mainstream media and the largest book publishers refuse to countenance conspiracy theories to begin with, so they belong in Category Three. We'll call them "passive debunkers."

The present author assumes his readers are interested in reasoned arguments only, pro and con. We'll examine the two most cogent rebuttals to conspiracy theories, with particular focus on the Kennedy assassination and 9/11/2001.

1) *"Too many people would have had to keep the secret. Someone would have spilled the beans by now."*

In the case of John F. Kennedy's murder, there are two incompatible possibilities. Either Lee Harvey Oswald acted alone, or JFK was caught in a cross fire. In the latter case a conspiracy is self-evident (Oswald might have been connected to it, as an active participant or patsy). If there was a conspiracy, could it all have been kept secret for 47 years? The best answer is, "It depends on who was in charge of the conspiracy."

Oswald was himself murdered by Jack Ruby, two days after JFK was shot, and while Oswald was in police custody in broad daylight. Unless we take the excuse offered by Ruby at face value ("I felt sorry for Jackie and the children"), Oswald's death was Step One in a cover-up. Oswald told the Dallas police he was a patsy. If that were true, he surely would have spilled a lot of beans in his own defense, both at his trial and beforehand. If Oswald had survived, there would have been no Warren Commission, because its findings would have conflicted with his right to a fair trial. Oswald's attorney would have attempted to deflect guilt toward others; whether the strategy availed or not, information embarrassing to the government could have been revealed.

If Oswald had been lying about being a patsy, he still could have concocted a story to support his claim. Given his various associations, Oswald plausibly could have drawn enough suspects into his saga to have kept the debate going for years, whatever his fate in court. It's entirely likely that, had Oswald lived, the full story of JFK's assassination would be public knowledge today.

But the Warren Commission decided Oswald had acted alone, and Oswald didn't live long enough to prove otherwise. Without imputing dishonest motives to the commission members and staff, it's safe to say that their finding effectively took everyone else off the hook. Save for the futile efforts of District Attorney Jim Garrison in New Orleans, there would be no further investigations, and *no arrests that could have led to a plea bargain and exposed the conspiracy.*

Plea bargains with suspects are a powerful law enforcement tool to uncover the full extent of a crime. "We've got you dead to rights. But tell us who was in this with you, and we'll charge you with a lesser crime." But as a practical matter plea bargains can't be utilized after a federal commission has decided that only one person did it. Regarding the Kennedy assassination, the debunkers' familiar "too many people would have had to keep the secret..." dissent dissolves into the question, "Would anyone confess to a crime or enter into a plea bargain agreement after the investigation had effectively ended?"

Because the Warren Commission's finding halted the efforts of most law enforcement, conspiracy theorists were left to speculate about who was behind the assassination. Was it a CIA coup? Were people in the military–industrial complex afraid JFK would withdraw from Vietnam and deprive them of major contracts? Was it a mob hit, in response to Attorney General Robert Kennedy's deportation of New Orleans Mafia don Carlos Marcello? Or was it the FBI, given that J. Edgar Hoover was worried that Kennedy's affair with Judith Campbell Exner (who was also Mafia kingpin Sam Giancana's mistress) might subject JFK to blackmail by the mob? Was it Texas oil barons, many of whom were LBJ's friends, or might it have been anti-Castro Cubans who hated JFK for calling off the Bay of Pigs invasion? Was it some combination of these; for example, anti-Castro vigilantes working with mob boss Santos Trafficante in Miami?

Books and articles proliferated, beginning soon after the assassination. Most had a specific villain in mind and built a case to suit. But that's not how cops solve a crime. CBS-TV analyzed the forensic evidence at length without pointing fingers at anyone except Oswald. In 1991 Oliver Stone's film "JFK" strongly hinted at a conspiracy, but was vague about who had orchestrated it. The issue remains opaque.

The CIA and Mafia are the two most frequently cited suspects. Could they have kept a secret like this since 1963? Well, yeah. That's what they do.

The CIA orchestrated the overthrow of Mossadegh in Iran in 1953, and nobody was the wiser until the late 1970s, when a book came out that forced the CIA to fess up. CIA operations in Chile and Guatemala took decades to become known, and other operations remain top secret. Secrecy and plausible denial are part of the CIA's modus operandi, and integral to its training methods. If the CIA were behind Kennedy's murder, it could easily have remained a secret, especially after the Warren Commission named Oswald as the lone assassin.

Organized crime uses the code of *omerta* (silence) to keep its activities secret. Anyone tempted to rat out others goes to the top of a hit list, and nobody in the mix is in doubt about how the system works. Those who doubt the mob's capacity to protect its secrets should ask themselves, "Who among Jimmy Hoffa's many friends has identified his killer?"

Cracks in the Mafia's ability to keep secrets began with the publication of *The Valachi Papers* in 1968, which gave law enforcement new insights into its methods. Greater use of witness protection programs and the creation of new identities have since weakened the mob. But in 1963 a possible hit on President Kennedy could have been kept secret, at least until the Warren Commission report was released. After that, the perpetrators would have had only conspiracy theorists and Jim Garrison to worry about.

A number of people talked openly about a conspiracy in JFK's murder, only to meet early deaths. Actress Karyn Kupcinet, daughter of columnist and TV personality Irv Kupcinet, predicted JFK's murder in a frantic phone call minutes before it happened. She paid with her life a few days later. Jack Zangretti predicted Ruby would shoot Oswald, and he was shot to death weeks later. Gary Underhill, a CIA agent who said the agency was complicit in the assassination, was found dead in May 1964 of a gunshot wound to the head. The ruling was suicide. Two reporters who had visited Jack Ruby's apartment the same day he shot Oswald, Bill Hunter and Jim Koethe, died in 1964. Hunter was "accidentally" shot by a cop. Koethe died from a blow to his neck, which might not have been self-inflicted. Teresa Norton, the last person to speak to Ruby before he shot Oswald, died of a gunshot wound nine months later. Did they all know too much, or do accidents just happen?

"Coincidence theory" is as commonplace as conspiracy theory. It's less tenable because it contradicts the laws of chance, but because it fits the purposes of those in power, it remains inside the mainstream. The laws of probability forbid as many inexplicable deaths as occurred after JFK's murder, but to connect those deaths automatically identifies one as a conspiracy theorist (and outside the mainstream). The truth is, it's dangerous to know too much, and even more dangerous to talk openly about what you know. This is especially true if you're a public figure with a wide sphere of influence.

Consider the mysterious death of reporter, radio personality, and "What's My Line?" panelist Dorothy Kilgallen, who had interviewed Ruby during his trial and later told friends she was about to "break the Kennedy assassination case wide open." Dorothy died on November 8, 1965, from either an accidental drug overdose or foul play made to appear like an accident. Coincidence theory allows for the former, but circumstances strongly suggest the latter.

Dorothy Kilgallen was a fearless reporter for the *New York Journal-American* (a Hearst newspaper), their gossip columnist, and the daughter of famed journalist James Kilgallen. In her early 20s she had covered the trial of Bruno Richard Hauptmann for the Hearst chain. Dorothy's investigative work in the Sam Sheppard murder case helped Sheppard obtain a new trial, at which he was acquitted. In the wake of the Warren Commission report, Dorothy cited discrepancies in the report in her column, violating a tacit self-censorship agreement among newspapers about the case. When she interviewed Ruby during a recess at his trial for murdering Oswald, Dorothy learned (according to friends in whom she confided) that Ruby and Dallas policeman J.D. Tippit (whom Oswald was first accused of killing) had met at Ruby's Carousel Club in Dallas two weeks before the assassination, in company with Bernard Weissman, a right-wing fanatic who had placed an ad in Dallas newspapers on November 22, 1963, stating that JFK was "Wanted for Treason." Also present at that gathering was a fourth person, identified only as a "rich Texas oilman." Dorothy also had established connections between Ruby and David Ferrie, between Ruby and figures in the New Orleans Mafia, including Carlos Marcello, and between Ruby and anti-Castro operatives in Florida and Texas.

Kilgallen told at least six people in New York that she was about to reveal the truth about JFK's murder. One was Lee Israel, who later wrote Dorothy's biography, *Kilgallen*. Others were her next-door neighbor, her hairdresser, her agent Bob Bach, her publisher, and Nick Vanoff, producer of the TV show, "Nightlife." Vanoff interviewed Dorothy on air, and at his request, Dorothy kept quiet about her investigative work in the Kennedy murder, even as she held a large file of notes on the assassination on her lap throughout the interview.

What's especially remarkable about Dorothy Kilgallen's demise is that all the major dailies in New York, including her own *Journal-American*, reported it without citing her investigation into the Kennedy assassination. That speaks volumes about press censorship, given that crime investigation had been Dorothy's métier since the 1930s. She was described posthumously as a columnist and game-show panelist who had died from ingesting a lethal combination of alcohol and barbiturates. That's all. Her folder of notes on the assassination had disappeared at the time of her death, but that fact wasn't cited either. Dorothy's body had been found in bed in the master bedroom of her house, a room she hadn't slept in for years, but nobody in the press wondered how that could possibly be. The death of Dorothy's friend Florence Smith two days later under unexplained circumstances passed notice until *Kilgallen* was published. Dorothy's notes were never found. One can infer they were stolen from her by whoever placed her body in the wrong bed, or more probably, she had passed them on to Florence Smith for safekeeping, a decision that proved unsafe for both the notes and Florence. Dorothy died a private death, because none of her newspaper colleagues had her passion for the truth. Florence died because she was Dorothy's friend.

All the circuitous pathways surrounding the murder of John F. Kennedy seem to have passed through Jack Ruby's nightclub. Ruby's history and his known underworld connections make his excuse for shooting Oswald, i.e., that he was overcome by sympathy for Jackie and the children, a bad joke. Still, debunkers would ask, "Could everyone connected to Ruby and to JFK's assassination have remained silent since 1963?" Answer: We'll never know, but we do know that those who did speak out didn't live very long.

What about 9/11? If it wasn't orchestrated by Osama bin Laden and executed by 19 Muslims, if in fact the Twin Towers and WTC 7 were blown up by nanothermite, could those behind the crime have kept it a secret for the past nine years? What about the hole in the Pentagon, and the plane that went down in Shanksville, PA? Were these faked, and was the fakery covered up successfully? To answer these questions it's important to distinguish between two broad categories of conspiracy theories in re 9/11.

Scenario One: Forces within our government planned and executed a clandestine plot, using terrorist attacks that occurred during antiterrorist war games as a cover. The war games allowed the attacks themselves and rationalized the non-response of our air defense system (NORAD).

Within this scenario exist opposing theories. Some believe no planes struck anything except the Atlantic Ocean that day. Others concede that two planes hit the Twin Towers, but that a missile, not a plane, struck the Pentagon, and that the jetliner in Shanksville was shot down to prevent it from crashing into the White House or the Capitol. This theory would require that one plane went down in the ocean or landed safely somewhere, because it's beyond cavil that four airplanes were hijacked. In either secondary theory, Scenario One requires that the Twin Towers and WTC 7 were deliberately blown up, and that the debris at three separate crash sites was confiscated to permit a cover-up.

Scenario Two: Everything happened as the official story says, but insiders in the Bush administration knew about it in advance and did nothing to prevent it. Vice President Dick Cheney allowed a jetliner to hit the Pentagon, even after being warned that it was on course to do so. President George W. Bush, who was reading a book to kindergarten children in Florida at the time, might or might not have known what was going on. Three giant skyscrapers collapsed vertically from heat within, including one that had never been struck by a plane, albeit in the history of office building fires, no skyscraper had ever collapsed in free fall before. No airplane debris, no aircraft black boxes and no human remains were found at any of the crash sites; that also had never happened before. But one passport, supposedly belonging to one of the named hijackers, was found intact in the wreckage at Ground Zero, sitting alone among debris that had been incinerated beyond recognition. Three anonymous Muslims, none of whom was an experienced pilot and none of whose names appeared on a passenger manifest, managed to execute extremely difficult aeronautical maneuvers in New York and Washington. In the case of the Pentagon, this meant flying a Boeing 757 at 500 mph a few feet off the ground while avoiding all buildings and utility poles nearby the Pentagon. Not a trace of any plane was found...at least, none that survived an initial cleansing of the crash sites.

From a criminal point of view, Scenario One implies mass murder on the part of those in charge, while in Scenario Two public officials would be guilty of a lesser offense, perhaps criminal negligence. That's a meaningful difference in legal terms, yet oddly the first scenario is far more credible than the second, given the physical evidence. Regarding the question, "Could the perpetrators have kept it all a secret for nine years?" the answer is, "In Scenario One, it would have been difficult but possible. In Scenario Two, it would have been a snap, unless someone had recorded a before-the-fact phone conversation between the perpetrators and someone in the Bush administration, one that proved the White House knew what was coming." That's a practical nullity, because any such person would have had to convince a news organization of the conversation's validity (assuming he lived long enough to do so).

On a practical level, Scenario Two is impossible for three reasons. No outside terrorist could have presumed that our air defense system would be non-responsive. Nor could it have guessed that some mysterious Mr. Clean would arrive on the scene and remove all forensic evidence from three separate crash sites, thus frustrating an honest investigation. And no planned attack by hostile forces could have contemplated the collapse of WTC 7 seven hours later, because it would have offered no identifiable benefit to the terrorists and because no such building had ever collapsed from reflected debris or internal fires before. So our analysis must focus on Scenario One.

We know that Operation Northwoods had the unanimous approval of every branch of the military in 1962. Such a complex plan would surely have included plausible deniability, in the event of a prior leak or if something had gone awry during the implementation. Just as the public would have been prepared to believe the worst about Fidel Castro, and willingly dismiss speculation about an inside job in 1962, it would have accepted any reasonable cover story about Muslim terrorists in 2001, especially given the total absence of media skepticism. The public still remembered the World Trade Center bombing in 1993. Only overwhelming evidence of treason would have sufficed to sway public opinion, and what brave newspaper reporter, working with the approval of what editorial superior, could have introduced such evidence? Could it have happened in 2001?

The debunkers' argument, "Somebody would have spilled the beans by now" sounds reasonable enough, but it presumes that whoever does the spilling would first survive to tell the tale, would attract mainstream media attention, would be believed, and would be given a platform. In point of fact, when a whistleblower spills the beans, the beans can end up in the whistleblower's lap.

Consider the fate of Sibel Deniz Edmonds, a Turkish-American woman who went to work as a translator for the FBI shortly after 9/11. Being fluent in Turkish, Farsi, and Azerbaijani, Edmonds was asked to translate messages intercepted by counterintelligence agents. She was also told to listen to wiretapped conversations involving FBI suspects, separate the crucial from the irrelevant, and translate the crucial. Edmonds was the daughter of an Iranian-born surgeon with liberal political ideals who had fled Iran for Turkey in 1981 to escape harassment from Ayatollah Khomeini's revolutionary guards, and she was eager for the opportunity to help her adopted country identify Middle Eastern terrorists.

Edmonds was quickly disillusioned. After 9/11 the FBI did receive a flood of information from foreign sources about possible terrorist suspects, all of which needed to be translated. Edmonds wanted to do her job, but almost immediately she was told to stop translating and let her work pile up. FBI agents in the field were as eager to do their jobs as she was, and wanted all the information they could get from Edmonds and other translators. But the FBI bureaucracy was more interested in creating a deliberate backlog that could justify asking Congress for bigger budgetary outlays.

Edmonds outlined this situation in a letter dated August 1, 2004 to Thomas Kean, chairman of the National Committee on Terrorist Attacks Upon the United States. By the time she wrote it, a lot had happened in Sibel Edmonds' life...all of it bad.

In the letter to Kean, Edmonds also said she'd discovered that Melek Can Dickerson, a fellow Turkish-American translator, was leading something of a double life...on the one hand translating messages to help fight the war on terrorism, on the other, maintaining a relationship with two FBI intelligence targets through their common association with the American–Turkish Council (ATC), an organization Dickerson had once interned with. This dual relationship was improper, and Dickerson clearly knew it, because she had concealed her relationship with the ATC during a background security check.

Things got murkier for Edmonds. Early in 2002 she met with Dennis Saacher, a special agent for the FBI who handled Turkish counterintelligence. Saacher had his own reasons for distrusting Melek Can Dickerson, and therefore wasn't surprised to learn from Edmonds that Dickerson had been designating telephone intelligence involving her ATC associates as "not pertinent" to her investigative work, meanwhile arranging to have all messages involving those same associates kept away from her colleagues, including Edmonds, and under her own watch. Edmonds also told Saacher of a Sunday morning visit Dickerson had paid to Edmonds at her home in Alexandria, VA, where Dickerson urged Edmonds to become involved herself in the ATC's business and social activities.

Edmonds and her husband had found Dickerson's visit unusual. Saacher went further. He said Dickerson's conduct amounted to "espionage." Meanwhile, Edmonds had translated wiretapped conversations during which one of the speakers boasted of a secret relationship with Speaker of the House Dennis Hastert. It involved payments of "tens of thousands of dollars" to Hastert, in exchange for political favors and privileged information. Edmonds' account of these conversations jibes with facts that came to light later, i.e., in the late 1990s the FBI wiretapped Turkish nationals as they attempted to bribe "[unnamed] senior American politicians" in Washington and Chicago. Speaker Hastert, at that time, represented a Congressional district near Chicago.

Edmonds' world was closing in on her. She tried to persuade her FBI superiors that beside Dickerson's questionable ATC activities, Dickerson had leaked secure information to at least one FBI target, and had tried to prevent Edmonds from hearing wiretapped conversations that would have implicated Dickerson herself. Edmonds asked for a full investigation. What she got instead was a pink slip at the end of March 2002.

Edmonds wasn't merely fired. She was told she couldn't discuss her case publicly because all the information was "classified." The Bush administration added to Edmonds' woes by invoking a rare legalism, "state secrets privilege," that precluded any civil action being heard in court (Edmonds had filed suit in her own behalf) on the grounds that such a proceeding, even if held in a secure setting, would threaten national security. To her dismay, Sibel Edmonds learned that "national security" means whatever the executive branch of government wants it to mean.

The other sensible-sounding argument used by debunkers of conspiracy theories in re the Kennedy assassination and 9/11 goes about as follows:

> 2) *"It would have been too difficult to execute. Somewhere along the way someone in the grand cabal would have screwed up."*

This argument presupposes that Lee Harvey Oswald, a man with no driver's license, no educational or work pedigree, and at best a mediocre marksman, was able to execute a high-profile murder that CIA agents trained in clandestine operations and/or experienced Mafia hit men could not have executed. And, that 19 Muslims with box cutters for weapons, none of whom was an experienced pilot, breached security at four separate airport locations and executed a suicide terror operation that highly motivated and well-trained operatives within a shadow government could not have carried out.

Killing a president is harder than it was in Lincoln's day, but as both Kennedy and Lincoln were heard to say often, "If someone is willing to give his own life to take mine, it can't be prevented." The president has to appear in public, and the Secret Service can't frisk everyone in a large crowd. So it doesn't take a grand cabal to kill a president. It just takes a little planning and a good marksman, like the guy who blew JFK's head open with the final shot fired at Dealey Plaza on November 22, 1963. As the Zapruder film shows clearly, that gunman could not have been Lee Harvey Oswald. He was less than a good marksman, and at the moment JFK's head exploded from the final shot, Oswald would have been firing through the branches of a tree, at a target moving away from him, and from an angle that precluded the possibility that he had fired it.

Even a deadeye Dick, firing from directly up range at the Book Depository, could not have managed to hit Kennedy in the right front of his head. A second gunman fired that shot, which automatically means a conspiracy, barring the one-in-a-million possibility that two separate assassins, acting independently of each other, decided to kill President Kennedy at the same time.

It does take more than one person to cover up a conspiracy and deflect the blame to a single conspirator, or to a patsy. Considering that he couldn't hold a job and didn't drive a car, Lee Harvey Oswald had been a pretty busy guy before the assassination. He traveled to and from Russia, commuted between New Orleans and Dallas, organized a local chapter of the Fair Play for Cuba Committee in New Orleans, showed up at the Cuban consulate in Mexico City seeking a visa to travel to Cuba, and supposedly tried to assassinate (retired) General Edwin Walker.

Walker was a right-wing extremist and virulent anti-Communist whose murder would have marked his assassin as a likely Castro supporter. Walker did live in Dallas, but far across town from Oswald's residence at the time. Ballistic evidence showed the bullet fired at Walker had come from a Mannlicher-Carcano rifle, like the one found at the Texas School Book Depository; together with Marina Oswald's statement that her husband had admitted firing at Walker, it made for a seemingly solid case.

But Oswald didn't drive, and would hardly have risked carrying a loaded rifle in a taxicab or on a cross-town bus. It has never been satisfactorily explained where Oswald hid his rifle en route to Walker's house and back, presumably on foot, or how a guy who couldn't hold a job and didn't drive could have traveled as freely as Oswald had before November 22, 1963.

One plausible explanation for Oswald's freedom of movement has been dismissed as a conspiracy theory, but it jibes with what we've learned about Operation Northwoods and about clandestine anti-Castro operations in the early 1960s. It suggests there were two "Oswalds," and that the person who tried to arrange passage to Cuba from Mexico was an impostor. This isn't a farfetched notion by any means. A similar ruse had been part of the Operation Northwoods planning.

Whether the "second Oswald" ever reached Cuba would have been irrelevant. The goal was to place the real Oswald in Mexico City, to label him a Cuban sympathizer, and later to tie the murder of Kennedy to him and Fidel Castro. Had the real Oswald lived to stand trial, of course, such a ruse would have failed, if Oswald could have proven he was somewhere other than in Mexico City on the date in question. Oswald also could have shown that he lacked the wherewithal to get to Mexico City in the first place, let alone to Cuba afterward.

A jury might also have wondered, "Why would [the real) Oswald, who was broke, didn't drive and didn't speak Spanish, have wanted to go to Cuba, anyway? What could he have accomplished there? Would Castro have accepted a complete stranger as a potential ally in a murder plot against John F. Kennedy...the same man who had aborted the Bay of Pigs invasion and enabled him, Castro, to remain in power? Or would Castro have suspected that Oswald was an undercover American spy, sent by the CIA for a malign purpose?"

When Operation Northwoods was finally exposed in 2000, we learned that military leaders had schemed to blame Castro for certain false-flag operations as a pretext for invading Cuba and overthrowing his regime. President Kennedy vetoed Operation Northwoods. Assuming only that the schemers didn't give up at that point, it's a very small leap of logic to imagine that by murdering Kennedy and framing Lee Harvey Oswald a year later, schemers could have achieved their desired goal of liberating Cuba while at once avenging JFK's failure to support the Bay of Pigs liberators. Afterward, they'd have made sure to rub out the real Oswald, while the impostor disappeared into the ether.

How farfetched is that? How hard would it be for clandestine operatives, practiced in deceit, to find a guy in a bar somewhere who looked like Oswald, and pay him a tidy sum for merely approaching a foreign embassy with a visa request? It wouldn't even have been necessary to tell the impersonator who it was he was impersonating, or why. The hardest part would have been persuading the real Oswald to carry a Mannlicher-Carcano rifle into his workplace on November 22.

There's no question that (the real) Lee Harvey Oswald brought a rifle to the Book Depository that morning, wrapped in paper. He told his traveling companion that the package contained "curtain rods." Nobody forced him to do it. Could it have been mind control, a Manchurian candidate-type operation? Had Oswald been mentally programmed to fire at Kennedy (or at Connally) while another shooter was poised behind the grassy knoll, unbeknownst to Oswald? Was Oswald a CIA asset who had been told to fire in the direction of Kennedy's motorcade but miss, on the premise that the agency wanted to show JFK how dangerous it was to appear in public? Oswald was broke...it wouldn't have taken much to persuade him.

Evidence linking Oswald to the CIA or military intelligence is flimsy, but any connection could explain how Oswald was able to travel with impunity, lacking a source of funds or a driver's license. It would also explain Oswald's claim of being a patsy ("Oh, now I understand what those bastards were up to!"), and the necessity of having Oswald killed before he could blow their cover.

The notion that a grand cabal was necessary to murder John F. Kennedy, and that someone would have screwed up, sounds more logical than it is. Someone only had to get Oswald to bring a rifle to work, place a deadly marksman behind the grassy knoll, and bump Oswald off before he could talk. The Warren Commission's finding was a bonus that made the cover-up easier.

Regarding 9/11, did someone screw up? In fact, a number of someones did, but it hasn't mattered a great deal in terms of public perception.

It's hard for patriotic Americans to conceive that people in their government would have conspired to murder thousands of innocent people in cold blood. But suppose for argument's sake that the planes that struck the Twin Towers had been late in arriving. Planes are often late. What if the collisions had been planned for an hour earlier, before business hours, when the buildings would have been almost deserted? There would have be no New Jersey widows to make life miserable for the Bush administration, because their husbands wouldn't have arrived at work yet. It would still have been a major news event, the public would still have been terrified, but a human dimension would have been absent.

Whoever failed to clear nanothermite from the rubble at Ground Zero screwed up, big time. There was no legitimate reason for a deadly substance used exclusively for military purposes to have been found anywhere in New York City, but there it was...evidence of the deliberate destruction of two skyscrapers. The clean-up crew either didn't know what nanothermite was, or they didn't notice it. Who could have guessed that those responsible for transporting a military-grade explosive to Ground Zero would never be called to account?

Theodore Olson, Solicitor-General of the United States under Bush, screwed up, too. His wife Barbara was aboard the plane that supposedly struck the Pentagon, which might explain why reporters have gone easy on

Olson over his phony claim that he spoke with her via her cell phone while the plane was in the air. Cell phones don't operate at high altitudes, which fact called Olson's story into question immediately. Eventually an FBI document proved that the claimed conversations (Olson told Fox Network and Larry King that he'd spoken to Barbara two separate times) never took place. Why would the second highest-ranking legal official in the country have lied about such a thing, except as part of a cover-up? See Chapter 28 for more about this.

The BBC screwed up when their newscaster broadcast news of the collapse of WTC 7 about a half-hour before it happened. Someday they might be forced to explain his x-ray vision. The mainstream media haven't been curious enough to inquire. Not even Clark Kent at the Daily Planet, who knows all about x-ray vision, has asked BBC for an explanation.

Whoever released the names of the 19 Muslim suicide terrorists must have screwed up, because at least six of those named have shown up alive overseas. One, in fact, has filed suit in an effort to clear his name.

Traders who bought put options (bets on a price drop) on airline stocks and reinsurance stocks on September 10, 2001, really screwed up. They bought so many puts that the huge increase in volume alerted regulators to the likelihood that the buyers had inside information. The trades were nullified, and nobody got to keep his profit. Regulators know who they are now, even if the public doesn't. Still, no charges for insider trading have been filed against anyone, which probably doesn't make Martha Stewart feel any better.

(Then) Transportation Secretary Norman Y. Mineta screwed up in his testimony to committee Vice Chairman Lee Hamilton. Mineta told the truth, but evidently without understanding the meaning of what he was testifying to.

Mineta said that on the morning of 9/11, at the command center in the White House basement, a radar technician in an adjoining room had been monitoring the progress of American Airlines Flight 77 as it approached the Pentagon, and was periodically reporting on its progress to Vice President Cheney. As the plane neared the Pentagon, according to Mineta, the technician asked Cheney whether certain standing orders were still in place, and Cheney angrily replied that they were, asking, "Have you heard anything to the contrary?" None of this is denied, but Mineta's testimony never established whether those standing orders had been to shoot down the plane or to allow it to continue in flight. If the former, it means someone failed to carry out an order, which failure might have been simple or criminal negligence, or possibly just bad luck (whether shooting down the plane would have been justified is a separate issue, and one the Bush administration certainly didn't want to deal with). If it were the latter, someone had given an order to allow a hijacked airplane to crash into a government building. That sounds like treason. In either event the Bush administration was vulnerable to lawsuits from the victims' families, so isn't surprising that no one has come forward to clarify the matter.

As Secretary of Transportation, with jurisdiction over commercial air travel in the United States, Mineta was responsible for knowing whether or not our air defense system had standing orders to shoot down a hijacked airplane. If he had been kept "out of the loop" on 9/11, which from his testimony appears to be the case, by the time Mineta testified before the commission in 2003 he certainly had to have known the facts. Yet the issue of what the "standing orders" were remains unresolved, and Mineta's lack of candor since 2003 can only be categorized as deliberate obfuscation.

Mineta also told Hamilton that Cheney and his wife Lynne were already at the command center when he (Mineta) arrived there at 9:20 a.m. Mineta was certain about it. But the Secret Service logged Cheney's arrival at 9:58 a.m., 21 minutes after Flight 77 had (apparently) struck the Pentagon. A reasonable person would infer that Cheney didn't want people to know that he had micromanaged the final stages of a doomed plane's flight. If Cheney had arrived at the command center at 9:58, the conversation with the technician, as described by Mineta, obviously could not have taken place. Either Mineta lied (without a reason), or the Secret Service deliberately misrepresented the time of Cheney's arrival at the command center (with a reason). The reader is invited to choose between the two possibilities.

It's a fallacy to assume a conspiracy has to run smoothly. The bigger the conspiracy, in fact, the less crucial it is to avoid errors, because a story can become "too big" for the mainstream media to investigate. Contradictions and enigmas vanish into the ether, or are assigned to the subalternate category of conspiracy theories.

As long as a majority of the public gets its news from daily papers and television, it will remain ignorant of stolen elections, renegade intelligence operations, and misconduct on the part of government officials. The Shah of Iran came to power in 1953, and 25 years passed before we learned a CIA coup had enabled the transfer of power from Iran's democratically elected leader to an American puppet. Operation Northwoods was conceived in 1962, and the secret was kept for 38 years. John F. Kennedy was murdered in 1963, very possibly for the same reasons that caused Operation Northwoods to be approved unanimously at the Pentagon a year earlier, but we still don't know the full story and might never know it. Someday, if our great-grandchildren are lucky, they might know that George W. Bush was twice elected president fraudulently, and that the most secretive administration in American history kept the ugly truth about a deadly terrorist attack from their progenitors.

Chapter 8. Deaths of the Rich and Famous

Four presidents have been assassinated since 1865—Abraham Lincoln, James A. Garfield, William McKinley, and John F. Kennedy. Two others, Theodore Roosevelt (after leaving office) and Ronald Reagan, were wounded in assassination attempts. Four other presidents—Andrew Jackson, Franklin D. Roosevelt (before taking office), Harry S Truman, and Gerald R. Ford (twice), were targeted for murder but escaped unharmed.

Of these eleven incidents, only the assassinations of Lincoln and Kennedy gave rise to enduring conspiracy theories. Why so? Did their unique celebrity put them in a separate category from say, Garfield and McKinley, in that intense public curiosity led to unwarranted speculation? Maybe... celebrity does have its own currency. The sudden deaths of popular culture icons Marilyn Monroe, Princess Grace of Monaco (née Grace Kelly), and Michael Jackson have attracted rampant theorizing about sinister plots.

Does this observation juxtapose cause and effect? Could it simply be that the higher one's profile, the more emotion one generates, positive and negative, and the likelihood that such a person would be murdered increases proportionately?

James Abram Garfield was a dark-horse Republican presidential candidate in 1880, relatively unknown before gaining the nomination on the 36th ballot in Chicago. He won the election by a whisker. Garfield had been in office only four months when Charles J. Guiteau, a disappointed office seeker with an unstable personality, shot him at Washington's Union Station. Guiteau could be heard shouting immediately afterward, "I am a Stalwart, and now [Vice President Chester Alan] Arthur is president!" Garfield lingered with his wounds throughout the summer of 1881 before dying in September, as much from inept medical treatment as from Guiteau's gunshot. Arthur became president.

The 1880 election had been conducted amid factional dissension among Republicans. Stalwarts (good name, not necessarily good people) were led by New York's political boss, Roscoe Conkling, and favored a third term for Ulysses S. Grant. Half-Breeds (don't ask) supported Maine Senator James G. Blaine. Congressman Garfield, a Blaine supporter at the convention, became the compromise nominee when neither Grant nor Blaine earned a majority. Arthur, who had a questionable reputation as a functionary in the New York political operation, became the vice presidential nominee as a sop to Arthur's mentor Conkling, notwithstanding that President Hayes had earlier fired Arthur as Collector of the Port Authority on ethical grounds. Garfield and Arthur barely knew each other, either before or after their inaugurations.

In light of Guiteau's outcry, "I am a Stalwart, and now Arthur is president," one might have expected suspicions to arise about possible links to the corrupt New York machine, if only on the basis of, "Who benefited?" But no conspiracy theories developed. Many questioned Guiteau's mental capacity, but a plea of insanity failed to sway the jury, and he was convicted of murder and hanged in 1882. Guiteau is the only presidential assassin to survive more than seven weeks after his crime, and no undue speculation followed in the wake of his execution.

Leon Czolgosz, assassin of President William McKinley in 1901, was a disciple of Emma Goldman, she a prominent anarchist of the fin de siecle era. Publicly, Goldman expressed sympathy for Czolgosz after his arrest, and she was briefly held as a suspected accomplice. But no evidence could be found that Goldman shared more than a common ideology with Czolgosz, who admitted to the crime, was convicted in one hour, and electrocuted a mere 45 days after McKinley's death. Czolgosz' refusal to consult with his court-appointed attorneys hastened his demise, but even allowing for that, the swift handling of his case was exceptional.

Given Goldman's notoriety and the country's almost obsessive animus toward socialists, immigrants, anarchists, and other radicals at that time in history, it's remarkable that the assassination of McKinley was never viewed as part of a conspiracy. On the contrary, Czolgosz' body was quickly buried on the grounds of Auburn Prison. Acid was poured into his casket to accelerate the decomposition process, as if authorities were eager to forget everything about the man. Czolgosz remains the least familiar of the four presidential assassins.

Guiteau and Czolgosz were loners and friendless ne'er-do-wells, which could partially explain why conspiracy theories never developed. Then again, Lee Harvey Oswald had a similar personal profile (to Czolgosz', especially), yet speculation has raged since 1963 about Oswald's possible ties to the CIA, FBI, pro-Castro groups, and anti-Castro groups. The contrast between the three assassins' post-mortems is stark, and begs the conclusion that John F. Kennedy's personal magnetism had something to do with it. Compared to JFK, Garfield and McKinley were dull as dishwater.

Few Hollywood stars were more magnetic than Marilyn Monroe. Her death in 1962 at the age of 36 has been the subject of endless speculation. Based on one's analysis of Marilyn's final hours, she died by 1) suicide, maybe a result of depression over the end of her affair with John F. Kennedy, 2) an accidental drug overdose, because two doctors treating her for mood swings and insomnia had failed to consult with each other about her prescriptions, or 3) a murder conspiracy, because JFK had revealed classified secrets to Marilyn in the heat of passion, secrets that endangered national security and which she had threatened to take public.

Marilyn had attempted suicide several times, so it can't be ruled out. At the time of her death, however, she had decided to remarry Joe DiMaggio, making it unlikely that JFK's decision to end their affair would have led to suicide. Marilyn was notoriously irresponsible when it came to appointments and rehearsals, but there's no evidence that she was ever vindictive toward anyone. Suggestions that she would have revealed classified secrets as an act of vengeance, assuming she possessed them to begin with, are a stretch. The most likely conclusion is that Marilyn died of an accidental drug overdose. The whispers will no doubt continue, however, because the premature death of a Hollywood icon adds intrigue to fascination for millions. People just love talking about Marilyn Monroe, as if the conversation itself transmutes her memory into current reality.

Grace Kelly was a Hollywood beauty and an Academy Award winner when her storybook marriage to Monaco's Prince Rainier in 1956 turned hero worship into fantasy for millions of adoring fans. Never before had a movie queen morphed into a real-life princess, so for decades afterward tabloid and mainstream media in both hemispheres fed public demand for gossip about her family, which just happened to feature two rebellious princesses whose un-royal behavior included romantic liaisons with continental *enfants terribles*. It was said that these romances were unacceptable to Her Serene Highness, Grace.

When Grace died in 1982 in what appeared to be a simple auto accident, it gave rise to conspiracy theories that still resonate throughout Europe. There was more to these rumors than idle speculation. Monegasques depend heavily on the casino at Monte Carlo for revenue. The Mafia has long been notorious for infiltrating gambling enterprises; its standard tactic is demanding a share of revenues in exchange for "protection." So it isn't farfetched to suppose that Prince Rainier, who publicly sought to distance Monte Carlo's casino from organized crime's influence, had refused to buy protection and had ignored warnings from the mob at his peril. It's entirely possible that Grace's demise resulted from someone having tampered with the brakes on her doomed vehicle.

Of course, conspiracy theories need not be rational. The mob angle was plausible, but more Europeans believed Grace had lost control of the car during an argument with her daughter, Princess Stephanie, over Stephanie's boyfriends. Others suspected that Stephanie had been driving and deliberately crashed the car in retaliation for her mother's constant nagging about her own lifestyle. If nothing else, this gossip proves that the celebrity status of the victim, more than motive, opportunity, or means, can inspire conspiracy theories.

The death of rock star Michael Jackson in 2009 is a matter of ongoing litigation as this is written, so the less said about a possible conspiracy the better. Whatever the outcome of lawsuits, expect the Jackson debate to linger for years, if only to keep his memory alive. Elvis Presley's death in 1977 was non-controversial at the time, but his frequent appearances at 7/11 stores since then suggest the original reports were false, and rumors that he faked his own death are accurate.

OK, we're kidding. The point is, some idols are so iconic that their fans won't let them die. Conspiracy theories grow like weeds in the graveyard of any major celebrity who dies too young.

CHAPTER 9. THE PECULIAR LEXICON OF CONSPIRACY THEORISTS AND DEBUNKERS

This imaginary conversation is between two old friends, senior citizens who meet on a park bench to chat. It is intended to sound realistic, and at once to demonstrate that unique language patterns inform arguments about possible conspiracies. Skeptics (conspiracy theorists) and debunkers don't talk like real people. Italics are used to highlight specific words and phrases that best illustrate the point.

DAN FOOL: "How have you been, Trey? Long time no see."

TREY COOL: "Been good, Danny Boy. What ya' been up to?"

DAN FOOL: "Oh, the usual. Been reading up on the Internet about 9/11."

TREY COOL: *"Still wearing that tin-foil hat, eh?"*

DAN FOOL: "No, seriously. *There are a lot of questions that haven't been answered.*"

TREY COOL: "You said the exact same thing about the Kennedy assassination."

DAN FOOL: "What do you mean?

TREY COOL: *"Oh, you said you weren't a conspiracy theorist; you were just asking questions that needed answers."*

DAN FOOL: "What's your point?"

TREY COOL: "You said you didn't know for sure who did it, you just knew Oswald couldn't have acted alone."

DAN FOOL: "He couldn't have, unless the laws of physics have been repealed. Have you looked at the Zapruder film lately?"

TREY COOL: "Danny, *it's so hard for some people to believe a pathetic loser like Oswald could bring down a president. So they hunt for conspiracy angles that don't exist.*"

DAN FOOL: "That's pop psychology, Trey. I look at it the opposite way."

TREY COOL: "What opposite way?"

DAN FOOL: "*It makes many people uncomfortable to imagine that sinister forces within their own government could conspire to murder their beloved president. By rejecting conspiracy theories out of hand, they relieve their own discomfort.*"

TREY COOL: "Wow! Talk about pop psychology!"

DAN FOOL: "I really believe that."

TREY COOL: "*Keep on drinking the Kool-Aid, Danny.*"

DAN FOOL: "Have you ever studied the facts about Kennedy's murder, Trey?"

TREY COOL: "I did for a while. It did sound a little fishy, I admit. But it was a dead-end street. Finally I decided that *if there had been some grand plot, we'd know about it by now. Somebody would have spoken out in the last 47 years.*"

DAN FOOL: "A number of people did speak out, and they wound up dead. Have you ever looked into the death of Dorothy Kilgallen?"

TREY COOL: "No, but it sounds as if *you're using a so-called conspiracy to explain another so-called conspiracy. You conspiracy buffs do that all the time.*"

DAN FOOL: "It's called CYA, Trey. Criminals want to cover their assets. That's why people who know too much wind up dead, especially when they speak out."

TREY COOL: "Danny, *the principle of Occam's Razor teaches us that in seeking a solution to a problem from among multiple possible explanations, the simplest explanation is the best. That tells us that Oswald acted alone, and it also means the Twin Towers collapsed because of burning jet fuel from the planes.*"

DAN FOOL: "Even though no skyscraper had ever collapsed vertically before?"

TREY COOL: "No skyscraper was ever hit by a jetliner going 500 mph before."

DAN FOOL: "What about WTC 7, which wasn't hit by any plane?"

TREY COOL: "Danny, *have you really thought about what it would take to pull off a project of that size? Do you honestly believe those bumbling fools in the Bush ad-*

ministration could have done it? They couldn't even protect New Orleans from Hurricane Katrina!"

DAN FOOL: "You didn't answer my question, Trey, old boy. What about WTC 7?"

TREY COOL: "It caught on fire and collapsed. Danny, *you conspiracy guys have had nine years to prove your case, and you haven't succeeded yet.*"

DAN FOOL: "I'd say it has been proven. The media just won't admit it. Nanothermite was found at Ground Zero. That's a substance used only by the military, and only for huge demolitions. It can't have gotten there by accident. Impossible. The Twin Towers were sabotaged by explosives. There's no doubt about it, Trey. There's a lot more proof than the nanothermite, but it's in the form of documents that remain classified. If we'd just declassify those documents, we'd know a lot more."

TREY COOL: "And so would our enemies. The one thing we should never do is give away our intelligence to people who want to kill us."

DAN FOOL: "Have you been listening to Dick Cheney on Fox Network, Trey? You sound a little brainwashed."

TREY COOL: *"Spoken like a true liberal, Danny."*

DAN FOOL: *"Trey, this has nothing to do with liberals and conservatives."*

TREY COOL: "What is it about, then?"

DAN FOOL: *"It's about whether we can trust what our government tells us. The Bush administration lied about everything else under the sun, so who's to say they told the truth about 9/11?"*

TREY COOL: *"You're not going to find the truth on the Internet. Anybody can put phony stuff out there. There's no fact checking, no journalistic filter."*

DAN FOOL: *"That's true, but those mainstream journalists you rely on for news refuse to even discuss 9/11. People who get their information from newspapers and television don't even know a 9/11 truth movement exists."*

TREY COOL: *"Truth movement? You mean liberal celebrities like Rosie O'Donnell and Charlie Sheen? They're just trying to attract attention to themselves by spouting off on a political issue. It's called keeping your face in front of the public."*

DAN FOOL: "No, I mean physicists with doctorates, engineers, architects, retired military officers, firefighters, clergy, witnesses. The movement is growing bigger every day."

TREY COOL: "What did Lincoln say? You can fool some of the people all the time...you know the rest."

DAN FOOL: "In Europe, it's common knowledge that 9/11 was an in-side job."

TREY COOL: "Europe is all socialists. You can make socialists believe anything bad about government. Well, I gotta go, Danny. The little woman always expects me home for lunch. *Keep drinkin' that Kool-Aid.*"

Etcetera, etcetera. Lost amidst the familiar colloquy is a simple fact. If and when rogue elements within a government conspire in a false-flag event, or an assassination, or some other criminal act, the only remedy citizens have is their justice system. But the Justice Department is part of the executive branch of that same government. The chickens have to trust the fox to protect them, but when government values secrecy over candor, trust is forfeited. At that point even the truth can sound like a lie.

The Freedom of Information Act was passed in response to public ire over the lies of Vietnam and Watergate. It's been valuable, but when an executive can conceal embarrassing information by invoking a states-secret privilege, and thus stifle a whistleblower like Sibel Edmonds, the act is helpless. It's up to Congress to fix it, but the current crowd in the Capitol can't agree on anything. That isn't a conspiracy theory.

CHAPTER 10. GRAND CONSPIRACY THEORIES WITH QUESTIONABLE MOTIVES

This book seeks to examine controversial events in history through the prism of conspiracy theories. It presumes that identifiable anomalies surrounding the events themselves, not presentiment or bias, have informed the efforts of conspiracy theorists to uncover hidden truths. The book's title implies that most conspiracy theorists are sincerely motivated; when they challenge the historical record they mean to stigmatize no one. Toward that end, skepticism about the Lincoln assassination, the Kennedy assassination, 9/11, et al., should be divorced from allegiance to wide-reaching conspiracy theories that span centuries and target secret societies such as the Illuminati, Masons, Elders of Zion, and family dynasties like the Rothschilds.

The Illuminati, also known as the Illuminati Order and the Bavarian Illuminati, grew out of the 18th-century Enlightenment period. Europe had been ruled by family dynasties for centuries. Royal children married royal cousins, mutually aggrandizing one another and perpetuating their sovereignty through incestuous cross-pollination. This pattern was offensive to freethinkers, Enlightenment intellectuals, and progressive writers, who organized in 1776 as the Bavarian Illuminati (more immodestly, the Perfectibilists), under the leadership of Adam Weishaupt, a law professor at the University of Ingolstadt. Weishaupt attracted Freemasons to the cause, also prominent writers including J.W. von Goethe and J.G. Herder, and even a few mid-level Bavarian royals who wanted to buck the system.

The Bavarian Illuminati didn't survive as a recognized entity beyond 1785, although literary conservatives Augustin Barruel and John Robison did link its activism to the onset of the French Revolution. The Bavarian Illuminati was a real organization, but it would be a footnote in the history books if not for conspiracy theorists who connected it with an imagined secret society, called simply the Illuminati, that extends chronologically from the Enlightenment to the present. This vast assembly of perfect people includes the likes of Winston Churchill, Prescott and George H.W. Bush, David Rockefeller, Barack Obama, Zbigniew Brzezinski, and the Rothschild banking family, all supposedly acting together in pursuit of world domination.

It's a tough sell. Obama was a year old when Churchill died. The Rothschilds did finance the Napoleonic Wars, but that was quite a while ago, and no record of any meeting between a Bush and a Rothschild exists anywhere. It isn't clear when banker David Rockefeller and diplomat Zbigniew Brzezinski, two men as similar as a pineapple and a frog, first became acquainted. The Illuminati is prominent among a number of real or fictitious aggregations that according to enduring conspiracy theories, seek a New World Order wherein global masses would be forced to live under a unitary government, use a single banking system, spend a common currency, and live according to a uniform lifestyle. Illuminati would be pulling the strings like benevolent wizards. We wouldn't be in Kansas any more, Toto.

The inclusion of the Rothschilds, a 19th-century banking dynasty, together with disparate statesmen of varying political philosophies in the 20th and 21st centuries, is curious. The family has become part and parcel of most grand conspiracy theories, the common denominator of which is a strain of anti-Semitism on the part of the theorists. There's no credible evidence of any collusion, or even a common political philosophy, among the (new) Illuminati.

Anti-Semitism seems to have motivated publication of a document titled *The Protocols of the Elders of Zion,* now considered the Rosetta stone of 20th-century (published) conspiracy theories. Possibly authored as early as 1868, it wasn't widely distributed until 1903 in Czarist Russia. That was a time of pogroms, a mass flight of Jews to Continental Europe and the West, and growing world awareness of Russia's persecution of Jews. It isn't clear that the Elders of Zion ever existed, and if so whether they were latter-day descendants of the Priory of Zion, a collection of monks in the Middle Ages that was cited by Dan Brown in his best-selling book, *The Da Vinci Code*.

Zion, of course, is the homeland promised to Jews by God (Yahweh) in ancient times. In the early 20th century the word became associated with a Jewish liberation crusade, Zionism, a movement that led to the Balfour Declaration in 1917. British diplomat Arthur James Balfour, acting for the government of King George V, delivered a statement of policy to the Second Baron Rothschild (scion of the banking family), endorsing a Jewish state in Palestine. Balfour's timing was unfortunate for the sake of its seizing by conspiracy theorists, who after the publication of *The Protocols* 12 years earlier, had already conceptualized a New World Order scheme involving royalty, diplomats, and financiers. The Balfour Declaration, in particular its personal delivery by a diplomat acting for a king to a Rothschild who called himself a baron, fit the theorists' conspiratorial paradigm like a glove. Balfour should have known better, but British diplomats exist on a higher plane than conspiracy theorists.

In the text of *The Protocols*, a recently conscripted Elder of Zion receives an instruction manual describing how his compatriots will seize control of worldwide media and banking, thus allowing Jews to dominate the globe. Its publication in Russia no doubt mirrored White Russian fears of the pending Russian Revolution (1905) and possibly the Bolshevik Revolution (1917). Regardless, *The Protocols* survived that period and later provided Nazis with propaganda ammunition for their purge of German Jews. It remains favored reading material for neo-Nazis and other hate groups. Despite its durability, most contemporary scholars consider *The Protocols of the Elders of Zion* a hoax.

The Rothschild rumors have too much staying power to have depended on a single fraudulent document. How could it be that the family became connected to conspiracy theories about planned world domination in the first place, given that its patriarch, Mayer Amschel Rothschild, was humbly born in a Frankfurt, Germany ghetto called "Jew Alley" in 1744? It might have to do with the family's habit of having cousins marry cousins, in the same manner as European royalty of the same period. It didn't help that the Rothschilds freely assigned themselves royal monikers like "duke," "baron," and "viscount." Whenever Rothschild offspring did marry outside the family tree, inevitably it was to other aristocrats and wealthy bankers. There were Rothschilds in Germany, Italy, England, Austria, France, and Switzerland, all operating under a coat of arms that included a clenched fist and five arrows, one for each of Mayer Rothschild's sons, and a Latin motto that translated as "harmony, integrity, industry."

When English and French bankers named Rothschild offered Japan financial help for the Russo-Japanese War (1904–1905), Russian nobility naturally supposed the family empathized with revolutionaries inside Russia. In 1909 British Prime Minister David Lloyd George added fuel to the conspiratorial kindling by referring to Lord Nathan Rothschild as "…the most powerful man in Britain." Given further that Queen Victoria's grandchildren included Kaiser Wilhelm II and a Russian Czarina, and that the Rothschilds all had royalist titles evoking a feudal era, it isn't surprising that egalitarians of the Belle Epoque Era saw them as an extension of European monarchies.

That was then, this is now. It takes great imagination to assume the Rothschilds were ever in cahoots with anyone in a grand plot to establish Jewish rule throughout the globe. In fact, the family wasn't even in cahoots with itself. Family dynasties eventually splinter into factions. For three examples, Franklin and Eleanor Roosevelt broke from the family's Republican roots and became Democrats. But their youngest son John became a Republican, like his great-uncle (on his mother's side) Theodore. John D. "Jay" Rockefeller IV, senator from West Virginia, is a Democrat, unlike his ancestors and unlike his uncle Nelson, the former vice president. Maria Shriver, niece of John F. Kennedy and daughter of Sargent Shriver (George McGovern's Democratic running mate in 1972), is married to the Republican Arnold Schwarzenegger, two-term governor of California. Where the Rothschilds are concerned, many individual family members did favor a Jewish state in Palestine and welcomed the Balfour Declaration, but others did not. If the Rothschild family had been part of any grand plot aimed at global domination, it first would have had to overcome divisions among the cousins. Dynastic families are like that.

Abraham Lincoln's murder gave rise to spectacular conspiracy theories. One that has lingered in the 145 years since is that he was assassinated with the encouragement, if not by the direct hand, of the Catholic Church. The extent to which anti-Catholic bias is responsible for the theory's durability depends on how one interprets history.

Hatred of Catholics was rife in the mid-19th century. A flood of Irish Catholics into the United States in the wake of the potato famine created competition for jobs and engendered virulent anti-Catholic sentiment. That in turn gave rise to the American (or "Know-Nothing") Party, a short-lived organization that in 1856 persuaded former president Millard Fillmore to run for president on their ticket. Fillmore carried only the state of Maryland, where nativistic sentiment was strong and where four years later Abraham Lincoln would win a paltry 2.5% of Maryland's total vote. Anti-Catholic sentiment was a bona fide political factor in the 1850s.

But when Lincoln ran in 1860, secession, states' rights, and abolition of slavery were the paramount issues, not religion. The American Party had dissolved. The case for the Catholic Church's involvement in the Lincoln assassination rests largely on the writings of a Canadian-born priest-turned-Presbyterian minister named Charles Chiniquy, who in 1886 published an autobiographical work titled, *Fifty Years in the Church of Rome*. Chiniquy had once been a priest in Illinois, where Lincoln helped him in a legal matter, and it was there that they cemented a friendship. In his book Chiniquy boldly asserted that the Catholic Church was responsible for Lincoln's murder.

Chiniquy's case is anecdotal, and quite weak. He asserted that Southern forces had attacked Fort Sumter only after an assurance of support from Rome, an allegation he supported with an apparently genuine letter written by Pope Pius IX to Jefferson Davis, president of the Confederacy. In that letter Pius reaffirmed his support for the Southern cause and decried rampant anti-Catholic bias in the United States. Chiniquy wrote further that John Harrison Surratt, a Catholic and a Confederate spy who once had been John Wilkes Booth's ally in an abduction plot targeting Lincoln, had been aided by priests in Quebec during his (Surratt's) flight from the United States immediately after the assassination. That much was factually accurate.

Surratt departed Quebec with the aid of Catholic priests. He sailed the Atlantic and eventually reached Rome, where he worked as a Papal Zouave, with or without the knowledge of Pope Pius IX. That was probably the only job Surratt could have found in Europe, given that he was a failed seminary student who had worked only as a Confederate spy during the Civil War. For his part, Booth had earlier visited Canada, where he consulted with officials of the Confederate shadow government there about a germ warfare strategy against the Union. But there's no evidence that Booth and anyone in the Catholic Church made contact during those visits.

Mary Surratt, John's mother, became the first woman executed by the United States government for her alleged role in the assassination itself (unjustly so, although Mary no doubt had been aware of the earlier kidnap plot, which had germinated at her rooming house with her son as Booth's chief lieutenant). Her cause attracted post-mortem sympathy when the priest who gave her the last rites of the church before her hanging complained publicly afterward that he'd been allowed to visit Mary in her prison cell only after promising not to publicly avow his belief in her innocence. In the wake of Mary Surratt's execution Catholic sentiment against Radical Republicans grew very strong, and Mary did become a martyr to the burgeoning women's movement of the 19th century.

All true. But John Wilkes Booth was an Episcopalian, not a Catholic. He did live in Maryland, but he wasn't motivated by religious issues, rather a love for the Confederate cause, a hatred of Lincoln personally, and a belief that Lincoln, who had suspended the writ of habeas corpus and truncated other civil liberties during the War Between the States, was a tyrant on a scale with Julius Caesar.

The assassination was an outgrowth of several quixotic kidnap plots Booth had concocted with Lewis Powell and others. One was planned for Ford's Theater in January 1865, where the gang intended to abduct Lincoln and haul him off by carriage to Richmond under cover of darkness. Booth's intent was to exchange Lincoln for Confederate war prisoners. That plot failed because Lincoln went to another theater on the night in question. Two months later a plan was devised to Shanghai Lincoln from a carriage, en route to an out-of-town theater performance. That also failed because Lincoln didn't appear.

At that point several members of the kidnap band told Booth they'd had enough. Starved for manpower, Booth shifted gears from kidnapping to murder.

It seems clear that Booth had help from unidentified persons on the inside in Washington, as outlined earlier. But how and where the Catholic Church could have entered the picture is hard to conceive. It's unlikely the Vatican hierarchy shed tears over Lincoln's murder, but even less likely it was part of a conspiracy.

In the big picture, unsubstantiated or poorly formulated conspiracy theories, especially those motivated by ethnic or religious biases, disserve honestly motivated conspiracy theorists. Badly motivated theories give ammunition to debunkers who can then say, "Don't believe the rantings and ravings of those conspiracy buffs." Using this line of argument, debunkers are able to draw attention to the political dynamics surrounding a case, and away from the evidence.

Anti-Semitism has motivated conspiracy theories in the past, but hatred of Jews should be divorced from honest criticism of Israel, and even from suspicion of Israel's motives. Regarding 9/11, the presence of nanothermite at Ground Zero, and the extreme unlikelihood that 19 Muslims with little or no flying experience could have executed complicated maneuvers aboard huge jetliners, strongly suggest that powerful forces formulated a clandestine plot aimed at achieving a specific goal, e.g., justifying the invasions of Iraq and Afghanistan.

Some conspiracy theorists believe the CIA, possibly with the active cooperation of Israel's Mossad, conceived and carried out the attacks, in the guise of a plot masterminded by al Qaeda. A full investigation of 9/11 could reveal the truth, and should be undertaken in the face of possible accusations of anti-Semitism on the part of the investigators. In the meantime, to simply ask, as some have done, "Who benefited from 9/11?" as if the question alone establishes a case against Israel, exposes the conspiracy theorist to at least the appearance of anti-Semitism.

Chapter 11. Sometimes Cops Are the Conspiracy Theorists

On the night of March 1, 1932, 20-month-old "Charlie" Lindbergh, first-born son of famed aviator Charles Lindbergh and author Anne Morrow Lindbergh, vanished from his second-story nursery bedroom at Highfields, the family's newly constructed home in the Sourwood Mountains region of Central New Jersey, near the town of Hopewell. The child's apparent kidnapping triggered a blizzard of police activity and a media frenzy that continued unabated for years.

Charles Augustus Lindbergh, "The Lone Eagle," had flown solo from New York to Paris in May 1927 aboard The Spirit of St. Louis, a tiny plane with no window in the front and no radio. A reticent Midwesterner who viewed his accomplishment purely in scientific terms, 25-year-old "Lindy" was unprepared for the public adulation and ceaseless badgering by reporters that began the moment he landed. When two years later he married the shy and bookish daughter of wealthy diplomat Dwight Spencer Morrow, the press dogged Lindy and Anne as they escaped on their honeymoon yacht. When their first child was born in 1930, and nicknamed the "Eaglet" by the press, he became a poster child for media excess. The public could not get enough of the Lindberghs, to the consternation of two private people who hoped to raise their child with some semblance of normalcy and who built their home in a remote area primarily to escape the media onslaught.

Then came the shocking news that the Eaglet had been kidnapped. Actually, nobody should have been shocked. The police certainly weren't.

In the Great Depression year of 1932, kidnappings were as commonplace as insider trading on Wall Street. The press invented a term for them...the "snatch racket." In 1931 more than 1,100 abductions had been reported, while thousands of others went unreported as anguished parents negotiated with kidnappers in confidence. Typically, the child would be returned after a few days in exchange for a ransom payment, one the kidnappers knew the parents could and would pay. Well-to-do families were always targeted. "Ho hum," said the man on the street, who was more worried about finding work amid the Great Depression. "Those rich people can afford it."

In New Jersey kidnapping was a minor crime in 1932, impossible as that might seem in the 21st century. In the Prohibition era organized crime ruled the streets, financed by bootleg liquor and enabled by crooked cops and under-funded law enforcement agencies. The New Jersey State Police, first responders when word of the Lindbergh kidnapping went out, were in fact a paramilitary organization that had been in business for barely ten years. Led by H. Norman Schwarzkopf Sr. (father of the Persian Gulf general), the NJSP were poorly equipped to solve all but the simplest criminal cases. Making things worse, Schwarzkopf himself idolized the much younger Lindbergh, and no doubt out of compassion for his hero Schwarzkopf allowed Lindy to run the investigation from the start. The tail wagged the dog.

But everyone seemed to agree on one point. It had been a carefully thought out crime by a gang working in concert. The Lindbergh family used the house only on weekends, repairing to the Morrow family estate in Englewood during the week. Anne's mother, Elizabeth Cutter Morrow, was a recent widow, and staying by her side also meant Lindy could commute easily to his work in New York City.

On this one occasion Anne Lindbergh decided to stay over in Hopewell, because the Eaglet had been suffering from a cold. March 1, 1932 would prove to be the only Tuesday night ever that the Lindbergh family stayed overnight at Highfields, a decision Anne hadn't made until midday. That fact led the cops to conclude that the kidnap gang had been tipped off about the family's change of plans. How could any random kidnapper(s), acting without inside information and coming from a distance, have known the child had been sick? Would he/they ever have chosen a night when the house was presumably empty?

Considering its remoteness only someone familiar with Highfields' precise location and its narrow access roads could have been running the show, the police reasoned. It had clearly been a team operation, as Lindy himself suggested when he said to his wife beside the empty crib, "Anne, they've stolen our baby."

Charlie Lindbergh's abductor had apparently climbed a crudely built ladder. It was found outside the house, with a cracked side rail that evidently had buckled under the combined weight of the kidnapper and the child as they descended. The ladder had been too short to reach the window, which fact dramatized the difficulty the kidnapper must have faced in entering the nursery, and especially in climbing back down with a child in tow. But investigators concluded that the kidnapper had jimmied a window whose lock didn't work, had taken the Eaglet from his crib, had left a ransom note demanding $50,000 on or beside the windowsill, had somehow managed to regain footing on the ladder, then apparently had fallen to the ground with the child in his arms when the ladder broke. He or she had then fled on foot to a parked car, carrying the (dead?) Eaglet, while leaving the ladder behind as evidence. A chisel that apparently had been used to pry the window open was also found on the lawn.

Remarkably, the abduction took place around 9 p.m., less than an hour after Lindy had arrived by car from New York and while he, Anne, and three family servants were wide awake and active inside the house. This fact alone seemed to rule out a lone kidnapper, who would logically have done the deed while everyone was asleep...assuming, that is, that he'd somehow learned the house would occupied on a Tuesday night. The evidence seemed to implicate someone on the inside, but among Lindbergh's first instructions to Schwarzkopf was, "Don't question my servants. They're above suspicion."

The window had been left open by the kidnapper. It was a cold and windy night, yet Lindy told the police he'd found the ransom note, apparently written by a German or someone pretending to be German, on the windowsill. That must have also aroused the cops' suspicions, because a piece of paper could easily have blown away there, while placing it inside the crib would have ensured that it was read. But Lindy was in charge. The cops might also have wondered why no fingerprints of any kind, not even innocent ones belonging to Anne, the Eaglet or his nurse, were found in the nursery. Someone had evidently seen fit to scrub the entire room clean...

walls, doors, furniture, everything. Who had done such a thing, and why it was done, remain a mystery 78 years later. Certainly it wasn't the kidnapper.

The Lindberghs employed a domestic couple at Highfields, Aloysius (Ollie) Whateley and his wife, Elsie, who worked at the Morrow residence during the week. The Eaglet's nurse, Bessie Mowatt (Betty) Gow, customarily cared for him in Englewood on weekdays, with Anne taking over on weekends, while Betty remained at Next Day Hill, the Morrow estate. But on Tuesday, March 1, Anne summoned Betty to Highfields to help her care for Charlie. Betty arrived there midday in a car driven by Charles Henry Ellerson, a Morrow chauffeur.

Anne's change of plans meant Betty Gow had to cancel a planned nighttime date in Englewood with one Henrik "Red" Johnson, a Swedish-born immigrant she had first met on the coast of Maine. The Morrows and the Lamont family, their neighbors in Englewood, also had neighboring vacation homes there. Johnson worked on the Lamonts' yacht in the summer of 1931, when a romance developed between him and Betty. After the summer Red followed Betty to Northern New Jersey, where he lived in a rooming house and continued to see her.

Police were understandably curious about how the kidnap gang could have known about Anne Lindbergh's sudden change of plans on March 1. Red Johnson provided a possible clue to the quandary. Before leaving Englewood for Highfields with Ellerson, Betty had left a message with Red's landlady that their date was off. Red returned the call, but too late to catch Betty. Violet Sharpe, a Morrow servant who answered the phone, confirmed to Red that Betty had left for Hopewell. Thus, the police figured, Red Johnson and Charles Henry Ellerson were two people of interest in the case, as they were privy to information helpful to a kidnap gang, i.e., the Lindbergh family would be staying at Highfields on a Tuesday night for the first time ever. Others who knew this were Violet Sharpe and Red Johnson's landlady. To the cops it seemed clear that whoever had planned the kidnapping had been in touch with at least one of these four people during that day.

The cops' interest in Johnson intensified after they learned that Red had placed a long-distance call to Highfields that evening. Red later claimed it was simply to confirm with Betty that their date had been broken, and to tell her he'd decided to visit his brother in Hartford, Connecticut. But Johnson had known the date was off since lunchtime, because Betty had left him a message to that effect before leaving Englewood, and Violet Sharpe had confirmed it to him. Besides, Betty was gone. Yet Red said he'd placed a toll call from 60 miles away to make sure, and to tell Betty he'd suddenly decided to go see a brother who lived almost four hours away by car, on a wintry night in the middle of the week. It all sounded fishy to the police, so they pursued Johnson and found him in his car in Connecticut. In the back seat was a milk bottle, which seemed to fit in with a young child's abduction. But Johnson convinced the cops he was devoted to milk, and because there was no direct evidence of his involvement in the crime, they let him go about his business. Several years later he was deported to Sweden.

Meanwhile, back at Highfields, the Lindberghs' garage had been converted into a temporary police headquarters. Lindy and the cops fielded phone calls from newspaper reporters, radio stations, other law enforcement agencies, and the public. Lindy remained in charge. Most of the calls were genuine, if not immediately helpful to the investigators. Others were obvious hoaxes. Finally a call came in from a retired educator in the Bronx named John F. Condon, who, acting on his own, had placed a notice in a local newspaper, *The Bronx Home News*, offering to act as an intermediary between the kidnapper(s) and the Lindberghs. Condon had received an immediate response to his notice, so he said, and over the phone he described an odd symbol that had been affixed to the kidnappers' message—three interlocking circles colored red, white, and blue.

Lindbergh glanced again at the ransom note he'd found and saved for the police. It had the same interlocking circles! Was there any way Condon could have known this? It seemed clear that Condon had connected with someone in the kidnap gang, so Lindy invited Condon to meet with him at Highfields. Condon agreed. Because Condon didn't drive, he summoned a friend and former prizefighter, Al Reich, to get him to Hopewell. He spent the night sleeping in the nursery from which the Eaglet had been abducted.

The cops were curious about Condon, and not merely because he might have been in touch with the kidnapper of the Lindbergh child. How could Condon have intuited that a random kidnapper in Central New Jersey would be reading a neighborhood newspaper like *The Bronx Home News*? What were the odds? If nothing else, it seemed to rule out the possibility that a single individual had committed the crime. And, the cops wondered, was Condon himself part of the gang?

Condon received several more communications from the apparent perpetrator, either by mail or by delivery to his home. He replied to each through follow-up ads in the newspaper, using the alias "Jafsie," a variation on his initials, JFC. Condon wanted to keep everything on the QT to avoid scaring his pen pal away, and finally he convinced the mystery man to meet him under the cover of darkness at nearby Woodlawn Cemetery, with nobody else present. The cops wanted to follow from a respectful distance and possibly make an arrest, but Jafsie, a long-winded man (to some a pompous blowhard) who had abiding faith in his own powers of persuasion, insisted that he be allowed to go alone. This was brave of the 72-year-old Condon, who for all he knew might have been facing a gang of desperate criminals half his age. But to the cops, Condon's bravura also suggested that he might have known exactly whomever he had agreed to meet, given that the individual had responded so quickly to his note in a local newspaper and had trusted him to come alone.

It turned out to be a medium-sized individual with a Teutonic accent. In the course of their conversation Condon asked, "Are you German?"

"No, Scandinavian," the man replied. He identified himself as "John," which Condon thought was an odd name for one of Scandinavian descent, probably an alias. But the name "Cemetery John" stuck, and has been used ever since in describing the person Condon negotiated with. John cited unnamed others as being in cahoots with him in the kidnap caper, which he said had been planned for many months.

Cemetery John was annoyed that Condon hadn't brought the ransom money with him, but agreed to meet him on the night of April 2 at St. Raymond's Cemetery, about ten miles to the south of Woodlawn, to make the transfer. By then Lindbergh had raised $50,000, which the authorities converted into gold certificates for identification purposes. Lindy insisted on driving Condon to St. Raymond's; Jafsie agreed, but he convinced Lindy to remain in the car, about 400 feet away, while he handed over the money in exchange for written directions to the spot where the Eaglet was purportedly being held. It turned out to be a boat named "Nelly," anchored near Martha's Vineyard in Massachusetts.

The writer of the directions wrote "Boad Nelly." "Boad" is a verbalism that a literate German familiar with English would never have used in writing the word. It seemed that whoever wrote the note had erroneously assumed the "d" sound that replaced "t" in Germanic speech would also substitute for it when writing the word. Not so...a German-born person might pronounce the word "boat" as "boad," but would still spell it "boat." That error made it likely the writer was not a German, but was pretending to be one for some reason. Lindy overrode Condon's protests and allowed Cemetery John to flee St. Raymond's, fearing that to capture him before the child was recovered would jeopardize the Eaglet's safety. Lindy chartered a plane and flew to the supposed site on the Massachusetts coast. There was no "Boad Nelly," and no Eaglet. Lindy had been duped.

About seven weeks later a child's body was found in the woods near Hopewell, alongside the main road between Hopewell and Princeton. Despite its extreme decomposition Lindy quickly identified it as his son's. The body was immediately cremated without an autopsy, and no funeral service was held. The nation mourned. All that remained, it appeared, was to find the gang that had murdered America's favorite little boy.

Appearances can deceive. The woods surrounding the village of Hopewell comprise hundreds of thousands of acres, yet a passing motorist named William Allen said he had found the child's corpse, 75 feet in from the road, after stopping to relieve himself. Because Allen was an African-American, who in 1932 would not have been allowed to use a public restroom in New Jersey, his excuse for entering the woods seemed credible at first blush.

But in May the trees are in full blossom in New Jersey, so Allen hadn't needed to walk anywhere near 75 feet to gain privacy. Fifteen or twenty feet would have easily sufficed. Yet Allen said he had continued to push his way through dense underbrush, seeking further privacy, until *voilà*, there lay a dead child! He had found a needle in a haystack.

Because everyone assumed Lindbergh would recognize his own child, even in a badly decomposed state, and as nobody wanted to intrude on his grief, only a few skeptical cops wondered about the odd circumstances surrounding Allen's discovery. It had been far too pat, some thought. And, why had the body been left near the most heavily traveled road in Hopewell? Would a kidnapper have risked being discovered in the process of disposing of a dead body there? Assuming the child had died in a fall from the broken ladder, wouldn't a kidnapper have ditched the corpse in a secluded place as quickly as possible?

Normally, yes. But there was good reason to suspect that the Eaglet's body had been deposited near the Hopewell-Princeton Road on purpose, and that William Allen had been recruited to find it there. The road was a main artery for bootleg liquor transport in 1932, and mobsters might well have become uneasy from seeing teams of volunteer investigators prowling the area for weeks, searching for clues. Better to end the mystery and chase away the crowds by having the body "discovered," then go on with your illegal business. Granted, that's a conspiracy theory...but history has proven J. Edgar Hoover wrong. There really is a Mafia, they were into bootleg liquor back then, and conspiracy is their modus operandi.

The case dragged on. A few ransom bills appeared in circulation, too randomly to be tied to one person. About a year after the kidnapping, and just prior to the (newly elected) Roosevelt administration's mandated deadline for turning in gold certificates, someone laundered (deposited) $2,980 in the Corn Exchange Bank in New York. The deposit ticket bore the name "J.J. Faulkner." This became the first large transaction involving Lindbergh ransom money. But by the time bankers realized the money was hot, the depositor had left the scene.

New York and New Jersey cops, and agents from the Bureau of Investigation (it wasn't yet called the FBI) launched a manhunt for J.J. Faulkner. They never found such a person. But in its search the BI did find the inscription "J/J Faulkner" on a dumbwaiter roster at the Plymouth Apartments in Uptown Manhattan. This intrigued them, because a recent superintendent of that building, one Duane Baker (Bacon), was an ex-con with a lengthy criminal resume. Baker had fled Plymouth with the rent receipts in his pocket on April 15, 1932, less than two weeks after the ransom exchange between Condon and Cemetery John at St. Raymond's Cemetery, and hadn't been seen since.

"J/J Faulkner" wasn't a real person. The letters stood for Jane and Jane Faulkner, a mother and daughter who had once lived together at Plymouth and whose names had never been removed from the dumbwaiter roster after they moved out. The mother had died before 1932, meanwhile the daughter had married a man named Carl Geissler and had relocated to Larchmont, New York, a Westchester County suburb.

The trail got hotter. It turned out that Carl Geissler worked for the same company as a man named Ralph Hacker, who turned out to be John F. Condon's son-in-law! What also fascinated investigators was that Baker had once worked as a driver for Armour Meat Packing Company, succeeding the very same Charles Henry Ellerson who had driven Betty Gow to Highfields on March 1, 1932. Baker and Ellerson had also been seen together at a Fort Lee, New Jersey speakeasy called "Sha-Toe," pronounced "chateau."

Even more suspiciously, a day before the discovery of the Lindbergh child's body near the Hopewell–Princeton Road, Ellerson's car had disappeared over a cliff along the New Jersey Palisades and burned beyond recognition. Ellerson escaped with his life at the last second by jumping from the car.

Were these mere coincidences, the Baker/Ellerson connection and the one involving Faulkner/Geissler/Hacker/Condon? Had Baker, needing a convenient alias under which to launder Lindbergh ransom money, seen "J/J Faulkner" on his dumbwaiter and used it as a single name, assuming it couldn't be traced to any particular person? Had Ellerson recommended Baker for his job at Armour, and remained friends with him afterward? Had Ellerson's car been used to transport a dead child to his final resting place for the reasons cited, after which it had been wrecked to destroy evidence? Was Baker a kidnapper, or merely an extortionist?

We never found out. The Geisslers were cleared after an investigation. Baker (whose wife was German) and Ellerson were never arrested. In fact, after having been fired by Mrs. Morrow for reasons having nothing to do with the Lindbergh case, Ellerson was later rehired.

In September 1934 a German-born carpenter living in the Bronx, Bruno Richard Hauptmann, passed a $10 ransom bill in payment for gasoline at a nearby service station. When the suspicious attendant recognized the bill as a gold certificate, he jotted down Hauptmann's license plate number on the back, and notified police. This chance event provided the cops with their first break in the case. They staked out Hauptmann's residence overnight, allowed him to leave it by car the next morning, then blockaded traffic and arrested Hauptmann.

The cops found approximately $14,000 of Lindbergh ransom money in the garage across a dirt road from the house where Hauptmann rented the second-story apartment. Some of the bills were hidden under boards that had been nailed down, in an obvious effort to conceal their location.

"Where did you get this money?" police demanded to know.

"I was holding it for a friend, Isidor Fisch, who went home to Germany," claimed Hauptmann. It turned out Fisch had died in Germany the previous year, so the carpenter's alibi wasn't verifiable. Hauptmann maintained that he and Fisch had been business partners, with Isidor trading fur pellets and Bruno (he preferred to be called "Richard") trading stocks for profit. But Hauptmann produced no business records to validate the partnership's existence. Even worse, he had made no effort to settle with Fisch's heirs after his death. Hauptmann had simply spent freely from the money Fisch had entrusted to him, claiming Fisch had owed him separately. It all sounded fishy...the press called it Hauptmann's "Fisch story."

The police were sure Hauptmann was somehow connected to the Lindbergh kidnapping. He had stopped working as a carpenter at about the same time. His story of how and when he had first met Fisch (he said it was after March 1, 1932) didn't square with the testimony of friends (who said it was before then). Hauptmann had spent quite freely since 1932, especially for someone who had passed his time trading stocks during the Great Depression.

But having a pile of Lindbergh ransom money in his possession, and cheating his friend's estate, made Hauptmann a possible extortionist and a disloyal friend. It didn't make him a kidnapper. Somehow Hauptmann had to be placed in Hopewell on Mar. 1, 1932, or directly connected to a gang that had abducted the child. The case had dragged on too long. The public wouldn't settle for the arrest of a mere extortionist after two-and-a-half years.

Finding witnesses in Hopewell proved to be a hard task for the cops, though they tried mightily. The two they found were unreliable. A local man named Millard Whited had a reputation so poor his own family didn't trust him, and he'd said back in 1932 that no, he hadn't seen anyone suspicious at the time of the kidnapping. Now, after being promised a share of the reward money, Whited gladly identified Hauptmann as one he'd seen driving near Highfields. The other "eyewitness" was one Amandus Hochmuth, a nearly blind octogenarian who identified a flowerpot as a woman's hat in the office of Governor Harold Hoffman, who interceded in the case following Hauptmann's conviction in 1935.

Hauptmann's own alibi witnesses were more credible. Several testified to having seen him at his wife's place of business in the Bronx on the night in question, which would have ruled out his being in Hopewell, at least four hours away by car, on the same night. None of these people were known to be liars, and none had vision problems. In the end, though, their testimonies carried less weight with the jury than those of Whited and Hochmuth.

Hauptmann's trial at Flemington, New Jersey began on Jan. 2, 1935. It became a three-ring circus, with a voracious press corps competing for hotel and courtroom space with celebrities, including Damon Runyon and Jack Benny. Hauptmann was indigent, ransom money not being legal tender, so the Hearst newspaper chain agreed to pay for his attorney in exchange for an exclusive on trial gossip. That lawyer turned out to be Edward J. "Death House" Reilly, a once redoubtable defender whose recent succession of convicted murderers had earned him the sarcastic nickname. Reilly had dissipated into an alcoholic state, and spent almost no time with Hauptmann, his client. But he was so expansive with the press during his nightly happy-hour news conferences that William Randolph Hearst easily got his money's worth.

Hauptmann clearly didn't. Both Lindbergh and Condon identified the carpenter as Cemetery John in court, which effectively sealed his doom. Their testimonies were very curious, because Lindy had heard Cemetery John utter only two words, "Hey, Doctor," from a distance of at least 400 feet at St. Raymond's Cemetery. Lindy had also expressed doubt at that time that he could identify anyone based on a single instance. Yet he did so in court, confidently. For his part Condon had failed to pick out Hauptmann in a police lineup just after the carpenter's arrest. But their emphatic testimonies in court outweighed all other factors. Other key prosecution witnesses testified that Hauptmann had written the ransom notes and had built the ladder found outside Highfields on the night of the kidnapping. The chisel found on the lawn was linked to Hauptmann's own toolbox. The jury found Hauptmann guilty of felony murder and sentenced him to death in the electric chair. The verdict was upheld on appeal.

What about the rest of the gang? Had Hauptmann suddenly become a lonely scapegoat for others? Hadn't everyone assumed all along that the kidnapping of Charlie Lindbergh was a team effort?

Governor Hoffman, who was already being mentioned as a possible Republican vice-presidential nominee in 1936, put his political future on the line. He wondered about Hauptmann's accomplices, and defied public sentiment by instituting a de facto appeal process. Hoffman appointed his own private investigator to the case, the legendary Ellis Parker, and against all established protocol Hoffman personally visited Hauptmann at his Trenton prison cell. From these meetings came an offer to Hauptmann. "Tell us who was in this with you and we'll commute your sentence to life imprisonment."

The German was intransigent. In the face of the evidence he proclaimed his absolute innocence. Since nobody believed that Hauptmann had merely held ransom money for a man who had died, one whose relatives he had never contacted after the fact about their supposed inheritances, it was impossible to imagine Hauptmann having been framed. Then again, would any sane person submit to a ghastly death in the electric chair when simply naming others (or inventing names, had he really been a lone kidnapper) could have saved his life?

A reasonable person might conclude that organized crime had hired a gang to kidnap the Eaglet, not to glom $50,000 but to get Al Capone out of jail, where he had been sent for income tax evasion, and that the ransom note had been a ruse. From his prison cell Capone promised to return the child to the Lindberghs in exchange for his freedom, a promise he never could have fulfilled had Hauptmann been a lone kidnapper, simply because Capone wouldn't have known who he was. Capone was hated and feared by many, but his worst enemy never accused him of being stupid. It would have been beyond stupid of Capone to make a promise he couldn't fulfill. What Capone didn't know was that the kidnap gang had screwed up, and the Eaglet had died.

The cops allowed Lindbergh himself to decide about Capone's offer, and he turned Big Al down. But had the kidnapping in fact been a mob escapade, it would go far to explain Hauptmann's decision to maintain total innocence and die in the electric chair. Mob tactics weren't well understood in the 1930s, but thanks to Joe Valachi and others we now know that organized crime unhesitatingly threatens the loved ones of anyone who rats them out from prison. It's entirely possible, even likely, that Hauptmann had received such a threat regarding his wife and infant son, and that he went to the chair to protect them from mob retaliation. The alternative for Hauptmann would have been spending a lifetime in prison without a wife and son to visit him.

There was another reason to suspect the mob in the case, but it never reached the jury's ears. After failing to identify Hauptmann as Cemetery John at the lineup, Condon had told B.I. agent Leon Turrou, "...They'll kill me. My life won't be worth five cents [if I make a positive identification]." Condon's reference was clearly to the mob. Only after realizing that Hauptmann would be going on trial as a lone kidnapper, and that the case would end with a guilty verdict, did Condon feel safe. He reversed himself, and with a melodramatic flourish testified, "...[Cemetery] John is Bru-no Rich-ard Haupt-mann!"

In prison, Hauptmann had pleaded to Hoffman and to anyone who would listen that he couldn't possibly have been Cemetery John. His argument was irrefutable. Condon had seen him twice at close range and had given the cops his description. Cemetery John was a marked man after April 2, 1932. He had been involved in the crime of the century. Yet Hauptmann moved freely about the Bronx for two-and-a-half years after the kidnapping, never once disguising himself, never growing facial hair, never in any way behaving as if he feared being identified. Hauptmann frequented City Island, a Bronx resort area where Condon lived in the summer. It's very probable that the two men saw each other there more than once. Meanwhile the cops were on constant lookout for a man matching Cemetery John's description. He was there in plain sight, and the cops were desperate to arrest someone, anyone...nevertheless Hauptmann, the most sought-after criminal in the country, was never once stopped for questioning in 30 months time.

The case remains a stain upon New Jersey's justice system. Anna Hauptmann spent the next 60 years trying to prove her husband had picked her up at work on the night of the kidnapping, an effort that drew compassion even from many who thought he was guilty as hell. Numerous efforts to reopen the case failed (the present author was politely turned down by Governor Christine Todd Whitman), prosecutor David Wilentz went on to become a prominent political figure in the state, and books proliferated that viewed the case from every possible angle.

Back in the day, even the governor's own skepticism wasn't enough to stem the tide of justice. Hauptmann wouldn't talk, so Hoffman gave up his inquiry, and Hauptmann was executed on April 3, 1936. By then the Lindbergh family had fled to England, sick to death of the endless press attention and fearful about repeated threats to the life of their second son, Jon.

For the purposes of this book it suffices for us to understand that the term "conspiracy theorist" doesn't apply only to people who challenge the conventional wisdom. In the Lindbergh case almost everyone was a conspiracy theorist...New Jersey and New York cops, the Bureau of Investigation, Al Capone, the press, Jafsie Condon, even Charles Lindbergh himself all assumed a gang had committed the crime. It was the majority belief, and the evidence supported it. Debunkers, those who thought Hauptmann had acted alone, constituted a small minority. They included prosecutor Wilentz, a psychologist named Dudley Schoenfeld (who never examined Hauptmann, or even met him, yet drew a profile of a remorseless lone-wolf killer that served Wilentz' purposes), and twelve jurors who accepted Wilentz' eleventh-hour argument that Hauptmann had pulled off the crime of the century, all by his lonesome.

CHAPTER 12. WHEN A RULING AUTHORITY BECOMES THE CONSPIRACY THEORIST

Any skeptic who questions his government's official explanation of a controversial event will be called a conspiracy theorist, often as an accusation. But cops are never called conspiracy theorists, nor are FBI or CIA agents, even though conspiracies are intrinsic to their work. When the government itself imagines a conspiracy against American interests, that's never a theory, either. It's a call to arms, or at least a convenient political argument. Iconoclasts who in turn question their government's conspiracy theories are called unpatriotic or worse.

Except dissent is not unpatriotic. If it were, we'd all be driving on the left side of the road and paying taxes to the Chancellor of the Exchequer.

Medieval kings who suspected conspirators of plotting against them had the scoundrels arrested and summarily executed. There was no need to prove an actual conspiracy to the masses. The Tower of London operated independently from Old Bailey. The Glorious Revolution in 1688 did lead England to a more democratic model called a constitutional monarchy, and the American and French revolutions a century later further distanced the world from divinely granted authority.

The Industrial Revolution of the 19th and 20th centuries, in particular technological advances in communications and travel, has made the world a smaller place. This was self-evident when John Glenn orbited the Earth in 1962 before a nationwide television audience; it's even more obvious today, when one places a telephone service call in Miami or Seattle and is connected to someone in India. The complexity of e-mail communications in a fiber-optic world can mean a message sent from Japan to Korea might be routed through Atlanta, and one between two neighbors in Florida can detour through New Zealand, all it a matter of seconds.

A subtle consequence of the shrinking world is that global conspiracy theories become easier to promote. A threat from a perceived enemy looms nearer, and in the hands of a demagogue seeking to consolidate power, declared threats (both genuine and contrived) can be used to inspire widespread fear and dictate national policy. This clearly happened after 9/11/2001.

The Soviet Union collapsed in 1991. For the preceding 72 years Communism had been the bogeyman of choice for American demagogues, beginning with the Red scare that followed World War I. But Marxist–Leninist ideology had never been compatible with durable economic prosperity. Single-party rule always invites corruption and societal stagnation. Communism was doomed to failure from the outset. Yet oddly, when A. Mitchell Palmer, J. Edgar Hoover, Richard M. Nixon, and Joseph R. McCarthy used anarchists, socialists, and Communists as political punching bags for five decades beginning after World War I, it wasn't Marxist economics or Stalinist brutality that was portrayed as the threat to the American way of life. Josef Stalin, we now know, wasn't a Communist ideologue. The threat was "Godless Communism," which supposedly had infiltrated government, labor, schools, even the military. In this construct anarchy equated with atheism, socialism and Communism were interchangeable nouns, and everyone in the 20th-century labor movement was in cahoots with all the rascals in a vast conspiracy to undermine traditional values.

Between November 1919 and January 1920 Attorney General Palmer responded to a series of building explosions in eight American cities the previous June (including one at his own home) by deporting over 500 left-wing radicals he suspected of being responsible. Palmer was the highest-ranking legal official in the country, yet he saw no need for pursuing the matter through the criminal justice system. He just shipped the suspects out without a trial. Palmer framed his actions as necessary against a growing cancer that threatened our way of life, one which American doughboys so recently had fought to preserve at Chateau-Thierry and Belleau Wood. Patriotism always sells.

The aftermath of a war seems to engender a search for new bogeymen. It happened again a generation later. The ink was barely dry on the Japanese surrender documents when the House Un-American Activities Committee (HUAC), first organized in 1938 by Republicans seeking to root out subversives while embarrassing Franklin D. Roosevelt, continued its work by targeting real and suspected Communists in the literary and entertainment fields. Left-leaning playwrights and screenwriters were summoned to testify before Congress and asked to identify colleagues who shared their political views. Those who asserted their Constitutional privilege and refused to cooperate found themselves blacklisted by Hollywood studios.

Meanwhile Winston Churchill, who had guided Britain's inspiring resistance to German aggression before Pearl Harbor and became America's staunch ally afterward, added fuel to the fire in a 1946 speech at Fulton, Missouri. Sir Winston lamented that an "Iron Curtain" had fallen over Eastern Europe. For HUAC and those who believed Communism was a worldwide conspiracy of evil, Churchill's speech was a godsend. A hero of the war had spoken out against the newest world evil, as if he'd undergone a sudden epiphany about Marxist–Leninist ideology and Josef Stalin.

Not really. Forgotten was that Churchill had previously consented to the division of postwar Europe in conferences with Roosevelt at Casablanca, with Roosevelt and Stalin at Teheran and Yalta, and with Truman and Stalin at Potsdam. The Allies had willingly (if misguidedly) conceded Soviet hegemony over Eastern Europe; given Stalin's brutal methods, an Iron Curtain was certain to fall, and Sir Winston was too savvy not to have known it all along. Also overlooked was that Churchill had been fighting England's real and imagined enemies since 1898, when he marched alongside Lord Kitchener at Omdurman in the (Anglo–Egyptian) Sudan, battling Mahdi warlords with crude weapons who represented no conceivable threat to the English homeland. And, that Sir Winston had led the doomed Gallipoli campaign against Ottoman Turks at the onset of World War I. And (as cited by BBC journalist Greg Palast in his book *Armed Madhouse*), that Churchill had once written, when England was preparing to draw a new map for the Middle East, "I am strongly in favor of using poisoned gas against uncivilized tribes to spread a lively terror...against recalcitrant Arabs as an experiment."

Churchill was always an eager warlord, and the Iron Curtain speech should be considered in that context. Like Abraham Lincoln and John F. Kennedy, Sir Winston was a master wordsmith, and also like them, he inspired the masses using eloquence. Unlike Lincoln and Kennedy, Churchill thrived on armed conflict. The "Empire on which the Sun never set" was at its apex when Churchill first built his reputation as a British imperialist in Africa, but by 1946 Britain had become a fading empire, a casualty of its own noble intentions. His Tory government, in fact, was voted out of office mere months after V-E Day, the glorious echoes of Dunkirk and the Battle of Britain having yielded to national disquiet over economic conditions.

But Churchill's Iron Curtain speech, delivered on American soil, melded with a grand conspiracy theory already extant in the United States, i.e., Communists were everywhere among us, and the threat could only be dealt with proactively. His timing was exquisite, and he was preaching to a choir of conspiracy theorists...not skeptics, that is, theorists within the United States government.

Domestic forces took it from there, aided by the new technological toy, television. As America looked on from its living rooms, a young Congressman from California, Richard Nixon, pursued a one-time fellow traveler named Alger Hiss through a maze of prewar associations, finally establishing that Hiss had lied about not having been a Communist back then. Being a Communist had never been a crime; in fact, when Hiss had been mixed up with the "wrong people," the Soviet Union was our ally and Franklin Roosevelt was admitting to cordial relationships with a number of Communists.

If religious zealots had gone after a former atheist who now believed in God, one whose crime was having sworn under oath he'd never been a nonbeliever, that would constitute perjury...but no prosecutor would have gone near it. Timing is everything. Hiss' self-protective lie cost him his freedom and at once jump-started Richard Nixon's career.

By 1950 a Communist takeover had forced the Nationalist Chinese government of Chiang Kai-shek onto the island of Formosa (now Taiwan). This fact gave Red-baiting ideologues in Congress added leverage. Nixon parlayed his successful pursuit of Hiss into a successful campaign for the US Senate against liberal Democrat Helen Gahagan Douglas. In the kind of slur that marked his political career, Nixon referred to Mrs. Douglas as the "pink lady," a pejorative that suggested she wasn't quite a Red sympathizer, only that she couldn't comprehend the dangers of worldwide Communism. Nixon's cause was advanced by the fact that his opponent was an ex-actress, married to actor Melvyn Douglas, at a time when Hollywood was seen as a primary locus of the grand conspiracy.

The Korean conflict had been underway for five months when Nixon and Douglas squared off. Korea had been under Japanese rule since 1910 (they called it "Chosen"), and in the wake of Japan's defeat in World War II the United States and Soviet Union agreed to a division of the country along the 38th parallel. When North Korean armies, backed by Communist Chinese forces, invaded the South, President Truman committed American troops under the generalship of Douglas MacArthur to the region.

As in the United States nine decades earlier and in Vietnam two decades later, the struggle was a civil war between two groups of Koreans, Northern and Southern. But they were all one people, fighting as patriots to control their homeland. The arbitrary 38th parallel, established by two countries that didn't even border Korea and had no reason beyond the spoils of war to determine its internal affairs, hadn't divided indigenous Koreans along anthropological lines. Except for the deadly fear of Communism that had already embedded itself in American political thought, together with the fall of China to the Communists the previous year, the United States would never have gone into Korea.

The Korean conflict ended with a truce agreement three years later, but the second Red scare of the 20th century continued apace, led by Sen. Joseph R. McCarthy (R-WI), who had been railing against Communist infiltration of the State Department since 1950. A snarling alcoholic who had first misrepresented his war record to get elected, in 1954 McCarthy held Senate hearings designed to expose thousands of Communists he claimed had invaded the Pentagon, all of whom were on a list McCarthy held "...right here in my hand..." but which he never showed to anyone. Television audiences sat transfixed as the Wisconsin senator interrogated a succession of lowly government clerks who, it came out many years later, had been chosen as witnesses not for any important information they had, or any left-leaning instincts of their own, but for their lack of sophistication and susceptibility to intimidation by McCarthy.

After being excoriated for his methods by CBS-TV newsman Edward R. Murrow, and challenged during an interrogation by attorney Joseph Welch ("At long last, sir, have you left no sense of decency?"), McCarthy eventually found himself censured by previously hesitant Senate colleagues. He lost his influence and died in 1957, a casualty of demon rum. The eponymic label "McCarthyism" has since applied to those who abuse power ruthlessly while defaming innocent people.

Notwithstanding McCarthy's fate, anti-Communist fervor remained a dominant factor in American politics. It led to a nuclear arms race with the Soviet Union, reciprocal spying and the U-2 incident, the Bay of Pigs fiasco and the Cuban missile crisis, and eventually the Vietnam conflict.

Our Vietnam policy was predicated on a corollary of anti-Communist doctrine called the Domino Theory. It went, "If we don't stop the Commies [here], they'll topple every neighboring country in sequence, and eventually they'll rule the globe." We didn't stop them in Vietnam, yet somehow Thailand, Malaysia and Singapore remained free from outside domination at every moment between the fall of Saigon (1975) and the collapse of the Soviet Union (1991). Theorists who suspected a grand plot to enslave the world might have first pondered the Soviet Union's headaches with satellite countries like Hungary and Yugoslavia, and its reciprocal mistrust of Communist China. But common sense doesn't necessarily motivate political action. Whenever logic contradicts imperatives like control of the world's oil supplies or the needs of the military–industrial complex, the profit motive and governmental conspiracy theories act together to contravene it.

Despite official denials, it's absolutely clear from the Downing Street minutes that the United States and Great Britain had been discussing an invasion of Iraq before 9/11/2001, and that intelligence was being manipu-lated to justify it. But discovering that Saddam Hussein had weapons of mass destruction (those weapons were never clearly defined, but the words "mass destruction" meant something more than low-yield bombs and deadly chemicals) might not have sufficed to sell the public on the need for a unilateral invasion of Iraq. After all, Saddam's brutality had been visited almost entirely on his own people, and toward that end Saddam had used weapons sold to him by the United States for use against Iran.

Even if dangerous weapons were to be found in Iraq, something more would be needed to ensure public approval of a more aggressive Middle Eastern policy (along the lines of the Project for a New American Century). If a "new Pearl Harbor" could be combined with a broad-brush conspiracy theory about a "Muslim caliphate extending from Spain to Indonesia," as articulated by Vice President Dick Cheney, Secretary of Defense Donald Rumsfeld, and President Bush himself (although Bush used the words "totalitarian empire" instead of "caliphate"), the package might sell. And, should WMD never be found in Iraq, the Muslim conspiracy notion could be a powerful substitute rationale, a kind of Plan B in the propaganda chain, ahead of "Saddam was trying to buy yellowcake uranium from Niger," "Saddam and Osama bin Laden are in collusion," and "We need to create a Western-style democracy in the Middle East."

The Muslim Caliphate Theory carried risks. One was that the public would realize that 15 of the 19 Muslims who were identified as 9/11 terrorists were from Saudi Arabia, a US ally, and that the Bush and bin Laden families had been connected for decades through the oil business. It's hard to demonize a whole religion, Islam, by claiming that one man controls a Muslim caliphate from Spain to Indonesia. That's a bit like alleging that the Irish Republican Army was reporting to the pope. It's even harder after President Bush has said publicly, six months after 9/11 and a year before the invasion of Iraq, "I don't think about Osama bin Laden any more." You don't think about a man who's directing a grand Muslim conspiracy extending halfway around the globe, Mr. President?

Another risk was that members of the Bush administration would tell conflicting versions of the story, thus reducing the caliphate theory's credibility. This happened, as a matter of fact. Secretary of Defense Rumsfeld claimed that "Iraq would serve as the base of a new Islamic caliphate to extend throughout the Middle East and which would threaten legitimate governments in Europe, Africa, and Asia." Iraq? If so, that would have taken Osama bin Laden out of the picture. Iraq couldn't possibly have served as the caliphate's base of operations, because in that paradigm Saddam Hussein would have been the man in charge. Except, bin Laden had called him an "infidel."

Saddam was a secular Muslim, closely aligned with the Sunnis, a minority in his own country. He was widely mistrusted, even hated, by Muslims of all sects outside Iraq's borders, especially Kurds and Iranian Shiites. Saddam Hussein would have been the least likely person for Muslims from Spain to Indonesia to ever anoint as their caliph, yet the Secretary of Defense saw fit to proclaim Iraq as the epicenter of a Muslim caliphate.

Of course, if Saddam were to be captured and executed, as did in fact happen, then no Muslim caliphate based in Iraq could possibly have existed, unless it were run by the same people the United States had approved as Saddam Hussein's successors. In that case the Bush administration would have had some explaining to do to the families of 4,000 dead soldiers. The Muslim Caliphate Theory is nonsensical on its face, bur it remains gospel

among neoconservative ideologues. No one connected to the Bush administration has publicly renounced it.

Logic and common sense are inimical to a hawkish foreign policy. It's
more important to inspire fear in the body politic, and toward that end to
define an enemy in the broadest possible terms, as in, "vast conspiracy of
evil [Communism]" and, "caliphate from Spain to Indonesia [Islam]". What
helps even more is a catalyzing event like 9/11, one that terrifies the majority
of the public and converts the rest into conspiracy theorists.

Chapter 13. Reinvestigating 9/11

This book assumes that a new investigation of the terrorist attacks of 9/11/01 is needed, one that is unbiased, unfettered by politics, and spares no sacred cows. The following questions and more must be answered for the sake of the historical record. If a conspiracy beyond what is currently believed is uncovered, those responsible must be called to account.

- How did 19 Muslims avoid security at four separate locations on the same day?
- Why didn't any of those 19 names appear on a passenger manifest?
- Why was nanothermite, a powerful explosive used exclusively by the military, found in the rubble at Ground Zero?
- Could steel-reinforced skyscrapers collapse vertically without having been undermined?
- Did our aeronautical defense system fail from treachery, or from mere incompetence, and how did the terrorists know it would fail?
- Was Mohammed Atta aboard Jack Abramoff's yacht several days before 9/11, as several witnesses have claimed?
- Why did Theodore Olson claim that he spoke with his wife (while she was aboard Flight 77) on two occasions, when neither conversation took place?
- Why did the owner of WTC 7 say the building should be "pulled" (destroyed by explosives)?

• Could four jetliner crashes have left no debris and no human remains behind at any of three separate locations, albeit an accused terrorist's passport was found intact amidst the rubble of Ground Zero?

• Was the damage at the Pentagon consistent with impact from a Boeing 757, or did a guided missile strike the building?

• Did Cheney insist on a stand-down posture as a plane approached the Pentagon, or was the plane supposed to have been shot down?

• How could BBC have broadcast the collapse of WTC 7 before it ever happened?

• Why, as Thomas Kean claimed afterward, did NORAD repeatedly lie to his commission?

• Why, in March 2002, did Bush say he wasn't thinking about Osama bin Laden any more, if bin Laden had been the mastermind of 9/11?

• Was the plane that crashed in Shanksville, PA shot down?

• Could amateur pilots have maneuvered huge jetliners that skillfully?

• Are some of the 19 alleged suicide terrorists still alive, as British sources have reported?

• Could Osama bin Laden have directed 9/11 from a cave in Afghanistan or a hospital bed in Pakistan?

• Exactly what records were stored in WTC 7, and what would they have revealed had the building remained standing?

• Precisely what was in the August 2001 terrorist warning to the White House?

Political realities stand in the way of a new investigation. As this is written in 2010, a midterm election campaign is underway amid an intensely partisan atmosphere. Democrats control the White House and both houses of Congress, but on 9/11/2001 Republicans controlled all three. If President Obama were to call for a revisiting of the facts, it would give the GOP an issue for future elections, including November 2012. Every Democrat would be tarred with the "conspiracy theorist" label and charged with trying to embarrass the Bush administration.

Already, past and future presidential hopeful Mitt Romney has claimed that Obama's diplomatic outreach toward the Middle East "...adds fuel to the fire of...the 'blame America' crowd...Even [Iranian president] Ahmadinejad is saying 9/11 is a fabrication. These sorts of voices should not receive any kind of support from the...president of the United States." By this logic, if a foreign leader hostile to the United States speaks out on a controversial issue, an American leader who negotiates with him isn't a patriot, and whatever that foreign leader says, regardless of merit, must be disregarded, otherwise the listener wants to "blame America." Romney's rhetoric is shallow and shamelessly political, but it does dramatize the practical obstacles to any new investigation of 9/11.

An even larger obstacle is President Obama himself. His appointment of former Harvard colleague Cass Sunstein as head of the Office of Information and Regulatory Affairs suggests his own general dislike of conspiracy theories. Mr. Sunstein once suggested that government operatives should infiltrate locations where these theories germinate in order to discredit them (see Preface). In other words, be afraid of what you might learn.

The president has a personal reason for being antipathetic toward conspiracy theorists. He's had to deal with the so-called Birthers, a group dedicated to proving he was born in Kenya, not Hawaii, and was thus ineligible to run for president. Birthers aren't discouraged by the existence of a 1961 birth announcement in a Honolulu newspaper for Barack Hussein Obama. For that announcement to have been faked, someone in Hawaii in 1961 necessarily foresaw that a mixed-race baby with an African name, born halfway around the world, would someday be running for president of the United States and would need a falsified account of his birth.

The president has called for "moving ahead" with a new agenda, rather than looking backward at possible wrongdoing by Bush administration officials. No one has been indicted for any crime, and no special prosecutors have been hired. It's clear that President Obama is an unlikely proponent of any new investigation into 9/11. Without his active encouragement, it won't happen from within the country unless a credible person with inside knowledge goes public with a smoking gun...and even then, only if the corporate-controlled media, acting contrary to the wishes of Washington, provide the microphone.

A new investigation might have the best chance of happening as an outgrowth of diplomatic initiatives. The official version of 9/11 is widely regarded as fantasy overseas, and not merely by the president of Iran and the former president of Italy. Conspiracies have been a fact of life in Europe, at least since Julius Caesar encountered a few supposed friends in the Forum one fine day in 44 BC. Europeans don't have a Pollyanna attitude toward politics, and unlike most Democrats and the mainstream media, they don't fear doubting the Bush administration.

Because 9/11 was by inference the Bush administration's reason for invading Iraq, lawsuits in England, or in any country that suffered casualties in Iraq, could prompt requests for classified information about the prelude to the invasion, as part of a discovery process. The Downing Street minutes, for one example, could be sought as evidence. In that case the State Department would have to choose between snubbing the courts of a foreign ally and declassifying data that could embarrass the previous administration. Cooperating with another country in a diplomatic spirit would not accrue the same political costs as would an inquiry by the Justice Department.

By the time this book reaches print, a trial of Khalid Sheikh Mohammed and four other alleged 9/11 conspirators might have unearthed information that could lead to a new investigation...irrespective of the guilt or innocence of the defendants. The print and broadcast media have focused entirely on the debate over whether civil or military trials should be held, without disguising the fact that a military court would be more sensitive to the government's desire to keep information classified. The Obama Justice Department originally called for civil trials in New York; since then, local objections on practical grounds, together with bipartisan sentiment in Congress in favor of military jurisdiction, have made military trials more likely as this is written.

If a defense lawyer openly claimed that 9/11 was an inside job, would the court allow that on the record? Would the mainstream press be able to censor such a comment, or would the allegation itself, once it was leaked, set in motion an investigative process? How many worms can fit in one can?

Those in favor of military trials for the five current defendants might consider the trial of John Wilkes Booth's alleged fellow conspirators in June 1865. When Booth murdered Lincoln that April, Robert E. Lee had just surrendered his Army of Virginia to Ulysses S. Grant, but General Joseph Johnston was still leading Rebel battalions in North Carolina and had not yet surrendered to William Tecumseh Sherman. The assassination was therefore ruled to be an act of war, and Attorney General James Speed approved military justice for Booth's friends. The ruling met with public approval, at least until the public got wind of what was in store for the defendants.

The strict protocol of a military proceeding barred all eight defendants from testifying in their own defenses, and also from conferring with their attorneys during the trial itself. To insure their silence, the seven male defendants were hooded during their imprisonment on Secretary of War Edwin

M. Stanton's orders, a form of torture that has was controversial in 1865 and has since been widely condemned. Guilty verdicts were a formality against the eight, though the court did spare the lives of four defendants deemed to have only conspired with Booth to kidnap Lincoln...Dr. Samuel Mudd, Samuel Arnold, Michael O'Laughlen, and Ford's Theater stagehand Edman Spangler. The other four were hanged, including Mary E. Surratt.

Gaining convictions wasn't uppermost in the mind of Stanton, a Radical Republican who oversaw the investigation and preparations for the conspirators' trial. His higher purpose was tying the defendants to the Confederacy, and to Jefferson Davis. Stanton failed in that effort because his key witness, one Sanford Conover, contradicted himself on the stand and was exposed as a liar. Davis had been arrested, but no credible evidence connecting him to Booth could be amassed, so he eventually went free. Radicals had to settle for "waving the bloody shirt" at the South during election campaigns for the next 30 years, which they did with consummate skill.

Two years later John Harrison Surratt, the Confederate spy who had been Booth's managing partner in the original abduction plot but was ignorant of his eleventh-hour decision to assassinate, was arrested in Egypt, whence he had fled after his betrayal by a fellow Vatican Zouave and after executing a Harrison Ford-like escape from Italy. Surratt was returned to the United States for trial, but by 1867 a military proceeding was out of the question. Surratt's civil trial ended in a hung jury, reportedly eight to four in favor of acquittal.

The government's case was weak. It included "witnesses" who testified they had seen Surratt in Washington on April 14, 1865, while Surratt was able to prove he was in Elmira, New York at the time. As with the conspirators' trial two years earlier, Edwin M. Stanton, who remained Secretary of War even though the war was over, was in charge of witness selection and coaching. This time Stanton didn't succeed. Notwithstanding the weak case against Surratt, the hung jury outcome was a surprise to many. Surratt remained the object of public scorn for having fled the country while his mother, who'd been less involved with Booth than he all along, went to the gallows.

In the case of Khalid Sheikh Mohammed and his compatriots, the matter of classified information being leaked is only one potential concern for the government. Prosecutors might not be able to gain a conviction without proving the defendants were in cahoots with Osama bin Laden. That could present problems, because there's strong evidence that bin Laden was seriously ill in September 2001, was being kept alive on kidney dialysis machinery, and that CIA agents knew where he was being treated. A defense lawyer would certainly provide the court with bin Laden's timeline in 2001.

A court might yet decide that a connection with bin Laden did exist, and convict the five defendants of murder on that basis, but that could prove embarrassing to George W. Bush, who declared six months after 9/11 that he wasn't thinking about Osama bin Laden any longer. Contrariwise, if no link with bin Laden were established in court, the five men might deserve an acquittal. Khalid Sheikh Mohammed would go free, the public would become enraged, and the mainstream media would be drawn kicking and screaming into the fray. All that can be said with certainty is that a new investigation into 9/11 would not end with anyone's acquittal in court.

The question of torture has hung over the Iraq debate like a sword of Damocles. If it were raised at Mohammed's trial (defense lawyers would be remiss not to do so), it could influence not only the court's verdict but the verdict of history, because evidence gained through torture is inadmissible in court. It didn't matter in 1865, but it might in 2010, given the publicity that surrounded Abu Ghraib. It would be hard for even a military judge to exclude it.

CHAPTER 14. DAN FOOL AND TREY COOL MEET AGAIN

It's a few weeks after their last meeting in the park. Dan and Trey pick up the conversation about where they left off.

TREY COOL: "What's the latest on your grand conspiracy theory about 9/11, Danny?"

DAN FOOL: "Actually, Trey, it's Dick Cheney who has the grand conspiracy theory."

TREY COOL: "Say what?"

DAN FOOL: "Cheney said there's a Muslim caliphate that extends all the way from Spain to Indonesia, and that 9/11 was an outgrowth of it."

TREY COOL: "I'd believe that before I'd believe 9/11 was an inside job, as you do."

DAN FOOL: "Have you ever studied Muslim history, Trey?"

TREY COOL: "You mean about the Prophet Muhammad?"

DAN FOOL: "He lived back in the sixth and seventh centuries. I'm talking about the stuff that went on in the second millennium."

TREY COOL: "The Crusades?"

DAN FOOL: "Yes, the Crusades. And the Spanish Inquisition."

TREY COOL: "I know about the Crusades. Catholics wanted to drive Muslims out of the holy land. They went too far, I agree. But what's this about the Inquisition?"

DAN FOOL: "In the early 16th century most Spanish Muslims had been converted to Christianity. They were called Moriscos. The Catholic Church was afraid Moriscos were practicing Islam secretly in parts of Spain. When the Ottoman Empire sent Barbary pirates to raid the Spanish coast, Moriscos were suspected of helping them. Eventually King Philip III ordered Moriscos expelled from the country. Some who resisted were executed, others had their property confiscated."

TREY COOL: "Assuming you have your facts straight, Danny, that wasn't very nice of the king. But what does any of that have to do with 9/11?"

DAN FOOL: "Ask Dick Cheney. The point is, Muslims have historical reasons for resenting Christians."

TREY COOL: "Sounds to me as if you're refuting your own conspiracy theory. The 19 guys who flew planes into the World Trade Center and the Pentagon were Muslims, Danny."

DAN FOOL: "So we've been told. But six of those 19 have showed up alive in Europe."

TREY COOL: "Danny boy, have you considered that our government might simply have made an honest mistake in identifying some of them? There could be more than one person named Khalid Mohammad, you know."

DAN FOOL: "It's possible. But how is it that none of those guys appeared on a passenger manifest? Not a single Muslim name was on any of the four lists."

TREY COOL: "Maybe they didn't have tickets. Maybe they used aliases. Maybe they boarded the planes by sneaking on! How do you know what transpired at the airports that day?"

DAN FOOL: "I don't. But I'd sure as hell like to know. That's one big reason why we need a new investigation."

TREY COOL: "We already had one. And it didn't reveal any inside job. When does all this investigating stop?"

DAN FOOL: "The Kean–Hamilton Commission didn't do its job, Trey. Thomas Kean admitted that NORAD lied throughout. They never found out why our air defenses failed. The commission didn't even examine WTC 7, which is the key to the whole mystery."

TREY COOL: "Danny boy, you're sounding more like Inspector Clouseau every day."

DAN FOOL: "We need a new investigation, Trey. That's all there is to it."

TREY COOL: "Really? Who would do the investigating this time? Rosie O'Donnell?"

DAN FOOL: "One Senator and one Representative from each party, chosen by the party leadership. Preferably, they wouldn't be running for reelection in the next cycle. One Cabinet official, chosen by the president, would be included. Two state governors, one from each party. That makes seven altogether. Give them subpoena powers. All testimony would be given under oath and subject to perjury."

TREY COOL: "That's four Democrats and three Republicans. Well done, Danny. You assured your committee of a Democrat majority."

DAN FOOL: "OK. Make it two Cabinet officials, one of which has to be a Republican. Secretary of Defense Gates would be a good choice as the Republican. Satisfied now?"

TREY COOL: "I'm not sure I want the Secretary of Defense to leave his job at the Pentagon to take part in a witch hunt."

DAN FOOL: "Witch hunt? I don't recall your using that term when Ken Starr chased the Clintons around Arkansas looking for a smoking gun in Whitewater, or when the GOP was demanding a probe into Vince Foster's suicide. A five-year investigation, and all they came up with was oral sex. That's a witch hunt for you. Nobody died in the Oval Office, Trey...but 3,000 people lost their lives on 9/11, and that was only the beginning of the death and destruction."

TREY COOL: "Hey, calm down, Danny. Don't get your blood pressure up. It's bad for your heart."

DAN FOOL: "I know it is. And I don't want to die of a heart attack before we learn the truth about 9/11. But being stonewalled on this is what raises my blood pressure."

TREY COOL: "What would you say if we had a new investigation, but it didn't uncover any conspiracy? Would you be satisfied? Would your blood pressure go back to normal?

DAN FOOL: "Provided they asked the right questions, I'd be satisfied with the outcome."

TREY COOL: "And what might those 'right questions' be?"

DAN FOOL: "How much time do you have, Trey? It'll take a while to list them all."

TREY COOL: "Save it for our next get-together, OK? I gotta' meet the little woman for lunch.'

CHAPTER 15. OF COVERT ACTIVITIES AND PARAMILITARY OPERATIONS

The Central Intelligence Agency was created in 1947 by mandate of the National Security Act, signed into law by President Harry S Truman. It succeeded a World War II intelligence gathering operation, the Office of Strategic Services (OSS). In its own words, the CIA's mission is as follows:

1. Collecting information that reveals the plans, intentions and capabilities of our adversaries and provides the basis for decision and action.
2. Producing timely analysis that provides insight, warning and opportunity to the president and decision makers charged with protecting and advancing America's interests.
3. Conducting covert action at the direction of the president to preempt threats or achieve US policy objectives.

The agency represents its core values as follows:

1. Service. We put country first and agency before self. Quiet patriotism is our hallmark. We are dedicated to the mission, and we pride ourselves on our extraordinary responsiveness to the needs of our customers [sic].
2. Integrity. We uphold the highest standards of conduct. We seek and speak the truth—to our colleagues and to our customers. We honor those Agency officers who have come before us and we honor the colleagues with whom we work today.
3. Excellence. We hold ourselves—and each other—to the highest standards. We embrace personal accountability. We reflect on our performance and learn from that reflection.

Former President Truman wrote on December 22, 1963, one month to the day after the assassination of President Kennedy but without reference to the events in Dallas, that he had created the agency because intelligence was arriving at his desk from the Departments of State, Defense, Commerce, Interior, and elsewhere, and that it often conflicted. Thus Truman saw a need for a *central* agency that would provide intelligence free from interpretation by its sender...in Truman's words, in its "natural raw" state. He continued, "I never had any thought that when I set up the CIA that it would be injected into peacetime cloak and dagger operations."

In terms of the agency's mission as described above, it's clear that the first two statements conform to Truman's stated objective in creating the CIA, but the third does not. Regarding core values, the first and third representations are consistent with reasons for the agency's creation, but the second is not. The phrase "...highest standards of conduct," by its broadest possible interpretation, cannot mean cloak and dagger operations, kidnapping, drug dealing, or murder. It cannot mean a coup d'etat that results in the overthrow of the democratically elected leader of a sovereign foreign country in peacetime, as occurred in Iran in 1953. It cannot be applied to the CIA's activities in Guatemala in 1954, or Chile in the 1970s.

Using the word "adversaries" in the mission statement paints with a broad brush, by failing to distinguish between declared and undeclared enemies. As President Truman no doubt understood, such vagueness allows for covert action in any foreign country whose socioeconomic policies differ from ours. Is a country that merely elects a socialist as president automatically our adversary? Truman concluded, "We have grown up as a nation, respected for our free institutions and for our ability to maintain a free and open society. There is something about the way the CIA has been functioning that is casting a shadow over our historic position and I feel that we need to correct it."

Precisely what Truman meant by "the way the CIA has been functioning" and "a shadow over our historic position" is lost to history. He might have been thinking about the Iran coup (1953), the CIA and the Arbenz regime in Guatemala (1954), the Bay of Pigs debacle (1961), or various plots to murder Fidel Castro. In any case, Truman's wish that the CIA change its methodology has not been realized. Things have gotten much worse.

In 1964 the agency used disinformation to help defeat the socialist candidate for president in Chile, Salvador Allende. In 1970, after Allende had been elected to the presidency on his fourth try, the CIA, at President Nixon's direction, arranged Project FUBELT, a military coup that resulted in Allende's overthrow, his eventual murder, and the succession to the presidency of a brutal military dictator, Augusto Pinochet.

Fear of left-wing governments in Latin America had long informed US foreign policy decisions before 1970, regardless of which party was in power. In 1982 Representative Edward P. Boland attached a restrictive amendment to a Defense Appropriations bill (the Boland Amendment), which barred the CIA from using taxpayer funds in any attempt to overthrow the socialist government of Nicaragua, then being openly demonized by President Reagan. In spite of this amendment the Reagan administration, using the National Security Council to circumvent the new restrictions on the CIA, secretly funded the opposition Sandinistas by selling weapons to Iran through Israel and funneling the profits to the Nicaraguan rebels. This became the Iran-Contra scandal.

Before the Soviet Union's demise, Cold War exigencies motivated most of what Harry S Truman called the CIA's "cloak and dagger operations." Since 1991, and especially after the bombing of the World Trade Center in 1993, its activities have been inspired by the so-called war on terrorism. But that undeclared war ignores international boundaries. A given terrorist might have been born in Saudi Arabia, live in Yemen, and work for a cell in Pakistan that's directed by the Taliban in Afghanistan. In that case any ambiguity about what the CIA's mission statement means by "our adversaries" becomes irrelevant. Wherever a suspected terrorist is thought to be hiding, that country becomes a US enemy (for "hiding him") and the CIA's objectives are validated. Covert action may then include bombing of suspected terrorist quarters, kidnapping, torture, extraordinary rendition (the transfer of detainees to countries that practice torture), and the operation of secret prisons. If anyone on Capitol Hill asks questions, the White House will lie to provide cover.

Strong evidence exists that the CIA has been financing its covert activities through large-scale drug smuggling activity in Colombia, Panama, Nigeria, and elsewhere, with profits estimated as high as $15 billion annually. CIA whistleblowers with proven intelligence credentials have provided detailed information about these operations, which are summarized in the book *Defrauding America*, by Rodney Stich. It's tempting to dismiss this out of hand, but to do so collides with the published statement of an unidentified but self-acknowledged CIA operative in February 2010. Asked by a reporter if a certain antiterrorism practice wasn't illegal, the gentleman replied, "Of course it's illegal. That's what we do." Assuming the quote was accurate, either this CIA operative doesn't understand English, or he's admitting that the CIA no longer adheres to "the highest standards of conduct."

Terrorism is a tactic. It isn't a country, or a despotic national leader who can be stopped only by military force. Declaring war on terrorism is like declaring war on blitzkriegs or torpedoes. Nor is terrorism the sole province of Muslims. There were no Muslims in the Irish Republican Army. Oklahoma City bomber Timothy McVeigh wasn't a Muslim, nor was the Unabomber, Theodore Kaczynski. The Nicaraguan Sandinistas that Ronald Reagan called "freedom fighters" and funded illegally were in fact terrorists in terms of their tactics. It's been said before, but it bears repeating...one man's freedom fighter is another's terrorist. The war on terrorism is a fallacy almost by definition, but its opaqueness does provide cover for extraordinary responses to random acts of terrorism. Such responses won't be found in military textbooks published before the CIA was created.

Could the CIA have been behind 9/11? If it seems a stretch, the fact is that 20 years ago grabbing people off the street in Rome and sending them off to secret prisons, merely on the suspicion of terrorist connections (maybe based on bribe-induced or torture-induced statements from another suspected terrorist), would have seemed impossible. Most Americans knew before 1990 that the CIA engaged in what Harry S Truman called cloak and dagger operations, but torture and drug smuggling would have been unthinkable. In a world where a single criminal act is rationalized by the victim's government as grounds for war, who is to say that people inside that government would not adopt extreme methods for fighting such a war?

Mossad is Israel's counterpart to the CIA. Its founding in 1949 was based on an identical need to the United States' in 1947, i.e., to assemble scattered intelligence information into a single efficient organization. Like the CIA, Mossad has engaged in extralegal activities over the years, all to serve Israel's perceived national interests. Unlike the CIA, Mossad has never pretended that it cares about high standards of conduct while carrying out these activities.

Mossad first attracted world attention in 1960 with its arrest and transfer to Israel of Nazi war criminal Adolf Eichmann, who had been living in Argentina under an assumed name. Israel wasn't a political entity when

Eichmann's crimes were committed, thus it had no legal authority to try Eichmann in Israel, let alone abduct him from another country first. But these were technicalities most fair-minded people overlooked because of the depravity of the Holocaust. Eichmann was convicted and hanged, and almost everyone outside Argentina cheered.

In peacetime, if one country seeks a crime suspect who lives in another, the normal procedure is to seek that person's extradition through established diplomatic channels. But Mossad wasn't interested in courtesy or diplomacy; it just wanted Eichmann. Argentina protested that Israel had invaded its sovereignty by entering the country illegally and kidnapping an Argentine citizen. The United Nations Security Council agreed, but it merely asked Israel to cease and desist in the future. A planned Mossad kidnapping of Josef Mengele was therefore abandoned.

Mossad has been implicated in renegade activities in Belgium, Bosnia/Herzegovina, Cyprus, France, Germany, Greece, Italy, Malta, Norway, the United Kingdom, and the Soviet Union, as well as in every country in the Middle East. These activities include murder and assassination, nuclear arms development, abduction, and passport forgery. Israel has been fighting its own war on terrorism longer than the United States has.

In a Belgian incident in 1990, Canadian engineer and ballistics expert Gerald Bull, who was then working for Iraq on a novel weapon called a "supergun," represented a perceived threat to Israel's security. Mossad feared that Saddam Hussein would be targeting Israel with this weapon someday, so rather than waiting to find out when, or seeking protection through the Belgian court system, it simply sent a team of hit men to Brussels. They murdered Bull in cold blood.

No credible evidence connects either the CIA or Mossad to the terrorist attacks of 9/11. But those who think it's farfetched to make such a connection should consider the timeline between 1991 and 2001.

While American air forces were chasing Iraq out of Kuwait in 1991, the Iraqis launched scud missiles toward Israel. President George H.W. Bush asked the Israelis not to respond in kind, and Israel showed commendable restraint in not doing so. The Persian Gulf War ended, and Bush, with the unanimous approval of his cabinet (including Secretary of Defense Dick Cheney, ironically), decided not to pursue Saddam Hussein individually. Kuwait was liberated, but Saddam remained in power.

As the decade proceeded suspicions grew that Saddam Hussein possessed weapons of mass destruction that could threaten his neighbors, especially Israel. Mossad had murdered a Canadian ballistics expert who was working on the development of a new weapon in behalf of Iraq in 1990, so these suspicions had a basis in fact. Everyone knew Hussein was cruel enough to use any weapon on any enemy. The United Nations sanctioned Iraq and demanded that its weapons inspectors be allowed to search for WMD. Hussein resisted, but eventually allowed inspectors in. They found nothing at first, but kept searching.

By 2001 Israel and her closest ally, the United States, faced a decision. What would they do about Saddam Hussein if no weapons were found? What if he were simply moving WMD around to frustrate the inspectors? In that event, would an invasion of Iraq be justified? Hawks in both countries would certainly support it...but what about public opinion generally? What about the United Nations? How could broad support for an Iraq invasion be mobilized in the absence of WMD?

See Chapter Six for a possible answer.

CHAPTER 16. WHAT DID IAN FLEMING KNOW, AND WHEN DID HE KNOW IT?

At the time Harry S Truman wrote critically about the CIA's methods in December 1963, Ian Fleming's James Bond novels were rapidly gaining in popularity in the United States. President John F. Kennedy, assassinated in November 1963, had been, according to Fleming biographer Donald McCormick in *The Life of Ian Fleming* (1993), responsible for the surge in readership by commenting earlier that year that *From Russia with Love*, a Cold War novel with a complex plot, a swashbuckling Bond and Flemingesque elan, was among his favorite books. At the height of Cold War tensions, a year after the Cuban missile crisis had threatened to bring on World War III, JFK's favorable review could only have enhanced the popularity of all Bond books and films.

Fleming, born in London in 1908, wrote 14 Bond books in all. In each he combined his rich imagination and writing talent with practical experience gained as an officer in the Royal Naval Volunteer Reserve in the early years of World War II. Fleming's appointment in 1939 as personal assistant to Rear Admiral John Godfrey, Director of Royal Naval Intelligence, is curious. Fleming lacked a success profile. He had dropped out of Sandhurst, the British military academy, and had failed in an effort to join Britain's Foreign Office. Just prior to joining the navy Fleming had been, of all things, a stockbroker...which proves, one supposes, that being a stockbroker can lead to great things, even if no great things ever lead to one's becoming a stockbroker.

Fleming's code name in the RNVR was 17F. That was fairly close to James Bond's 007, but perhaps too suggestive of a hotel room or the Jolly Green Giant's shoe size to suit Fleming's love of intrigue.

It might have been Fleming's background as a stockbroker that inspired Operation Ruthless, a quixotic plan he conceived in 1940. In grand style worthy of a 007, Fleming imagined British operatives stealing a German plane and *deliberately crashing it* into the English Channel. Wearing Luftwaffe uniforms, Britons would exit the crashed plane and float on the surface, waiting to be rescued by a German patrol boat. They would then turn on their rescuers and murder them. The crew would commandeer the boat and maintain control of top-secret intelligence known to be onboard the vessel. Smashing!

Alas, the plan was never implemented. In 2008 Ian's niece Lucy Fleming told a British Broadcasting audience that someone in the Royal Air Force had informed her uncle's staff, in the nick of time, that the Heinkel bomber targeted for theft would have sunk to the bottom immediately. That sort of thing never happened to James Bond. Still, the episode proves that 61 years before 9/11/01, it wasn't unthinkable that deliberately crashing a stolen airplane belonging to a foreign country might achieve a desired purpose, or that highly motivated men would agree to do it.

The secrecy required to carry out a plan like Operation Ruthless might well have required that Prime Minister Churchill and King George VI be kept in the dark about it...even as a covert plan to crash planes into skyscrapers on 9/11/01 might have been unknown to President Bush, a far less experienced leader than Churchill and one in office less than eight months. President Truman's ignorance of the Manhattan Project upon taking office proves that in high-stakes intrigue, there's no point in devising a covert plot without keeping it top secret.

Author Henry Chancellor wrote in *James Bond: The Man and His World* (2005) that Ian Fleming and John F. Kennedy had met for dinner in March 1960. JFK, it was said, first enjoyed the Bond novels in 1955, while he was recovering from surgery. The 1960 dinner apparently became something more than a social occasion.

According to Chancellor's account, Fleming passed on to Kennedy his thoughts about potential covert operations aimed at discrediting Fidel Castro, who had just come to power in Cuba. Kennedy was still a US Senator in 1960, but was running for president. It's known that Fleming's ideas did reach the desk of Allen W. Dulles, head of the CIA, who supposedly considered them seriously, though it isn't known if JFK was the conduit.

It is undisputed that Dulles was a committed cold warrior, brother of Secretary of State John Foster Dulles, and had been instrumental in the Iran and Guatemala coups in 1953 and 1954. He was still in charge of the CIA while the Bay of Pigs invasion, aimed at Castro's overthrow, was being plotted. We'll never know if Ian Fleming's ideas became part of the Bay of Pigs plot, but the timeline is suggestive.

Within the next four and a half years, a lot would happen in the lives of John Fitzgerald Kennedy and Allen Welsh Dulles. Kennedy was elected president. The Bay of Pigs operation was implemented, but it failed because JFK declined to provide air support. This infuriated anti-Castro rebels and CIA operatives working with them. Kennedy, angry about the CIA's involvement, fired Dulles. Kennedy blockaded Cuba, rebuffing the Soviet Union's effort to install missile infrastructure there. Dulles authored a book, *The Craft of Intelligence*, which emphasized the Soviet menace and the tactics Dulles thought had been necessary to combat it (Sean Connery, as James Bond, could be seen reading Dulles' book in the 1967 movie "You Only Live Twice," based on the Fleming novel). Kennedy was murdered in Dallas. Rumors circulated about the involvement of CIA and/or anti-Castro rebels in the assassination. The Warren Commission, which included Allen Dulles, decided that Lee Harvey Oswald, acting alone, had assassinated John F. Kennedy. The commission made no mention of several CIA plots to assassinate Castro that had been formulated during Dulles' years as director, or their possible connection to JFK's murder by those seeking revenge for his betrayal of the Bay of Pigs operation.

By the time the Warren Commission issued its report, in September 1964, Ian Fleming had died at age 56 in England. His legacy was convincing millions that covert action by spy organizations, legal and otherwise, had no limits except within one's imagination.

CHAPTER 17. WOULD PEOPLE IN OUR GOVERNMENT DO SOMETHING LIKE THAT?

Millions of conscientious citizens dismiss out of hand the thought that people working for the US government might orchestrate or acquiesce in a terrorist attack like 9/11. They reject theories of conspiracy in presidential assassinations. Many refuse to accept the idea that a presidential election would be rigged in favor of one candidate. A sense of patriotism, combined with a belief that leaders sworn to uphold American values would be above such things, keeps people from comprehending the worst. They ignore history, which shows that governments have often sought desired ends using extra-legal means.

Average folks are faced with the question, "Does the end justify the means?" in their daily lives all the time. Is spanking a child a justifiable means to enforce discipline, a desired end? Is speeding on the highway defensible if one is late for a doctor's appointment? May a worker go on strike out of loyalty to his union, even if public safety is endangered and a judge has ordered him back to work? The answer might be "yes," wherever one's desired end carries more weight than the available means.

People who aren't average have faced the same quandary. President Truman decided that dropping the atom bomb on Japan was a justifiable means toward the end of shortening the war, avoiding an invasion of Japan, and saving lives. Dr. Jack Kevorkian broke the law by helping end the lives of terminally ill patients, as a means to the desired end of ending their pain.

Highly motivated people have always used extreme means to justify desired *political* ends. John Brown caused death and destruction at the US garrison at Harpers Ferry in 1859, seeking to advance the cause of abolition. John Wilkes Booth murdered Abraham Lincoln in 1865, to eliminate a man he saw as a tyrant who had prosecuted a war against half the country while truncating civil liberties. Carrie Nation took a hatchet to saloons in the 19th century to call attention to the cause of temperance. Leon Czolgosz, an anarchist, assassinated William McKinley in 1901 because in Czolgosz' words, "No man should have that kind of power." Puerto Rican nationals tried to murder Harry S Truman in 1950, the better to dramatize their campaign for Puerto Rican independence. We read of zealots bombing abortion clinics, even murdering doctors who performed legal abortions, to defend the right to life of fetuses. Killing one doctor or destroying one abortion clinic, so goes the rationale, saves multiple lives and is therefore justified.

Such acts by individuals are often explained away as the work of deranged minds. Because it's difficult to imagine any wide conspiracy made up entirely of madmen, conspiracy theories are often rejected perfunctorily. But those who act according to the end-justifies-the-means principle need not be deranged. With the possible exception of John Brown, none of those cited above were insane.

Casual students of the Lincoln assassination have characterized John Wilkes Booth as a madman, when in fact he was a cunning and manipulative extremist, driven by a devotion to the Southern cause and hatred of Lincoln. Booth wasn't close to insane. On the contrary, he honestly expected a hero's welcome in Virginia for killing a man he perceived as the nation's worst enemy. Booth's daybook entry (written during his escape), with the words, "I have almost a mind to return to Washington to clear my name, which I feel I can do..." suggests there were unnamed others in Washington who could have aided him because they also thought Lincoln needed eliminating. These men would not have shared Booth's Southern sympathies or his hatred of Lincoln, but they knew Lincoln represented a benevolent attitude toward the South as part of Reconstruction. Lincoln's inherent kindness, as revealed through his second inaugural speech, in which he called for "...malice toward none and charity for all," was anathema to Radical Republican politicians who wanted to punish former Confederates and thereby marshal political power. Lincoln was assassinated six weeks later.

A "greater-good-for-a-greater-number" philosophy is often a corollary to a worthwhile end justifying illegal means. John Brown had been a passionate crusader for abolition for years when he raided Harpers Ferry. It was easy for him to rationalize away limited casualties at the Union fort if thousands of slaves could be set free. Carrie Nation was a temperance advocate, acting in behalf of thousands of women who had been abused by alcoholic husbands and boyfriends; in her mind the destruction of a few booze parlors was an easy tradeoff. Leon Czolgosz had been persuaded by hearing anarchist Emma Goldman's speeches that concentrated power in the hands of a few government leaders was tyranny, and therefore antithetical to a greater-good-for-a-greater-number matrix. Czolgosz was stupid not to understand that in a republican form of government assassinations don't change the leadership structure, but stupidity is not insanity. The would-be assassins of President Truman felt Puerto Rican independence would benefit everyone on their home island, and sacrificing one life to that cause was well worth it.

"The end justifies the means." "A greater good for a greater number." Spoken or unspoken, either can be an irresistible lure for anyone who imagines that criminal acts can be justified. If insanity isn't integral to such reasoning, then who is to say sane forces within government could not join in criminal conduct to achieve a common goal?

In the case of a stolen election, a desired end that would justify using crooked means might simply be not allowing "those rascals" in the opposition party to take control. That's more than enough, especially if partisan operatives convince themselves that the other side is planning to cheat, also. Stolen elections aren't rare in American history, and the public's cynicism about politics sterilizes the conscience of pragmatists who do the stealing. The sharp rejoinder from newly elected Senator Barack Obama about the 2004 presidential election, "Get real. There was fraud on both sides," inadvertently but accurately portrayed the partisan gridlock in Washington at the time. Both parties thought that the greatest good for the most people would lie in victory for their side. In fact, the two parties always think that.

Assassinating a president is more extreme than election fraud, but it's a matter of degree only. The end-justifies-the-means thinking that motivated John Wilkes Booth and the Puerto Rican nationals still applies, subject only to the self-restraint of the conspirator. Could highly motivated operatives have assassinated John F. Kennedy? Consider the reasons for group enmity toward JFK that could have inspired his murder.

1. He pulled the plug on the Bay of Pigs invasion, infuriating anti-Castro rebels.

2. Like Harry Truman he wanted to curb the CIA's covert activities, and he fired CIA chief Allen W. Dulles over the agency's involvement in the Bay of Pigs.

3. He wanted to exit Vietnam, thus posing a threat to the military–industrial complex.

4. Attorney General Robert Kennedy, a dedicated foe of organized crime, deported Carlos Marcello.

5. J. Edgar Hoover thought JFK's extramarital affairs could expose him to blackmail, thus jeopardizing national security.

6. JFK vetoed Operation Northwoods, aimed at Castro's overthrow or murder, in which decision Kennedy was at odds with the leaders of every branch of the military.

The Joint Chiefs of Staff approved Operation Northwoods unanimously, but Kennedy's refusal to implement it, on top of his failure to provide air cover for the Bay of Pigs operation, allowed Fidel Castro to remain in power. JFK then fired Allen Dulles. If the CIA were a Boy Scout troop and Kennedy were a scout, he was building up demerits quickly with the troop leaders. Given the anti-Castro sentiment that prevailed in 1963, and the Soviet Union's evinced desire to aid Cuba militarily, would anyone argue that powerful forces might not have decided that killing JFK (a means) and bringing Lyndon Johnson to power (an end) would be at least contemplated? Considering the CIA's history of ignoring the law in its covert activities, who can rule out the possibility that murdering JFK was the means to a more direct end, i.e., its very survival as an organization?

As far as organized crime's possible motives are concerned, when has the mob ever shied from committing murder, for revenge or merely to enforce silence on witnesses? Mafia dons order people killed with as little compunction as they order a pepperoni pizza.

And what of 9/11? Could the crashing of jetliners into skyscrapers and government buildings have been a justifiable means to an end? It's instructive to revisit the stated goals of the neoconservative think tank, Project for the New American Century (PNAC), and to consider these objectives in the context of desired ends justifying extraordinary means.

PNAC's Statement of Principles (1997) calls for "increased defense spending" and "[carrying] out our global responsibilities for the future." Note the words "global responsibilities." That means we have an *obligation* to police the world, not merely that it's morally upright or in our national interest to do so. We are obligated. The corollary of that presumption is that it would be *irresponsible* to do anything less than what was required to meet those obligations. It adds that we must "*accept responsibility for America's unique role in preserving and extending an international order friendly to our security, our prosperity, and our principles.*" There, PNAC eliminates any ambiguity about what's responsible and what isn't. All that remains ambiguous are the tangential questions, "What higher power elected America to police the world, and when was the election held?"

In implementing its principles PNAC said in 2000 that it wants to "*defend the homeland*" and "*fight and decisively win multiple, simultaneous major theater wars.*" These are listed first and second in the document "Rebuilding America's Defenses: Strategies, Forces and Resources for a New Century." We should consider them sequentially in connection with a possible insider plot on 9/11.

It has always been our government's core mission to defend the homeland. Why mention it in a policy statement, unless to make the second goal, fighting multiple major theater wars, sound as if we'd be doing so in self-defense? Was PNAC giving its motives away by first positing America's unique policing responsibility throughout the globe (sanctioned neither by treaty nor by any doctrine except its own), then suggesting we have to defend ourselves in order to fight wars in several major theaters at the same time? Wouldn't self-defense, in the form of unilateral wars, be a justifiable means to the end of meeting our stated responsibilities?

PNAC's Statement of Principles calls for "...[strengthening] our ties to domestic allies [*sic*] and [challenging] regimes hostile to our interests and values." It then talks about an international order friendly to our security, prosperity, and principles. The phrase "domestic allies" sounds like an oxymoron (a foreign country can't exist inside our borders), but it clearly references friends like Israel who represent a democratic model in the Middle East and who feel threatened by its hostile neighbors. An international order friendly to our prosperity has to mean that our multinational companies, in particular oil companies, must be allowed full access to foreign countries, whether the local citizenry wants them there or not.

In solving crimes, detectives consider means, opportunity, and motive. Any discussion of means and ends in connection with a stolen election, a presidential assassination, or a false-flag terrorist attack involves motive only, i.e., "*Would* sinister forces steal an election, murder a president, or destroy buildings and kill innocent people as part of a false-flag event aimed at stigmatizing a potential enemy?" The author believes the evidence is strong that national leaders in the neoconservative movement were more than adequately motivated to have orchestrated 9/11. In the next chapter we will discuss means and opportunity. Not *would* they have done it, but *could* they have?

CHAPTER 18. OPPORTUNITY, MEANS, AND A HUGE DILEMMA

In an earlier chapter two hypothetical 9/11 scenarios were presented. In Scenario One, sinister forces within our government orchestrated it all from the beginning. In Scenario Two, a planned attack was discovered in advance, could have been dealt with, but wasn't. With respect to opportunity and means, how likely is either scenario? We'll consider opportunity first, because without it no means are possible.

The most extreme theory within Scenario One is that none of the hijacked planes struck the Twin Towers or the Pentagon, or crashed in Shanksville, but were replaced by drone planes or missiles, while the four jetliners went down in the ocean or at some other remote place. It's not implausible; a similar tactic had been considered as early as 1962 as part of a false-flag strategy (see Chapter 6: Operation Northwoods). In that plan, the passengers (CIA agents posing as college students) were to have landed safely at Eglin Air Force Base. In the case of 9/11, it's not conceivable that four jetliners had been filled with secret agents who would have landed somewhere safely, because a list of victims was published and hasn't been contradicted by the victims' families. Furthermore, an occupied plane is known to have crashed in Shanksville, Pennsylvania, presumably because several passengers managed to overcome the hijackers. No body parts were found at the site, and no other debris, but there was communication from the plane that proved it had contained passengers. Further, it's illogical to assume any plot would have involved substituting drones or missiles for three of the four hijacked jetliners, but not for the fourth. As a practical matter, the idea that drones or missiles struck the Twin Towers and Pentagon may be disregarded.

OPPORTUNITY

Under Scenario One, all four planes were susceptible to being redirected because the hijackers had been assured NORAD would be standing down. It would have taken no more than one traitor, or one zealot in one branch of the US government, to tell the suicide hijackers the coast would be clear in order for the plot to have moved forward.

Getting the hijackers aboard the planes would have been a more involved matter. There's no evidence that gate attendants in Boston, Virginia (Dulles), or Newark had been told to suspend normal security procedures, and it's safe to assume one or more would have spoken out by now (to a foreign media source, if necessary) if such a suspension had led to the disaster. It's possible false IDs were provided. No Muslim names appeared on any passenger manifest, yet we're told every passenger was accounted for. Only a new investigation could reveal the truth.

Under Scenario Two, it's possible an accidental leak of NORAD's stand-down posture reached the plotters. Otherwise their decision to hijack planes on 9/11 would have been a matter of blind luck...very improbable. Equally unlikely is that the plot would have been undertaken to begin with without the hijackers having foreknowledge that our air defenses would be down. If the plotters benefited from a leak, a new investigation might reveal the source of the leak.

Scenario Two is even less plausible with regard to the gate/entry question. Viewed from the hijackers perspective, how likely is it that 19 dark-skinned men would have been allowed to sneak through four separate gates at three different airports on the same morning? Wouldn't the hijackers have insisted on knowing beforehand that deliberate action had been taken to clear their paths? Would they have tried otherwise? In sum, Scenario Two fails the smell test with respect to opportunity, thus means can be disregarded.

MEANS

If only Scenario One is viable, what about means? If people in our government had been running the show, would they not have recruited pilots with experience in flying large aircraft? Was any one, let alone all four of the 19 hijackers competent to pilot a Boeing 757? We're told that's what really happened, but if traitors in our government had planned the whole thing, would they have assumed amateur pilots could have maneuvered large aircraft expertly? Could anyone who hadn't flown anything larger than a Cessna have managed to circle the Pentagon at several hundred miles per hour and zoom in a few feet above sea level without crashing first? The unlikelihood of this renders the official story implausible, but no less the notion that 9/11 was an inside job.

If we assume that three jetliners struck the Twin Towers and Pentagon, right on target, and a Muslim hijacker with little or no flying experience was at the controls in each case (whether according to the official story or as part of Scenario One), then how did they gain actual control? Their only weapons were box cutters, we've been told, so we have to assume they used them to slash the throats of the pilots. Still, questions abound. It's not a simple matter to overpower a captain and a first officer, kill them both instantly with box cutters, clear the cockpit of their corpses, and assume control of a huge plane you've never flown before in time to find your bearings, alter your course, and aviate with precision. What were the passengers and crew of Flights 11, 77, and 175 doing all this time? The crash of Flight 93 in Shanksville supposedly resulted from a rebellion by passengers. Did the passengers and flight attendants on the other three planes all remain in their seats and passively wait for their collective doom?

If the most brilliant detective who ever lived were asked to solve the riddle of 9/11, he or she could not do so using a motive/opportunity/means matrix. And 9/11 is a riddle. Once again...the official story requires 1) that 19 Muslims, directed by someone in a cave or hospital halfway around the world, evaded security at four separate airport locations on the same morning (none of their names were on a passenger manifest), 2) that they seized control of three Boeing 757 planes, using no weapon more threatening than a box cutter, 3) that after gaining control of the cockpits, three of the hijackers (none with any experience in flying large aircraft) reversed course, executed intricate flying maneuvers, and struck three targets dead on, and

4) this was all done in such a manner that no debris or human body parts were left behind anywhere. That story is incoherent. It's a wonder that a majority of Americans still believes it.

But that doesn't tell us what did happen. Existing conspiracy theories are plausible as to motive, but fail regarding opportunity and/or means. All this proves is that the 9/11 riddle shouldn't be left to detectives, especially not Internet detectives. A truly independent panel with subpoena powers must investigate from the bottom up.

CHAPTER 19. DID THEY REALLY SAY THAT?

At 4:54 p.m. Eastern Daylight Time on 9/11/2001 (9:54 London time), Gavin Estler of BBC Worldwide issued the following on-air report (italics added): *"We're now being told* that another enormous building in New York has collapsed. It is the Salomon Brothers Building, [also known as] World Trade Center Building 7...." This report wasn't incorrect. But it came in 26 minutes too early. WTC 7 didn't collapse until 5:20 pm. No kidding.

Estler's use of the passive voice, i.e. "We're now being told..." was convenient for BBC, in that the source of this report remained unidentified. Who advised them that a skyscraper that was soon to implode in its own footprint had already done so? Was it Nostradamus, or maybe the Amazing Kreskin? Britons tend to use couched language like "We're now being told..." a lot, more out of a preference for formal speech than to conceal information. So please don't call us conspiracy theorists for wondering how this could have happened. BBC never cleared up the quandary; instead it claimed that their tapes of the broadcast had been lost somehow. Oh.

In an interview with *Parade* magazine in October 2001, Secretary of Defense Donald Rumsfeld was quoted as saying that terrorists had used "...a missile to damage this building," referring to the Pentagon. Was it a Freudian slip? Regardless, Rumsfeld's statement puts the former defense secretary in league with the most extreme conspiracy theorists concerning 9/11.

On December 27, 2004 Rumsfeld said that terrorists had "shot down the plane over Pennsylvania," which claim puts him in a league of his own regarding outlandish theories. Did he mean terrorists shot down Flight 93 from *inside the aircraft*? Didn't the hijackers have only box cutters for weapons? Supposedly Flight 93 was headed for Washington when rebellious passengers overpowered the hijackers and brought the plane down. Was this also a Freudian slip, i.e., Rumsfeld's unintentional acknowledgement that Flight 93 had been brought down on purpose?

Since leaving office on January 20, 2009, former Vice President Cheney has been doing the TV interview circuit with his daughter Liz, their central theme being that President Obama isn't doing as good a job of keeping the country safe as the previous administration had (supposedly) done. It was interesting, then, that on May 11, 2009, in an interview with Bob Schieffer on CBS' "Face the Nation," Cheney asked the audience to remember that Khalid Sheikh Mohammed had blown up the World Trade Center on 9/11/01. The former vice president didn't tell us how Mohammed had managed to obtain nanothermite, the deadly explosive found at Ground Zero. Nanothermite is a rare substance used only by the military to blow things up, so that's a real mystery.

It should be reassuring to know that Cheney realizes burning jet fuel wasn't responsible, but somehow it isn't. Chances are he simply misspoke, and had momentarily confused 9/11 with the 1993 bombing of the World Trade Center. It remains to be seen if lawyers at the upcoming trials of 9/11 suspects will attempt to use Cheney's odd locutions to their clients' advantage, and if so, if the court allows them on the record.

Former President George W. Bush was known for verbal gaffes, but on March 13, 2002 he might have topped himself. Asked by a reporter about the supposed mastermind of 9/11, Osama bin Laden, Bush answered, "...You know, I just don't spend that much time on him, to be honest with you. I truly am not that concerned about him. I was concerned about him when he had taken over a country." Bush never told us what country bin Laden had taken over...or why, in the space of six months' time, he (Bush) had ceased to be concerned about the most sinister terrorist who ever attacked the United States. Was this a tacit admission that bin Laden had not orchestrated 9/11 after all, or was it simply an example of Bush's known impatience with detail? The press chose not to seek the answer.

Bush 43 might have inherited his gift for awkward speech from his father, Bush 41. When asked by a reporter where he was on November 22, 1963, the day John F. Kennedy was assassinated, the elder Mr. Bush replied,

"I think I was in Houston." He remains the only American over the age of 60 who doesn't remember precisely where he was at that time.

John Farmer, a lawyer for the Kean–Hamilton Commission, put the following in writing in a recent book, regarding the commission's failings: "At some level of the government, at some point in time...there was an arrangement not to tell the truth about what happened." The key word is "arrangement." It separates self-serving ("CYA") testimony from an actual collusion to hide the truth...in point of fact, Farmer was alleging a conspiracy of lies.

Richard M. Nixon, who wasn't John F. Kennedy's closest friend, nevertheless must have had severe doubts that Lee Harvey Oswald had been a lone assassin. On the White House tapes Nixon's view about the Warren Commission's findings can be heard: "It was the greatest hoax that has ever been perpetuated [*sic*]."

J. Edgar Hoover must have agreed with Nixon. Asked if Oswald had been a lone assassin, Hoover replied, "If I told you what I really know, it would be very dangerous to this country. Our whole political system could be disrupted."

Howard St. John Hunt was the son of Watergate burglar H. Howard Hunt, who had told the younger man that he had declined an offer from the CIA to participate in Kennedy's murder. In an interview to *Rolling Stone Magazine*, Howard St. John Hunt quoted his father as saying in a deathbed confession, "There was a French gunman firing from the grassy knoll."

Bill Clinton, asked by a reporter why he had agreed to ride with President Bush 43 on Inauguration Day 2005 in light of the recent Congressional challenge to the 2004 election, replied, "He won the election fair and square." Clinton surely knew better. But his response strengthens the argument that the United States is a one-party nation regarding election fraud. Historians will note that Soviet Russia was a one-party nation when Josef Stalin famously said, "It isn't the votes that count...it's who counts the votes." They'll also remember that Ferdinand Marcos, in his final election "victory" in the Philippines, explained away a 10,000-to-zero margin in his favor in one remote district with the words, "I have a lot of cousins living there."

Mark Crispin Miller, author of *Fooled Again*, a book that detailed the fraud by which John Kerry was denied the presidency in 2004, told Kerry, "You were robbed." Kerry replied (according to Miller), "I know." When a brave reporter who overheard the conversation described it in print the next day, Kerry sent his press aide to deny that he'd agreed with Miller.

Larry Silverstein, owner of the World Trade Center complex, admitted during a Public Broadcasting System documentary in September 2002 that a decision had been made to "pull it" on 9/11, meaning WTC 7. Controversy has raged ever since over what "pull it" meant, and Silverstein has added fuel to the fire, if you'll pardon the expression, by remaining silent ever since.

Skeptics with knowledge in demolitions have stated that in construction industry argot, to "pull" a building is to bring it down with explosives. They further point out that WTC 7 collapsed in an identical manner to the Twin Towers, too similarly for it to have been an idle coincidence. The background circumstances were entirely different, yet the end result was the same. The Twin Towers encountered white-hot jet fuel and the impact of two jetliners traveling about 500 mph, while WTC 7 supposedly fell from scattered debris and reflected heat. Yet the buildings collapsed in identical fashion. Silverstein's use of the phrase "pull it" therefore fits the skeptics' assumption that all three buildings were demolished.

Obviously, this was a politically incorrect admission on Silverstein's part. In the absence of a clarification from Silverstein, his spokesperson, Dara McQuillan, countered by saying that "pull it," in the case of WTC 7, meant to "[evacuate] *a contingent of firefighters* [from the building]," and that people who suggest "pull it" referred to a deliberate destruction of the building are mistaken. Obviously, the singular predicate noun "it" can't be used to refer to the plural noun "firefighters" without violating the rules of grammar. But Ms. McQuillan explained that away by telling us that the unspoken collective noun "contingent (of firefighters)" had been implied, thus Silverstein use of "it" meant "more than one firefighter."

Well, that just isn't the way normal people talk, especially not people from the Big Apple. If New Yorkers mean to say, "let's pull firefighters (from a building)..." they don't say, "pull it," and assume people will understand that the word "it" stands for more than one person. They might say, "Let's get those guys outta' there," or maybe, "Let's pull them guys out." The reader is invited to imagine hearing Larry Silverstein, a born and bred New Yorker, saying, "Maybe we better pull it" on the afternoon of 9/11, referring to a decision about WTC 7, only to be told a year later that Silverstein had used the word "it" to connote a contingent of firemen, not the building itself.

Silverstein owned the building, but he wasn't in charge of the New York City Fire Department. Silverstein lacked the authority to order firefighters from the building in the first place. Yet intelligent people still believe that his statement, "Maybe we'd better pull it" meant, "Maybe we should pull a contingent of firemen out of there." That's enough to make one proud to be a conspiracy theorist.

Chapter 20. The Gospel According to the History Channel

The History Channel reviewed the evidence in the Kennedy assassination and decided that anxious Americans haven't needed to worry about all those conspiracy rumors that have been circulating for the past 47 years. It seems the Warren Report, issued in 1964, was right all along. Lee Harvey Oswald was indeed a lone assassin, and we'd all believe this except for Oliver Stone's 1991 film "JFK," which is to blame for all the gossip that still circulates in 2010 AD.

A cultural and generational gap is involved here. Decades before the History Channel made its first appearance on cable television, indeed from the beginning, a majority of Americans has disbelieved the Warren Commission. Long before Oliver Stone first imagined himself a filmmaker, citizens have been arguing among themselves about the ballistic evidence. They've viewed the Zapruder film again and again, watched Jack Ruby's trial on television, read books on the case, and visited Dallas to recreate the crime of the century in their own minds' eyes. For anyone of school age or older in 1963, the movie "JFK" appeared 28 years later as a tableau vivant of an all-too-familiar horror show. The film might have confirmed their suspicions, but it didn't arouse them.

The author recognizes that millions of younger viewers were first introduced to the topic of the Kennedy assassination via Stone's film. And therein lies the rub. Movies transform fantasy into reality; this makes them appealing as escapist fare, dangerous when dealing with historical events.

Stone's film has been roundly criticized, and not without good reason. It hinted at a wide conspiracy, but failed to identify specific conspirators. It made a hero out of New Orleans District Attorney Jim Garrison (played by Kevin Costner), when in fact the real-life Garrison managed to indict only one person, New Orleans businessman Clay Shaw, who was quickly acquitted for lack of evidence. Stone took creative license by assigning to Costner courtroom dialogue that Garrison had never used.

It's undeniable that Stone failed to make his case for a conspiracy in the film. Should we conclude, therefore, that Lee Harvey Oswald was a lone assassin? Only if we believe that when Benjamin Franklin's first experimental kite failed to get airborne, his failure rendered the laws of aerodynamics impotent.

How did the History Channel handle the matter of the Zapruder film, in particular the final gunshot that blew JFK's head open and drove his brain matter backward and to the left, onto Jackie? The question since 1963 has been, "Could this shot have come from Oswald's location at that moment, directly up range from the motorcade?" According to the History Channel, it could have, and did. The History Channel's scriptwriters reminded us that one's bodily movements after being struck by a projectile need not correspond to its path...as if that fact had anything to do with the path of JFK's scalp fragments. The program further cited the autopsy report, which showed that the final shot had caused a crater in the back of JFK's head. There again, the History Channel didn't discuss the direction of the fatal projectile, no doubt aware that doing so would have been counterintuitive to their analysis and conclusion. If the crater had resulted from *first impact*, then obviously Kennedy's scalp and brain tissue would have been driven *forward*, not backward and to the left.

The autopsy has been criticized over the years, no less roundly than Oliver Stone has been since 1991. The History Channel never cited the controversy that erupted after its release, or the contradictions in it that have been highlighted in numerous books. Two doctors who treated JFK at Parkland Memorial Hospital originally noted (as did an attending nurse) that Kennedy's throat showed an *entry wound*. After being told this was impossible, that it had to have been an exit wound because Oswald was up range from the motorcade at that point, the doctors reversed their opinions to conform them to the autopsy report. The nurse never changed her testimony, however; if she's right, and if the doctors were right in their initial conclusions, Oswald can't have been a lone gunman.

The author isn't qualified to analyze forensics, but he understands enough about physical science to know that a projectile that enters the back of a man's head (at six o'clock relative to the Book Depository in JFK's case) will not drive the bulk of his brain matter backward and to the left (toward eight o'clock). But a shot fired from the grassy knoll area (at two o'clock) would do exactly that. A majority of witnesses in Dealey Plaza reported hearing a shot from the grassy knoll area, another fact the program failed to mention in its eagerness to prove the Warren Report correct. Also omitted from the History Channel's account was the fact that the first news report from Dallas on November 22, from the Associated Press, stated that the "shots apparently came from a grassy knoll in the area."

The History Channel did cite Jack Ruby's mob connections, but swiftly dismissed them as a motive for his having killed Oswald. It focused instead on Ruby's violent temper, on his ranting and raving over how the loss of a president had harmed the country, and on how sorry he felt for Jackie and her children. Ruby was described as a tempestuous, small-time strip club owner, a lowly individual with delusions of grandeur that the Mafia would never have bothered with.

"Naivete, thy name is broadcast journalism." Is it possible that every historian who appeared on camera was ignorant of the fact that men with Ruby's shadowy personal history are those *most likely to need the mob's financing help*? Businessmen rely on borrowings, and the Mafia specializes in providing credit to people who can't qualify for it elsewhere...men just like Jack Ruby.

Assassination skeptics had long since established links between Ruby and the mob, going back to his days in Chicago. For the History Channel's experts to argue that Ruby wasn't worth the Mafia's time was just silly. That said, precisely what motivated Ruby on November 24, 1963, remains a matter of conjecture.

The most seductive argument against a presumed contract hit by Ruby on Oswald is that the mob would have had to eliminate Ruby next, and Ruby would have known it. Then, whoever killed Ruby would have become the next victim, ad infinitum. Maybe. Things would have gotten messy. But the same argument can be put forth against the existence of any contract killing, yet they happen all the time. The dark truth is that if Ruby had been in deep hock to the Mafia, they would already have threatened him, physically and/or through destruction of his place of business. Threats are only the beginning of the nightmare when someone owes money to the wrong people and doesn't pay it back on time.

If Ruby knew he couldn't pay what he owed, his days were numbered as long as he remained a free citizen. In prison, Ruby would have been safe from the mob's hit men, and possibly could have convinced a jury he had been temporarily insane when he shot Oswald. By shooting Oswald in broad daylight while surrounded by police, Ruby at least guaranteed himself that he'd be beyond the reach of the mob from that moment forward.

The History Channel never told us that Dorothy Kilgallen, who interviewed Ruby during his trial and told friends she was about to blow the cover off the case, had died under suspicious circumstances just before she could do so. The program never mentioned Dorothy at all, or her close friend Florence Smith, who died mysteriously a few days later, very possibly while in possession of Dorothy's voluminous notes on her investigation.

Those notes were never found among Dorothy's belongings. But somebody ended up with them. Had it been the police, and had the notes failed to support her claim of being able to break the case wide open, we'd certainly have been told this by now. We've heard nothing about the notes since 1965, which suggests that whoever did end up with Dorothy's assassination file has long since destroyed it, because it did in fact support her claim.

How did the History Channel treat the single-bullet theory? Not a problem. Using schematic drawings, it traced a clear path for the magic projectile, from the back of President Kennedy's neck to Governor Connally's torso, and beyond to his wrist. The narrator explained that the two men were positioned in the limousine in such a way that one bullet could have traversed both bodies easily.

The program never cited the doctors or the nurse at Parkland Hospital, who upon initially examining JFK, agreed that the hole in his throat was an entry wound, which would have been consistent with a shot fired from the railroad overpass. It dismissed claims out of hand that the magic bullet had been planted on Connally's stretcher by Jack Ruby, but never offered an explanation for how Ruby could have gotten to Parkland from his club (or wherever he was when JFK was shot) in less time than a speeding limousine containing the president had gotten there. It's certainly possible that the witnesses who placed Ruby at Parkland were mistaken or lying, but the program was of no help in that area. None of the witnesses were identified, even as their evidence was being dismissed.

Most glaringly, the History Channel ignored the averments of Mrs. Nellie Connally, who never wavered from her insistence that JFK and her husband had been hit by two separate shots. Mrs. Connally has always represented a problem for JFK assassination debunkers, because she was the closest person to her husband when he was struck. Nellie Connally was a charming woman of spotless reputation who had no reason to lie, and she never backed away from her testimony, which if accurate renders the single-bullet theory hopeless. If the single-bullet theory fails, then the portrayal of Oswald as a lone gunman also fails.

The History Channel might have benefited from the input of Bruce G. Richardson, who spent 40 years in the retail firearms business. Richardson worked for the US Information Agency in Afghanistan in 1986, and for two years he was a domestic consultant to the FBI's International Terrorist Team. After 1986 he visited Afghanistan as a free-lance journalist on several occasions. Richardson authored *Afghanistan: A Search for Truth* (Free-Form Press, 2009).

He told the author that the Mannlicher-Carcano rifle tied to Oswald (which at first was mistakenly identified by Dallas police as a Mauser) was in fact a 6.5 x 52 caliber Terni-Carcano, a World War II-vintage Italian weapon. Richardson says that based on his personal experience and the FBI's own tests, the recoil energy from that rifle would have disabled the sight attached to it (a side-mounted Ordnance Optics 4 x 18 telescopic sight) unless shims (thin metal plates) had been attached as stabilization devices. No shims were found on the rifle or among Oswald's possessions, which fact casts doubt on his ability to have practiced with the rifle.

Theoretically, Oswald could have used the rifle and sight without practicing first, thereby making a difficult task virtually impossible. But the Warren Commission said that Oswald, a mediocre marksman firing a cheap mail-order rifle with an incompatible and unreliable sight, through trees and at a target moving away from him, somehow managed to connect twice...and that, in defiance of the laws of Newtonian physics, the second connection struck Kennedy on the right-front of his head, driving his brain matter backward and to the left, even though the presidential motorcade was directly down range from the Book Depository at that precise moment.

Bruce Richardson repeatedly stated his case to FBI agents over the course of two years. Alas, all of them were wedded to the Warren Commission, even 35 years after the fact, preferring the conclusions of lawyers and government bureaucrats to those of a recognized expert in the field, one with no ax to grind.

Lyndon B. Johnson told intimates, according to the History Channel, that he believed Fidel Castro had been behind the assassination. Johnson's personal conspiracy theory went as follows: Castro had gotten wind of plots to kill him, supposedly being directed by Robert Kennedy; so he, Castro, arranged to have JFK killed first. Thus, Oswald was Castro's hit man. Kill or be killed.

This was the only conspiracy theory the History Channel lent any credence to, yet it's the most farfetched of all when one examines the history of Kennedy's presidency. Unless LBJ lied to his friends about his own suspicions (he had no reason to), or he was ignorant of what had been going on between JFK and the CIA while he was vice president (highly unlikely), the History Channel deserves to be called the Fantasy Channel for having turned history upside down.

Let's go over everything again. It was the CIA (and the Joint Chiefs of Staff, in Operation Northwoods) that plotted against Castro. It was the CIA that allied itself with anti-Castro rebels in re the Bay of Pigs operation, possibly acting in concert with Mafia boss Santos Trafficante. It was JFK who denied air cover to the Bay of Pigs rebels and left them high and dry. It was JFK who later fired Allen Dulles as CIA boss on account of the Bay of Pigs, and it was JFK who vetoed Operation Northwoods. It's arguable that Fidel Castro owed his very survival to John F. Kennedy's decision-making as president. Would anyone seriously argue, then, that Robert Kennedy was plotting to murder Castro at the same time his brother, as president, was calling off the dogs? Doesn't this notion qualify LBJ and the History Channel as avant-garde conspiracy theorists?

The History Channel's documentary on the Kennedy assassination did exactly what critics have accused the Warren Commission of doing. It cherry picked evidence that supported a preconceived conclusion, and dismissed or ignored evidence to the contrary. Until a more complete history is shown, the debate will go on.

CHAPTER 21. CONSPIRACY THEORISTS, DEBUNKERS, AND ANONYMOUS
TROLLS

The Internet has replaced the mainstream media as a battleground of choice for people who debate hot-button issues. Because all big-city newspapers and broadcast networks in the United States have become oligopolies through consolidation, they are allergic to any controversy that could annoy their stockholders and advertisers. The corporate-controlled media no longer investigate election fraud, possible false-flag events, or even the legality of unilateral war and torture. They only discuss them when forced to do so by revelations from overseas, as filtered through the Internet. The term "investigative journalism" carries little or no meaning in the 21st century, unless we apply that label to the contributions of supermarket tabloids, scandal sheets, and "entertainment TV" programs that tell us more than we'll ever need to know about the private lives of Tiger Woods, Michael Jackson, or Britney Spears.

The Internet has plenty of gossip, too. It has plenty of everything. Nothing is taboo on a site except for whatever the manager chooses to censor, such as hate speech, profanity, or whatever topic he or she chooses to avoid. The Worldwide Web lacks a journalistic filter, so it's up to the surfer to separate fact from fiction. It invites extremes of opinion, and produces a full spectrum of contributors, who tend to divide into three categories with respect to controversial events: 1) serious researchers without a predisposition toward a given conclusion (the most objective group), 2) sincerely motivated conspiracy theorists and honest debunkers with a point of view and a love of argument (the largest group), and 3) "trolls," hecklers who seek only to discredit other contributors they disapprove of, often for political reasons (the smallest group). Trolls tend to operate anonymously or hide behind clever nicknames, and use ad hominem attacks and gratuitous sarcasm in lieu of honest debate. They're the Internet counterparts of certain modern radio and TV "journalists" who shall remain nameless.

The Lindbergh Kidnapping Hoax Forum was created to discuss an old case, but it brings these three classifications into the clearest focus. Begun in 1998 by Ronelle Delmont, a book reviewer and erstwhile dancer from Florida by way of New York City, the forum revisits the 1932 kidnapping of Charles Lindbergh Jr., for which crime Bruno Richard Hauptmann was convicted in 1935 and executed in 1936. Ms. Delmont herself is predisposed to the view that Charles Lindbergh Sr. staged the kidnapping to cover up the prior death of his son, either from an accident growing out of a prank or at the hands of his sister-in-law, and that Hauptmann had been at worst an after-the-fact extortionist. This theory had been advanced in *Crime of the Century*, by Gregory Ahlgren and Stephen Monier (Branden Books, 1993), and suggested by Noel Behn's book *Lindbergh: The Crime* (Penguin, 1994). Since 1998 Ms. Delmont has welcomed any and all contributors to her site, regardless of motivation or viewpoint. Here follow personal profiles of frequent contributors to the Lindbergh Kidnapping Hoax Forum, with names changed to safeguard privacy and ensure the author's continued good health.

"Larry Rubin" is a diligent researcher who maintains a separate website for information and debate on the case. He has delved into New Jersey State Police archives and uncovered new facts that never came out at Hauptmann's trial, some of which shed doubt on his solitary guilt. Rubin belongs in Category One, because he is knowledgeable and willing to let the evidence speak for itself.

"Pete Leone" is another Category One forum participant. He once worked as a researcher for a prominent Lindbergh case author, and together with his friend "Sally Collins" is an excellent source of archival material. Leone firmly believes Hauptmann was guilty as charged, but is respectful toward other viewpoints and cordial toward everyone.

"David Cooper" has organized annual bus tours of Bronx, N.Y. sites associated with the Lindbergh Kidnapping Case, including Hauptmann's former residence, the nearby garage where Hauptmann secreted Lindbergh ransom money, Hauptmann's wife's place of business (where Hauptmann claimed to have been on the night of the kidnapping), and John F. Condon's former residence, which was the subject of an FBI stakeout during the two-and-a-half year investigation. Cooper belongs in Category One for his open-mindedness and thoroughness of research. He is also a student of the Lincoln assassination.

"Anne Riley" is a descendant of one of the key figures in the case, and has provided helpful family anecdotes. She's a truth seeker who doesn't favor any particular theory, is curious and dependably polite toward other posters, and therefore belongs in Category One.

The present author places himself in Category Two. I visited Highfields (the former Lindbergh home in Hopewell) twice and participated in a mock trial of Hauptmann in 1999, which was conducted in the Flemington, NJ courtroom that had been used in 1935. I've read most books on the case, but have done less hands-on research than many Category One forum participants. I have a clear point of view, i.e., Hauptmann at worst aided and abetted a gang hired by the mob, whose goal was to extricate Al Capone from prison and which used a $50,000 ransom demand to create the appearance of a normal kidnapping. I'm convinced Hauptmann did not abduct the Lindbergh child, and cannot have been Cemetery John for the reasons cited in Chapter 11.

"Bill Barringer" passionately claims to be Charles A. Lindbergh Jr., now age 80. He belongs in Category Two. Barringer's theory of the case is complex, involving switched children and Charles Lindbergh Sr.'s desire to protect his family's interests in a trust fund established for his first-born son by the child's Morrow grandparents. According to Barringer, the child whose body was found near the Hopewell-Princeton Road in May 1932 was the one for whom he was exchanged and whose name he assumed. Barringer rejects the conventional wisdom about the case out of hand, and can be thin-skinned if confronted with evidence that he isn't the Eaglet.

Harold Olson (his actual name) died a few years ago. He also claimed to be the Lindbergh child and argued his case on the forum, but with less vehemence than Barringer does. Olson's story, including his adoption by a family who once lived in Escanaba, Michigan, near a house owned by Al Capone during Prohibition, was well documented in Theon Wright's 1981 book, *In Search of the Lindbergh Baby*. Photos of Olson as an adult show an eerie resemblance to Charles Lindbergh's children, especially to his daughter Reeve. Olson was a Category Two forum participant.

"Gloria" uses her first name only. She argues vociferously, and doesn't always express herself lucidly, so it isn't clear exactly what she thinks happened in 1932. Unlike a troll, though, Gloria usually speaks to the facts in the case, and is unafraid of telling us who she is. She belongs in Category Two.

"Anonymous" is the personification of a troll (Category Three). He once used his real name, but no longer does. Long-standing forum participants know Anonymous as the same guy who was once "Alvin Goodman," because his style gives him away every time. If someone offers an original theory about the Lindbergh kidnapping, Anonymous will compare it to a theory he eschews about an unrelated case, e.g., the Lincoln assassination, even absent any logical basis for a comparison. His postings are always brief, usually devoid of facts or reasoned argument, and heavy with sarcasm.

Not exactly a troll, but belonging in Category Three, is "Dick." His methodology is unique. Dick will disappear from the forum for months on end, leaving behind a promise that he'll return someday with information that will render all prior speculation meaningless. He has the "goods." Eventually he returns without the goods, but with the same self-assurance and eagerness to belittle others. Dick will demand that other forum participants speak to a particular aspect of the case; if they demur because they lack the technical knowledge to argue against a recognized expert in the field of say, wood science or graphology, Dick will claim that they've been "called out." He isn't the forum's moderator; he isn't even around most of the time, but he referees the debate whenever he chooses to participate.

Visit any site that deals with controversial events in recent history, such as 9/11, the invasion of Iraq, the Valerie Plame affair, or the 2000 and 2004 presidential elections, and you'll find angry trolls who defend the government's version of events. Their approaches are similar. If one posits a theory the troll dislikes, that person is called a "lib" (liberal), a "wing nut" (extremist), or a "Kool-Aid drinker" (gullible). Trolls attack people, not the merits of their arguments, and invariably use Internet jargon as a substitute for clear English. Everything is black or white; viewpoints containing nuance are too much for a troll, and most have a poor command of spelling, grammar, and punctuation. "You're" will often come out as "your" in their postings, and "they're" as "their."

In the aftermath of the 2004 election, an army of right-wing trolls played the role of conspiracy theory debunkers (a misnomer, because claims that the election was stolen were never based on theory). If someone posted evidence demonstrating election fraud, that person was a "lib" or a "nut job." The facts were irrelevant. Trolls use a common lexicon and the same talking points, in fact use them so uniformly on various Internet sites as to suggest their arguments had been micromanaged by a higher authority. As practiced by the likes of Karl Rove, Dick Morris, Lee Atwater, and Roger Ailes, such tactics fall under the rubric of "spin control." They've been observed in the mainstream media since the 1980s.

George Orwell called it "group think." Political operatives serving both parties use the talking-point discipline to a fault, aided and abetted by talking heads on TV who know that complexity and nuance are incompatible with the need to summarize a controversial issue in time for the next commercial break.

Chapter 22. Gresham's Law of Conspiracy Theories

Sir Thomas Gresham was a monetarist and an adviser to Queen Elizabeth I in 16th-century England. In 1558 he wrote Her Majesty a letter that lamented the fact that earlier monarchs, including her late father, King Henry VIII, had allowed the country's metallic currency to reach what Sir Thomas called "an unexampled state of badness." This neglect, so wrote Gresham, had prompted British citizens to hoard coins containing silver and gold and spend the cheaper stuff. According to Professor George Selgin at the University of Georgia, Gresham outlined the dilemma to the queen more formally, to wit: "...all your ffine gold was convayd ought of this your realm."

Good Queen Bess lacked the prickly temperament of her father, fortunately for Gresham. Her mother Anne Boleyn had lost her head; according to historians of the period this misfortune filled Elizabeth with a visceral distaste for bloodshed, thus Sir Thomas managed to survive his moment of impudence with his torso intact. Exactly three centuries later economist Henry Dunning Macleod observed that bad money does indeed drive good money out of circulation. He named this phenomenon "Gresham's Law," in honor of Sir Thomas.

The same pattern exists with respect to conspiracy theories. Bad theories precede good ones, and they linger even after being recognized as bad. Whenever something shocking happens, the public is susceptible to believing misguided or even outlandish explanations out of fear, anger, and confusion. Years later, after the shock wears off, evidence of a conspiracy that was ignored or repudiated at first is looked at with a fresh perspective; by that time the original theory has survived as a myth, and because most of the suspects and witnesses have died, it's too late to revise the historical record. Call this phenomenon "Gresham's Law Revisited." People who enjoy this book might even decide to name it "Mills' Law."

Abraham Lincoln was murdered less than a week after Lee surrendered to Grant at Appomattox Court House. Public elation at the end of the Civil War turned to grief and outrage toward Rebels, so it isn't surprising that Booth's act of vengeance was seen as an extension of the war. Cries went out for the scalp of Confederate President Jefferson Davis, who was arrested and held for two years after the trial of Booth's fellow conspirators (Booth had been shot to death by a Union soldier while hiding from the posse in Virginia).

Belief in Davis' guilt was based on passion, not reason. In our context it was a "bad" conspiracy theory. This was recognized from a legal standpoint. The evidence against Davis was nonexistent, so after two years' imprisonment he was set free. But Radical Republican politicians who controlled Congress (analogous to 21st-century neoconservatives in that they employ uber-patriotism as a political weapon) used the assassination and the initial suspicion of Davis to marshal political power. Radicals branded all Democrats as erstwhile Rebel sympathizers for decades thereafter, in a tactic called "waving the bloody shirt." It won elections (Grover Cleveland was the only Democrat elected president between 1856 and 1912), and had the tangential effect of negating suspicion of other possible allies of Booth for three generations.

In 1937 a chemist and historical researcher, Otto Eisenschiml, wrote a best-selling book titled *Why Was Lincoln Murdered?* The book postulated that suspicion of Vice President Andrew Johnson or Secretary of War Edwin M. Stanton was consistent with certain facts in the case that had been overlooked in 1865. Eisenschiml lamented that preceding historians hadn't explored alternate angles.

Eisenschiml is dismissed as a conspiracy theorist by the current Lincoln historical community, in particular by academics who eschew his tactic of raising questions without having definitive answers. But Eisenschiml wrote *Why Was Lincoln Murdered?* 72 years after the event in question. Questions that should have been asked in 1865 had not been (because "everyone knew" those dirty Rebels had done it), and answers that might have been available at the time of the assassination no longer were. Had Eisenschiml written his book in 1870, when the only conspiracy theory the public could accept would have blamed the Confederate hierarchy, Eisenschiml's patriotism would have been called into question. Very possibly *Why Was Lincoln Murdered?* would have been banned from libraries north of the Mason-Dixon line or even burned, not because the author's logic was flawed but because the country wasn't ready for a book that cast suspicion on people in the Union government. It would have been "politically incorrect" at a time when Lincoln was a martyr to the cause of preserving the Union and when war hero Ulysses S. Grant had been elected president by a landslide.

Anticipating an objection, the author recognizes that in 1866 Congress did initiate an investigation into President Johnson's possible involvement with Booth. Although Booth had left a calling card at Johnson's hotel on the afternoon of the assassination, and some evidence exists that he had earlier sought (Vice President) Johnson's help in arranging safe passage out of Washington, the Congressional investigation produced nothing definitive. It seems to have been motivated more by Radical Republican anger at Johnson (a Southerner by birth and a former Democratic Senator from Tennessee who eventually fired Edwin M. Stanton as Secretary of War and was impeached for it) over Johnson's Reconstruction policies than by hard evidence. In truth, the probe of Johnson by Northern Senators in the Republican majority was of a piece with suspicion of Jefferson Davis, albeit it took the passage of time for historians to acknowledge it.

Gresham's Law Revisited showed up again in 1892. Lizzie Borden, a 32-year-old spinster who lived with her father, stepmother, and maiden sister in Fall River, Massachusetts, was arrested on murder charges after Abby and Andrew Borden had been brutally hacked to death with a hatchet one hot August morning in their home.

The savagery of the killing shocked the nation. Newspapers and magazines were the public's only sources of information in 1892, but from Fall River to San Francisco people read and talked of little else for months. Lizzie was an inconspicuous Sunday school teacher who according to custom stayed home. She fed pigeons and had no history of aberrant behavior, so the actual evidence in the case yielded to rampant speculation about what could have provoked a killer to such violence. Everyone had a theory. *The Boston Globe*, normally a paper that observed rigid journalistic guidelines, free-lanced the task of behind-the-scenes investigating to a reporter named Henry Trickey.

Trickey, who was aptly named, produced a bad conspiracy theory for the *Globe*. He "discovered" that Lizzie was pregnant. It seems her stern father had caught wind of it, and Andrew had demanded that Lizzie identify her lover or else forfeit her substantial inheritance (Borden left no will, so how Lizzie could have been denied inheritance rights has never been explained). Borden was 70, the second wealthiest man in Fall River, and an obsessive skinflint who chose to confine his family to a claustrophobic house in a working-class neighborhood and refused to buy a telephone.

The *Globe* plastered Trickey's story on its front pages without verifying his facts or speaking to Lizzie directly. This provoked an immediate backlash of public sympathy for the girl, who quietly proclaimed her innocence without exhibiting much grief over her parents' demise. Pro-Lizzie sentiment increased exponentially when it became clear she had never been with child as claimed, was in fact as pure as drifted snow. Trickey's story line had been bogus.

The case went forward without the tawdry angle. Ten months later Lizzie was acquitted by an all-male jury, amid wild cheers of approval in the courtroom. *The New York Times* even editorialized that the case should never have been brought.

The Globe published an apology to Lizzie. The case remained officially unsolved, left to the vagaries of public sentiment, which gradually turned from sympathy for Lizzie to widespread belief in her guilt. A careful examination of the evidence, much of which had been excluded from the original inquest and trial because the mayor of Fall River had prematurely informed Lizzie that she was under suspicion, demonstrates that nobody could possibly have killed Andrew and Abby Borden except Lizzie. She should have been convicted of murder, and might well have been but for *The Boston Globe's* rush to judgment.

More than seven decades later a Fall River native, Victoria Lincoln, who as a child had known the aging Lizzie Borden, probably solved the mystery in her book, *A Private Disgrace: Lizzie Borden by Daylight.* Anyone unfamiliar with the Borden case might wonder why it took so long, but such is the power of Gresham's Law Revisited: that old myths die slowly.

Victorian Era delicacy had precluded mention of Lizzie's menstrual cycle at her trial, by mutual agreement between the attorneys. Ms. Lincoln, after consulting with medical specialists who know far more about certain maladies than doctors in the 1890s knew, made a persuasive case that the murders, and also an unsolved burglary of the house several months earlier, had occurred when Lizzie suffered spells of temporal lobe epilepsy brought on by her periods. Lizzie's behavior tended to be normal for 27 days out of every month and something less than that on the other days. As far as motive was concerned, Lincoln discovered that Andrew Borden had been preparing to transfer property in his own name to his wife on the day of the murders, thereby enriching Abby at the expense of Lizzie and her sister Emma, both of whom disliked their stepmother intensely. It seems Lizzie had learned of Andrew's plans when she overheard a conversation the previous day between Andrew and her late mother's brother, John Vinnicum Morse ("Uncle Morse"), who was visiting from his home in nearby Dartmouth, Massachusetts. A similar property transfer to Abby five years earlier had enraged Lizzie and Emma and compelled Andrew to compensate the sisters equally. Andrew had neither learned his lesson nor had he read *King Lear*. He paid with his life for his stubbornness.

Lizzie was fortunate (or fiendishly clever) to have killed Abby first, be- cause if Andrew had died first his fortune would have passed to his wife under the laws of intestacy, and thence to her relatives, leaving Lizzie and Emma as Victorian maidens without portfolio. As it was, Lizzie bought a large house in a fashionable section of Fall River, named it "Maplecroft," and lived out her life there in comfort, ignoring town gossip.

The forensic evidence against Lizzie was overwhelming. Her alibi of being outside in the barn, looking for lead to make fishing sinkers at the moment Andrew was hacked to death, was contradicted by the absence of footprints in heavy dust that had collected since the barn had last been vis- ited. Some suspected Emma of being in cahoots with Lizzie, given that nei- ther sister could stomach Abby, and that neither would have countenanced Andrew's enriching Abby at the girls' expense for a second time. But Emma had been staying with friends out of town on the day of the crime, which gave her an airtight alibi. If there had been any conspiracy, it came after the fact and involved Lizzie and the Bordens' live-in maid, Bridget Sullivan, who was the only other person in the house at the time of the murders and almost certainly knew what had happened. Bridget left town after testify- ing at Lizzie's trial (having revealed nothing helpful to the prosecution), and returned to her family's home in Ireland. According to local legend in Fall River, Lizzie paid Bridget handsomely from her six-figure inheritance, out of gratitude for Bridget's helpful testimony and to ensure her continued silence.

The present author tried to prove the "Fall River Legend" through Irish historical sources about 20 years ago. Had the lowly domestic worker invested a large sum of money upon her return home, money that could only have come from Lizzie? It was impossible to tell (Bridget Sullivans in Ireland are more plentiful than leprechauns), although the search did indicate that Bridget was three years older than she had been telling people. For the record, she moved from Ireland to Montana around 1897, married a copper smelter named John Sullivan, and died a childless widow in 1948 at the age of 83. Bridget had outlived her bosses Andrew and Abby Borden by 56 years, and Lizzie and Emma Borden by 21 years. The sisters had long since been estranged from each other when they died a week apart in 1927, Lizzie in Fall River and Emma in New Hampshire.

Bad conspiracy theories in the Lindbergh Kidnapping Case preceded the arrest of Bruno Richard Hauptmann in September 1934, two and a half years after the crime, and they might have delayed the efforts of lawmen and historians to unravel the truth. Gaston B. Means, who made something of a career out of defrauding people, convinced a wealthy Washington matron named Evalyn Walsh McLean (who owned the Hope Diamond) that he had been in touch with the kidnappers of Charles Lindbergh Jr. Mrs. McLean gave Means $100,000 from her petty-cash account to deliver to the bad guys in exchange for the Eaglet's return. Means said he turned over the money, but that the kidnappers now were asking for more, at which point Mrs. McLean smelled a rat and turned Means in to the cops. In the meantime the public had been treated to a fable about a nonexistent kidnapper hiding somewhere in South Carolina.

Mrs. McLean had a lot more money than common sense. She had been a close friend of Florence Kling Harding, the former First Lady, and knew full well that Means had written a provocative book claiming that Florence had poisoned Warren G. Harding in 1923. In spite of this she entrusted Means with a six-figure sum.

A few months after the kidnapping police investigators in New Jersey contrived a bad conspiracy theory of their own. They questioned Violet Sharpe, a maid who worked for Anne Lindbergh's mother, Mrs. Elizabeth Morrow, in Englewood, about her whereabouts on the night of the kidnapping. Violet gave evasive answers that sounded fishy. It seemed she had gone on a date with a man she had just met and knew only by his first name ("Ernie"). She couldn't remember exactly where they and a second couple (whose names she couldn't recall) had gone that night. Meanwhile a guy with a suspect history named Ernest Brinkert was arrested in White Plains, New York and erroneously connected to Violet's evening on the town with "Ernie."

In fact Violet had never been to White Plains and didn't know Ernest Brinkert. She had told the truth (her date's name turned out to be Ernest Miller), but when the cops told her she was still under suspicion, Violet committed suicide with poison. The newspapers had a field day with the tragedy.

There was good reason to believe Violet had aided the kidnappers, if only unwittingly, but her premature death closed that avenue of inquiry. In a phone conversation on the day of the kidnapping, Violet had confirmed to Betty Gow's boyfriend, Red Johnson, that Betty had gone to Hopewell to assist Anne Lindbergh with the child, and thus their planned date for that evening was off. This meant that the Lindberghs would be staying over in Hopewell on a Tuesday night for the first time ever, something the kidnappers couldn't have known without inside information. This was a logical (or good) conspiracy theory, but it was driven out of circulation by a bad one, Violet's imagined connection to a man she had never met, Ernest Brinkert.

By the time Hauptmann was arrested, the public had become disgusted with cops on both sides of the Hudson River for their lack of progress in the case. Walter Winchell ridiculed them on his nightly radio broadcasts, and editorial writers asked what was taking so long. Whatever the extent of Hauptmann's guilt, the evidence suggested a conspiracy by definition (two or more people working together). But two and a half years filled with hoaxes and disproved theories was too long to wait...someone had to be convicted in the case, and if other guilty parties went free, so be it.

Gresham's Law Revisited might have saved Lizzie Borden from prison or the hangman's noose in the 1890s. It probably postponed Bruno Richard Hauptmann's arrest. But bad conspiracy theories need not favor either the guilty or the innocent. The law had the opposite effect on Dr. Sam Sheppard, who was arrested and charged with the July 4, 1954, murder of his pregnant wife Marilyn at their home in Bay Village, Ohio, a suburb of Cleveland on Lake Erie.

Sheppard was a prosperous osteopathic surgeon and the father of a young son. He told police that he had fallen asleep on the living room couch after a Saturday night dinner party, only to be awakened by a "bushy-haired intruder" who knifed his wife to death in her upstairs bed, then attacked Sheppard before fleeing the house. Dr. Sam claimed he had chased the killer to the lakefront and struggled with him, only to pass out from a loss of blood.

From a newspaper standpoint, the Sheppard case was Lizzie Borden redux, the difference being that Marilyn Sheppard had really been pregnant. Cleveland's newspaper editors made no secret of their belief in Sam's guilt. Investigative reporters probed into his personal life and discovered that Sam and Marilyn had belonged to a wife-swapping club; also, that Sam had a girlfriend who had moved to California but still had Sam on her dance card, so to speak.

The papers took a populist tack. They assumed the editorial stance that just because Sam was wealthy and could afford the best attorneys, he didn't deserve to get away with murder. This was a new kind of conspiracy theory...a rich doctor and his unscrupulous lawyers were combining to frustrate justice. How dare they? It occurred to almost no one at the time that Sam Sheppard might have been innocent.

Sam was found guilty of second-degree murder and sentenced to life in prison. Dorothy Kilgallen, who covered the case for the *New York Journal-American* (a Hearst paper) opined in her column that the evidence hadn't come close to justifying a conviction. For this heresy Dorothy's column was banned in Cleveland.

Sam pressed his case from behind bars. After twelve years, and with the help of power attorney F. Lee Bailey and a sympathetic US Supreme Court, Sam obtained a new trial, at which he was acquitted. He died in 1970, having enjoyed only four years of freedom. Sam's son Samuel Reese Sheppard continued to pursue his father's cause for years after the acquittal, as if hoping to convince diehards who still thought Sam had done it. They included the judge at his first trial, who according to Dorothy Kilgallen had said privately that Sam was "guilty as hell."

Forensic tests suggested that Marilyn's killer had been left-handed (Sam was right-handed), and DNA tests pointed to a man serving a life term for a separate murder, one Richard Eberling, who it turned out had worked as a handyman for the Sheppard family in the weeks before Marilyn's death.

Eberling denied that he had been the killer, but rendered the issue moot by dying in prison soon thereafter.

Gresham's Law Revisited begs to distinguish between bad and good conspiracy theories. Between 1963 and 1968 the government rendered the law irrelevant in three high-profile cases by sidestepping all conspiracy theories, good and bad. John F. Kennedy, Martin Luther King, and Robert F. Kennedy were assassinated in succession, and in each instance a single assassin was blamed while prosecutors eschewed circumstantial evidence of a conspiracy.

The evidence in JFK's murder has been discussed in earlier chapters. Whatever one's view, it's beyond cavil that Lyndon Johnson convened the Warren Commission for the purpose of discrediting conspiracy theories and identifying Lee Harvey Oswald as a lone assassin. Lyndon Johnson admitted it, and his insistence on receiving the Warren Report before the 1964 election attests to the political background. In the other two cases, the government's reasons for narrowing the focus to a single assassin are less clear.

James Earl Ray pleaded guilty to shooting Martin Luther King in Memphis, and the evidence showed he did have the means and opportunity. Similarly to Oswald, Ray was at the scene of the crime and owned the rifle that had been fired. Ray's motive remains vague, however, and also as with Oswald, his wide travels in the months preceding the murder and during his escape (Ray got as far as England before being apprehended) suggested someone had been paying his way. Ray might well have pleaded guilty because of Tennessee's odd criminal law that mandated life sentences for accused murderers who admit their guilt, but allowed death sentences for defendants who plead innocent to murder and are later convicted in court.

As Jesse Ventura reminded us in *American Conspiracies*, when the King family sued for wrongful death in Dr. King's murder, a Tennessee court ruled in its favor in less than three hours, determining that governmental agencies had been involved. The court's finding somehow passed notice in the mainstream press, which otherwise would have had to acknowledge that a so-called conspiracy theory had been validated by a jury's verdict.

Sirhan Bishara Sirhan remains in prison for Robert Kennedy's murder. The official investigation ended with his arrest and conviction, and it's clear from the evidence that Sirhan did fire several shots at RFK that night in Los Angeles. But witnesses reported hearing more shots than Sirhan's pistol was capable of discharging, and an analysis of the murder scene confirmed that at least one other person had to have fired a gun. Sirhan insists he remembers nothing from the night in question, which claim has given rise to speculation that he was a victim of mind control.

Gresham's Law Revisited is still valid in principle, but the arrest and speedy prosecution of a single individual renders any distinction between bad and good conspiracy theories meaningless. Convict a Hauptmann, a Ray, or a Sirhan, and forget about whomever he was associated with.

Before leaving the subject of bad and good conspiracy theories, the author acknowledges that he hasn't discussed UFOs or extraterrestrial beings in this text. Other discussions of conspiracies have begun and ended with the UFO sightings in Roswell, New Mexico in 1947 and real or imaginary "flying saucers." This avoidance was deliberate. For the purposes of this book, UFO sightings can be called "bad conspiracy theories," at least to the extent that they make honest conspiracy theorists easier to discredit. If the planet Earth isn't the only terrestrial body home to what we call intelligent life, it's entirely possible that aliens with a level of intelligence we can't comprehend have been here. The author accepts as fact that Neil Armstrong and Buzz Aldrin walked on the moon in 1969 (a small but vocal minority of conspiracy theorists insists the moon landing was faked), and we've landed probes on Mars since then. But until scientists prove or disprove the possibility that life exists elsewhere, the author believes the debate belongs in their hands. There are enough dangerous things going on in the world. Let's not obsess over matters beyond our control.

The author has also chosen not to explore unresolved questions about The Loch Ness Monster, a fearsome subterranean creature that allegedly has been terrorizing innocent fish in Scotland since the Pleistocene Epoch, or about The Abominable Snowman (also known as Yeti), an itinerant simian who prowls the Himalayan wilderness in search of Maureen O'Sullivan and Fay Wray. It's not that these controversies don't belong in a book about conspiracy theories. In a sense they do, but the conspiracy would involve only tourist boards overseas, acting in concert with travel agencies around the globe.

CHAPTER 23. CONSPIRACIES AND ONE-PARTY SYSTEMS

A blatant act of conspiracy ended Julius Caesar's reign via murder in the Roman Forum, albeit the plans had been made in secret. Les Miserables plotted in Paris basements before storming the Bastille in broad daylight to doom the reign of Louis XVI and Marie Antoinette. Bolsheviks executed Czar Nicholas and his family, which took some doing, but there was no doubt that a revolution had already begun when they were done. In each case, rumors about the conspiracy would have doomed it, because in a totalitarian state a dictator acts to quell rebellion before the fact, using whatever means he deems necessary. After the fact of a despot's overthrow by force, a conspiracy becomes self-evident, so in a totalitarian state there's no such thing as a conspiracy theorist.

It's supposed to be different in a democratic republic. We don't have emperors, kings, or czars. We elect presidents every four years according to one man, one vote, and we assume our votes are fairly counted. We elect Congressional representatives, who write laws and, in the Constitutional framework, act as a balance wheel against overreach by the executive branch. Provided only that the public has faith in the system, revolutions are unnecessary if the president steps out of line...the power of impeachment and/or the upcoming election provide built-in remedies. A presidential assassination is as close as we get to violent overthrow in America, but in that case the vice president takes over, the assassin goes on trial (unless somebody gets to him first), and the legislative and judicial branches of government remain unaffected. Life goes on.

When something goes wrong within the system, the United States is supposed to have checks and balances at the ready to fix it, short of a Constitutional crisis. The media are presumed to be independent and a watchdog for the public, and government officials are expected to provide truthful answers to tough questions about public policy at press conferences. The two-party system should suffice to guarantee that a stolen presidential election, an assassination, or a false-flag event that enables a shadow government to gain de facto power, be revealed through Congressional oversight.

It hasn't worked that way for the last 70 years or so. The United States has progressively moved away from democratic republicanism toward autocracy and plutocracy. The Manhattan Project developed an atom bomb in secret, so covertly that President Truman wasn't even aware of its existence until after he was sworn in. The CIA that Truman authorized gathered intelligence according to its mandate, but went beyond the mandate by staging coups in sovereign countries and committing murder and other criminal acts in the name of national security. Truman lamented this, but it continues as we speak. Whenever necessary according to their own perceived interests, the CIA and other intelligence agencies have lied to Congress.

When he left office in 1961, President Dwight D. Eisenhower, hero of D-Day, warned about a growing threat from the military–industrial complex. In spite of Ike's warning, the Pentagon and its corporate brethren in the defense industry now function as virtually an independent government.

Since the end of World War II, the United States has fought five wars (called conflicts, because that sounds better), in Korea, Vietnam, the Persian Gulf, Iraq, and Afghanistan. The total becomes nine if we add Lebanon, Grenada, Somalia, and Kosovo, and ten if we include the war on terrorism. The one common thread between these initiatives is that Congress never declared war.

It isn't a partisan matter. The steady erosion of democratic-republican principles since the 1940s has occurred under both Democrat and Republican presidents and under Congresses controlled by both parties, or divided. Whatever philosophical differences separated Democrats and Republicans since World War II, there was a consensus about the development of deadly bombs (we need them to be "safe"). Political differences didn't preclude coups d'etat, drug dealing and murder by people hired to gather intelligence. As Eisenhower understood, they didn't prevent oil companies and military contractors from shaping our foreign policy behind closed doors, all the while avoiding Congressional or media scrutiny.

Not unlike banana republics and totalitarian states throughout history, the United States has become, effectively, a one-party nation. A president was assassinated in 1963, and the Warren Commission (comprised of Democrats and Republicans) honored the new president's mandate to declare that the assassin had acted alone, and to do so before the 1964 election. The Warren Commission's haste to meet its deadline meant that a full investigation into possible CIA or Mafia involvement in the assassination was never undertaken, even though a majority of Americans has always disbelieved the Warren Report. Lyndon Johnson, having been safely reelected, staged a false-flag event in the Gulf of Tonkin, which effectively vacated his predecessor's (unannounced) plans to exit Vietnam. The opposition party didn't object, thus the Vietnam Conflict accelerated without a declaration of war. That's not how our system is supposed to work.

Until 1980, at least, the national media held up their end of the bargain. Antiwar protests, fully covered by newspapers and television, weakened President Johnson, who declined to run for reelection in 1968. His successor, Richard Nixon, who had been at war with the media since early in his political career, was driven from office by the Watergate scandal, which would have remained a minor political skirmish but for the efforts of reporters Woodward and Bernstein at the *Washington Post*. Nixon's successor, Gerald R. Ford, pardoned him, engendering editorial protests and public anger that enabled Jimmy Carter, a relative political unknown, to defeat Ford in 1976.

Then even the media capitulated. While Americans were being held hostage in Iran in 1980, TV networks demonized Ayatollah Khomeini and his government without once reminding us that Iranians had been angry at the United States since 1953, when the CIA orchestrated the overthrow of its democratically elected leader, Mossadegh, in favor Shah Reza Pahlavi. Later in the decade television made a star out of Oliver North, who had admitted to aiding and abetting the illegal transfer of monies to Nicaraguan rebels in behalf of the National Security Council. The Contras would have been called terrorists based on their violent tactical approach to dissent, except for the fact that they'd been opposing a Socialist leader the Reagan government disliked, Daniel Ortega. Newspapers and TV went along with

Reagan's characterization of the Contras as "freedom fighters." North didn't go to jail on account of Iran–Contra, in fact became a popular radio personality. When the United States drove Saddam Hussein out of Kuwait in 1991, the action was covered live, with General H. Norman Schwarzkopf and other military pundits in TV studios adding pithy comments about how our air assault had caught the Iraqis by surprise, and wasn't it all wonderful. No mention was made of the fact that Saddam's supposed cache of deadly weapons included those sold to him by the United States for use against Iran. The enemy of our enemy does not automatically become our friend, a lesson our government has been slow to learn, and one too nuanced for the mainstream media to handle.

Fast forward. The national media obsessed over President Bill Clinton's affair with Monica Lewinsky, which led to Clinton's impeachment for lying under oath about his prior affair with Paula Jones. Clinton was acquitted and remained in office.

Meanwhile an obscure Congressman from California, Gary Condit, had been carrying on after hours with an attractive aide named Chandra Levy, who was suddenly found dead of unknown causes one night in Washington. Having sold a ton of newspapers, magazines and commercial airtime over Clinton's misbehavior (which didn't involve national security and thus exempted reporters from accusations of being unpatriotic), the media played the morality card for all it was worth in the Condit matter. It sent reporters to his home district to interview constituents who didn't have the faintest idea what Gary had been doing in his spare time in Washington, but who did seem to enjoy their moments in the California sun. Condit became a celebrity, and the press became gossipmongers. The Condit–Levy story only disappeared from the media's radar screen because of 9/11.

Meanwhile the country had held a presidential election, in which former Texas Governor George W. Bush opposed Vice President Al Gore. Gore was well ahead in the popular vote, but the Electoral College outcome hinged on Florida's canvass, which was close. That is to say, the tallied vote was close. What the newspapers and TV networks never told us (it came out later, through the Internet) was that tens of thousands of eligible voters had been disenfranchised by the Republican power structure in Florida, according to a carefully orchestrated process that included falsely accusing legitimate voters of being former felons (and thus ineligible to vote under Florida law). In one typical case, an African-American named James Johnson, who had never committed a crime, was denied the right to register because he couldn't prove he wasn't the same James Johnson who had committed a felony years earlier.

The other vital element of the Republicans' strategy was to provide too few voting machines in Democratic-leaning precincts. This strategy would also serve Republicans well in 2004.

The print and broadcast media ignored all this. They chose instead to focus on a raging controversy in Southeast Florida over "butterfly" ballots. This was more entertaining, so it was worth covering. Many Democrats (albeit not enough to swing the state to Gore) had found themselves accidentally voting for third-party candidate Pat Buchanan, because of a confusing paper ballot that senior citizens had a hard time deciphering. This secondary issue resolved into a televised charade, as election officials tried to decide whether each individual ballot had reflected the voter's true intent. "Hanging chads" became catnip for viewers, all of whom the networks deemed incapable of understanding complex election fraud strategies by venal political operatives. These viewers enjoyed watching election volunteers hold tainted ballots up to a light, however. If controversy takes the form of an outtake from a sit-com, television will cover it.

Bush was declared the winner. The Florida Supreme Court ordered a recount, but after a heated legal battle the US Supreme Court overruled Florida, just in time for Bush to be inaugurated. Justice Antonin Scalia, speaking for the 5–4 majority, declared that to allow Florida to recount the votes would prejudice George W. Bush's "rightful claim" to the presidency, even though only a recount could have determined whether or not Bush's claim was in fact rightful. It wasn't, of course.

Scalia's argument was disingenuous. He had told a reporter, two days before hearing arguments from lawyers, what the final vote would be. Five justices had decided in advance, without the need for lawyers, that Bush had a rightful claim to the presidency.

What was left unsaid (thanks to the media, which were still talking about hanging chads) was that the Electoral College grants to states, not the federal government, final authority over all elections, even national elections. The Supreme Court had, in effect, decertified the Electoral College through its decision. Al Gore had won the popular vote, but the Supremes reigned supreme and Bush took office.

You know the rest. Eight months later came the nightmare of 9/11, one month after the Bush administration had been warned of a pending attack and done nothing in response. After that warning, in fact, Bush himself went on an extended vacation. The print and broadcast media made heroes out of Bush and New York Mayor Rudy Giuliani after 9/11, meanwhile neglecting obvious questions about how 19 obscure Muslims with little or no flying experience and box cutters for weapons could have commandeered four jet-liners and flown three of them expertly. Bush's popularity soared in polls.

Three years later Bush was reelected, in a manner of speaking. After the 2000 debacle, one might have expected investigative reporters to be on guard for a repeat of election fraud. No such luck. Democrat John Kerry conceded the election quickly, leaving it to two minor parties, the Greens and Libertarians, to challenge the outcome in Ohio, which had replaced Florida as the pivotal state. The media had nothing to say about any election fraud until two weeks later, when a presidential election in the Ukraine brought protestors out into the cold in Kiev to challenge the results. The press decided it was OK to talk about rigged elections, as long as they happened somewhere else.

Senator Barbara Boxer (D-CA) challenged the certification of Bush's victory in the Electoral College, citing clear evidence of fraud in Ohio and elsewhere. She got zero support. Newly elected Senator Barack Obama (D-IL) even saw fit to belittle the effort.

Four years later Obama was inaugurated as the 44th president. We're still in Iraq, and troop levels in Afghanistan have increased. The prison at Guantanamo remains open, in spite of Obama's promise to close it. No misdeeds committed by Bush administration officials have been prosecuted by the Justice Department. Nobody in the Obama administration seems concerned about unanswered questions about 9/11. As this is written Obama, who campaigned on a promise of more open government after eight years of secrecy and falsehoods, has gone even further than Bush in ordering the prosecution of whistleblowers who leak classified information about illegal conduct within government.

Many of the same financial wizards who failed to anticipate Wall Street's financial collapse that led to a taxpayer bailout are still on the scene in Washington. It's a one-party country.

Will a third party emerge, perhaps under a libertarian/truth banner, one that can separate itself from the Washington plutocracy? By the time this book is in print, we might know the answer to that question.

Chapter 24. Karl Popper and Conspiracy Theories, Scientific and Otherwise

Sir Karl Popper (1902–1994) is widely recognized as a leading philosopher of science. Born and educated in Vienna, Popper was influenced at a young age by hearing Albert Einstein lecture. He worked with psychoanalytic pioneers Sigmund Freud and Alfred Adler in behalf of disadvantaged children early in his career. Popper flirted with Marxism while still a teenager, but quickly rejected its philosophy as being overly doctrinaire. After World War II he moved to England and taught at the London School of Economics, which led to his knighthood. According to the Stanford Encyclopedia of Philosophy, Popper was "a self-professed 'critical rationalist,' opposed to all forms of skepticism, conventionalism, and relativism in science and in human affairs generally, a committed advocate and staunch defender of the 'Open Society,' and an implacable critic of totalitarianism in all its forms."

That's quite a resume, but for our purposes it suffices to understand that Popper revolutionized the manner in which scientific theories are evaluated. In a nutshell, he regarded a theory as genuinely scientific only if it could be disproved in any particular, in which event it would be rendered false altogether. Einstein's Theory of Relativity appealed to Popper because it entailed risk, i.e., it was susceptible to being disproved. The corollary to Popper's reasoning, one he articulated, is that a theory that cannot be disproved is by definition nonscientific.

If one applies Popper's logic to conspiracy theories, at first blush it would seem to discredit them perfunctorily. For example, if a conspiracy theorist were to claim that the CIA was behind the assassination of John F. Kennedy, that theory would be immediately subjected to a test of provability. Could we ever know to a moral certainty that people in the CIA had not suborned murder, or that a CIA operative hadn't been the gunman? The answer is no. As a practical matter, any competent spy organization would know how to cover its tracks, and would include plausible denial as part of its planning. Even if a tape recording were found in which a CIA agent admitted to having shot JFK from the grassy knoll, the agency could always claim the recording was faked, perhaps as follows: "That wasn't Agent James Bond speaking on tape, it was the notorious counterspy, Dr. No, who disguised his voice to implicate Bond. We know James Bond to be a hero, so he can't have been a killer." A theory of CIA involvement couldn't be proved or disproved.

Applied to 9/11, any claim that it was an "inside job" (first assuming the claim would be even considered by government leaders, a court, or the mainstream media) would be countered immediately by plausible denial, with a few words thrown in about the unpatriotic nature of the accusation and how it represented an insult to the memory of 3,000 people who died. The burden of proof would naturally fall on the claimant. But he or she would lack access to the evidence necessary to prove the allegation, because the government would argue that to yield it would "threaten national security." Based on precedent, a court would almost certainly side with government, and the legal process of discovery would never begin. The theory would remain in limbo.

So a claim of government involvement in 9/11 can't be proved, but can't be disproved, either. That's a classic Catch-22. Can any conspiracy theory, then, meet Popper's test of scientific validity? If not, does it mean all conspiracy theories should be disregarded?

The author suggests turning conspiracy theories upside down. If we know two and two doesn't equal five, but we can't prove it equals four, must we agree that it equals five? Likewise, if we know in our hearts that the official account of the Kennedy assassination as rendered by the Warren Report is wrong, but like Oliver Stone we can't choose between alternate theories of who killed JFK, must we then accept that Oswald was a lone assassin?

Suppose we think the government's story about 9/11 is equine excrement, but can't figure out how unknown bad guys managed to plant explosives under three skyscrapers in Manhattan, and can't imagine how a guy who had trouble flying a Cessna could pilot a Boeing 757 as expertly as he had to have done. Must we then kowtow to the bizarre idea that 19 Muslims under the direction of a guy in a cave (or a hospital) halfway around the world pulled it off alone...merely because people in power with a vested interest in hiding the truth want us to believe it?

In other words, let's shift the burden of proof. Let's first concede that Sir Karl Popper has a valid point, and that all conspiracy theories are nonscientific by definition because they can't be disproved. But let's not agree that two and two equals five, either...if it did, we'd be wearing two and a half shoes on our feet and the game of bridge wouldn't exist. Let's argue instead that the official version of the Kennedy assassination, as set forth in the Warren Report, is itself a mere theory. Isn't it that, in fact? Were any members of the Warren Commission in Dallas on November 22, 1963, to witness the event? Didn't the commission's conclusion that Oswald acted alone itself hinge on a dubious theory that a single bullet had passed through JFK's body and clothing, altered its course and passed through Connally's body and clothing, yet was barely scarred in the process?

Isn't the government's version of what happened on 9/11 merely a theory? If it were verifiable fact, physical evidence in the form of airplane debris, black boxes, and human remains would have been found. But none was, for the first time in the history of air crashes. It must be a theory, and not even a good one, if six of the 19 Muslims who were identified as suicide bombers are still alive in Europe. It's assuredly a farfetched theory that WTC 7, which wasn't struck by a plane, collapsed in its own footprint, identically to the Twin Towers, as the result of scattered debris and reflected heat from Ground Zero, albeit none of the pedestrians or rescue workers who strolled between the buildings in the course of seven hours suffered so much as heat prostration.

Aye, there's the rub...a conspiracy theory, as distinct from the "official" account of a controversial event, can only be called a conspiracy theory if it's advanced by a skeptic. If the people suspected of wrongdoing are on the inside, their explanation for what happened, however implausible, cannot be a theory and therefore isn't subject to Sir Karl Popper's test of theories.

Two and two must equal five in the brave new world. Unfortunately, Sir Karl is no longer with us to resolve the conundrum.

CHAPTER 25. MRS. FOOL MEETS MRS. COOL

The wives of Dan Fool and Trey Cool have been friends for years, and meet for lunch once in a while to catch up. Here follows an imaginary account of their latest conversation.

TIPSY FOOL: "What's new, Misty? It seems like months since we got together last."

MISTY COOL: "I know, Tips. But it's tough getting out of the house. Trey has this thing about my being home to serve him lunch. He doesn't cook, you know, so I'm Chef Julia."

TIPSY FOOL: "Let's get some wine and make this a real treat, then. I'm luckier than you are. I can get out anytime I want, because Dan's always on the Internet, investigating stuff. It might sound as if I'm feeling sorry for myself, but Dan mostly ignores me these days."

MISTY COOL: "You two have always been such a romantic couple, Tips. What's so important that he'd rather surf the web than have lunch with you?"

TIPSY FOOL: "Oh, Dan has this idea that 9/11 was what he calls an 'inside job.' He's passionate about it. Talks about nothing else. He's also upset that they never mention 9/11 on TV or in the newspaper."

MISTY COOL: "Maybe we haven't heard anything because they haven't caught Osama bin Laden yet."

TIPSY FOOL (to the waitress): "We'd like a bottle of Kendall-Jackson Chardonnay, please. (To Misty) You won't believe this, Misty, but Dan doesn't think Osama bin Laden had anything to do with 9/11. He thinks bin Laden is dead, in fact."

MISTY COOL: "Dead? I heard a recent recording of his voice. He admitted to doing it."

TIPSY FOOL: "Dan thinks that recording was faked, and that bin Laden has been a scapegoat all along. He also thinks Osama was once a CIA operative. I doubt that. But Dan's right about one thing. At first bin Laden denied being the mastermind, then suddenly a tape appeared where he confessed to it. That's passing strange. Why would anyone deny something, then voluntarily admit to it without being forced to do so?"

MISTY COOL: "Oh, dear, dear. I wasn't going to say anything, Tips, but Trey did tell me the other day that Dan was a wild conspiracy theorist. Now I can understand what you've been going through at home, the agony you've been suffering. I'm really sorry. This lunch is on me."

TIPSY FOOL: "Don't be ridiculous. I drink more than you do. We'll split the check, as always. Would you pass the bottle over, please?"

MISTY COOL: "Sure. You know, Trey likes Dan a lot, but he once told me he thought Dan might have emotional problems. Do you think possibly Dan's acting out repressed anger toward his mother, or maybe resentment toward a teacher he once had? Please don't take that personally, Tips. I'm only trying to help."

TIPSY FOOL: "I know you are, Misty. Look, Dan is a brilliant guy. He has two Masters degrees and reads three books a month. He speaks four languages fluently, and we've been around the world together twice. He's always been a wonderful husband and provider, but our lives are out of balance now because of his obsessive focus on this 9/11 business. Our son won't even speak to him at this point, because he thinks his father is a disloyal American. Our granddaughter told her teacher what Grandpa thought about 9/11, and guess what? She and our daughter-in-law were summoned to the principal's office for a conference. They live in a very conservative community, and this business has disrupted their lives."

MISTY COOL: "What exactly does Dan think happened?"

TIPSY FOOL: "That's the strange part. He isn't sure. He just knows that 9/11 couldn't have happened the way the Bush administration says it did. He says there are too many things that don't add up...too many coincidences."

MISTY COOL: "Then he really isn't a conspiracy theorist. He's just a skeptic."

TIPSY FOOL: "That's exactly right. But people he's never met on the Internet call him a conspiracy buff, a Kool-Aid drinker, or a tin-foil hat wearer, whatever the hell that means. One guy online called him 'Pinko Dan, the Conspiracy Man.' That insult made him more determined to prove his case."

MISTY COOL: "Except he doesn't really have a case to prove, does he?"

TIPSY FOOL: "Letch us order some more wine, Mitsy. Looky here, thish is what Dan said to me last night. 'All the evidence that could make the case for us was destroyed by the same people who pulled it off (hiccup). They schtole the black boxes and removed all the debris and body parts. Dan sesh we gotta' start over from the beginning with a new investigation. But the Obama people aren't interested. They only want to look forward.'"

MISTY COOL: "I guess Obama thinks the official story is right, then."

TIPSY FOOL: "Not necessarily, Mitsy girl. Danny says Obammer (hiccup) might well realize there was a conspiracy, but heesh afraid to have the truth come out because the stock market would (hiccup) tank and he'd get blamed for it. And, it would give the Republicans an issue in the 2010 and 2012 elections. Dan says ish all about (hiccup) politics."

MISTY COOL: "When he says 'make the case for us,' which 'us' is he talking about?"

TIPSY FOOL: "The American people, thash' who. Dan sez we've been betrailed (hiccup) by a group of neoconservative zealots who want to control the Middle East, and that 9/11 was done on purposh cuz' it gave them an excush to invade Iraq."

WAITRESS (entering): "Would you ladies like to look at a dessert menu?"

TIPSY FOOL: "No, we don' wan' no dessert, no how (hiccup). But lissen up, sweetie, I wan' ya' ta' bring us yer' bes' bottle of crème de menthe and two pony glashes."

MISTY COOL: "Are you going to be OK to drive, Tips?"

TIPSY FOOL: "I'm jush fine, Mitsy. Whadda' ya' think about that Middle Eastern oil business? Or d'ya think mebbe ish all about protectin' Ish-rael?"

MISTY COOL: "To be honest, it does make perfect sense to me now. I was reading one of Trey's old magazines, published before 9/11. Trey's a staunch conservative, you know. He subscribes to a lot of stuff from right-wing groups. Anyway, the magazine talked about how important it is for America to fulfill its obligations in the Middle East. Obligations! The guy who wrote the article actually said we'd have to fight several wars at once in order to shape that part of the world according to our own needs and fulfill our responsibilities. Responsibilities! The writer didn't mention oil in the article, but the more I think about it, it's clear that's what he was talking about. He also didn't mention Israel, but if we get control of the Middle East militarily, that will help them."

TIPSY FOOL: "Now yer' talkin', Mishie ole girl. You got it now."

MISTY COOL: "The article also talked about how we couldn't start a war without an excuse...something like Pearl Harbor all over again. You know what, Tipsy? I think Dan might be right about 9/11 after all. Maybe 9/11 was the new Pearl Harbor those neoconservatives had been hoping for."

TIPSY FOOL: "I'll drink to that." (to the waitress) "Check, please."

CHAPTER 26. WHAT MAKES A GOOD CONSPIRACY THEORIST?

There are good conspiracy theories and bad conspiracy theories (see Chapter 22). It follows that there are good and bad conspiracy theorists. What qualities do good conspiracy theorists share?

This is a subjective question. The author has been a skeptic (and hopefully, a good conspiracy theorist) since first questioning the conventional wisdom about the Lincoln assassination while an adolescent. A live TV special on the assassination back in the 1950s, with Jack Lemmon playing John Wilkes Booth, made me wonder how Booth could have simply waltzed into Lincoln's theater box uninterrupted and carried out a perfectly timed murder plot. Shouldn't he have expected interference from a guard? Clearly he hadn't, because he had only one bullet in his revolver, which he was saving for Lincoln. And as I learned later, Booth's only shot had to be timed perfectly, with a specific line of dialogue from the stage, and with the simultaneous attack by his co-conspirator, Lewis Powell, on Secretary of State Seward. I was only a teenager then, and I'd never heard the expression "conspiracy theorist," but it seemed reasonable to ask, "Would Booth have left all of this to chance, or did someone assure him Lincoln would be unguarded?"

If the author may be considered an authority, the following traits are necessary to be a good conspiracy theorist:

Persistence: Sir Karl Popper (see Chapter 24) told us that to be scientific, any theory must be susceptible to error. If he's right, then a conspiracy theorist must be unafraid of being wrong. The scientific method calls for continued testing of a theory, and this requirement would logically apply to conspiracy theories, just as it would to Einstein's Theory of Relativity or Newton's Laws of Motion. In fact, it applies even more firmly if the danger of being wrong could backfire on the conspiracy theorist.

Robert Woodward and Carl Bernstein sensed that Watergate had been something more than a two-bit burglary. But to prove a full-blown scandal, they had to challenge a president who had just been reelected overwhelmingly, and no less the skepticism of the *Washington Post's* executive editor, Ben Bradlee, who didn't necessarily trust Nixon but knew the risk to the *Washington Post* of going out on a limb and being wrong. The *Boston Globe* had jumped to conclusions in the Lizzie Borden case and very probably caused a miscarriage of justice. Cleveland newspapers had convicted Sam Sheppard of murder in print in 1954 and might have unduly influenced the jury that sent Sheppard to prison for 12 years.

Their careers were at stake, but Woodward and Bernstein kept digging. A tipster, then known as Deep Throat, fed them information grudgingly at nighttime rendez-vous in a parking garage, as if parceling out dog snacks to a ravenous Great Dane. Woodward and Bernstein's challenge was to apply each new piece of information against their latest theory in the case, almost like scientists in a laboratory. Often the theories didn't prove out. Because they were persistent, they convinced a skeptical Bradlee to wait, and wait some more, before killing their story. Woodward and Bernstein won.

Dorothy Kilgallen was nothing if not persistent. She earned her stripes as a young reporter in the Lindbergh Kidnapping Case and used that experience to advantage in helping Sam Sheppard obtain a new trial 30 years later. In doing so, she had to persist even after her Hearst column criticizing the guilty verdict was banned in Cleveland.

After John F. Kennedy's murder, Dorothy intuited that Jack Ruby had been motivated to murder Lee Harvey Oswald by something more than sympathy for Jackie and the children. Dorothy felt a personal interview with Ruby was crucial. That was easier said than done, because Ruby was under round-the-clock guard in prison. No reporters were allowed in. Dorothy persisted, and finally convinced the judge at Ruby's trial that an interview in court, during a recess, would not compromise security. She was only allowed a few minutes, but the information she obtained from Ruby prompted her to tell friends back in New York that she was about to break the Kennedy assassination wide open. Sadly, it also prompted certain other folks to "make her commit suicide" while they stole her voluminous notes on the case. In death, Dorothy Kilgallen had earned the label of good conspiracy theorist.

Brad Friedman might balk being called a conspiracy theorist. He's a dogged advocate for election integrity at the website he created, Bradblog, and his investigative work in the wake of the 2004 presidential election earned him praise from the *Los Angeles Times*, a mainstream paper that isn't warm toward conspiracy theories but still described Friedman as California's "most persistent blogger-watchdog on the dangers of voting technology." Brad would have to admit that to allege election fraud in today's highly charged, partisan political atmosphere does in fact make one a conspiracy theorist. So we'll use him as an example here.

He's too modest to take the credit, but Friedman's investigative work resulted in the resignation of former Diebold Systems CEO Wally O'Dell in 2005. Bad publicity about Diebold's election machinery, much of which originated in Bradblog, also led to the spinoff of the company's subsidiary, Diebold Election Systems, into Premier Election Solutions.

As a major fundraiser for the Bush–Cheney ticket in 2004, O'Dell had famously promised to deliver his home state to the Republicans, and didn't seem the least embarrassed that Ohio turned out to be the state that attracted the greatest number of fraud allegations. Those allegations, of course, were dismissed as conspiracy theories in the mainstream press after the election. Brad Friedman, fortunately, knows the difference between fraud and a conspiracy theory.

Ohio Secretary of State Kenneth Blackwell had even a greater conflict of interest than O'Dell's, which was also described in detail by Brad Friedman. Blackwell's office ran the election process, from the certification of voters to the appointment of election officials to the allocation of voting machines to Ohio's precincts. Meanwhile Blackwell was head of the Bush–Cheney campaign in the state, and a religious conservative who shamelessly described his political mission as an extension of his faith. A court rebuked Blackwell (an African-American) for attempting to decertify legitimate registrants in minority districts, even as Blackwell was touring the state giving lectures about leadership and business ethics as a prelude to his upcoming gubernatorial campaign. Thanks largely to Brad Friedman's persistence in speaking truth to power, Blackwell's lack of ethics was brought to light in time. His Democratic opponent won a landslide victory.

Gradually, if belatedly, the media were catching on. In 2006, Court TV's Catherine Crier told viewers, "If you want to learn about the state of our election process, I urge you to visit BradBlog.com." In a 2008 interview with Friedman, Blackwell's successor as Secretary of State, Jennifer Brunner, referred to the state's findings in its report on the security of electronic voting systems as "awful." She said, "...[Ohio] will be ready for the 2008 election."

A Thick Skin: Imagine that you're Mark Lane in 1965. You're 38 years old. You've been a successful lawyer, a member of the New York State legislature, and a Congressional candidate. You were New York manager for John F. Kennedy's presidential campaign in 1960. After JFK's murder, you're asked by Lee Harvey Oswald's mother to represent his interests posthumously before the Warren Commission, but the commission turns you down. Undaunted, you postpone other legal work to write a best seller, *Rush to Judgment,* which criticizes the Warren Commission. You should be riding high. But you're accused of having been partially funded by the Soviet KGB in your research for *Rush to Judgment.* Other assassination authors, possibly out of jealousy over your success, criticize your work and accuse you of taking quotes out of context and misrepresenting statements of witnesses.

As the years go by you become involved in other controversies. You align yourself with organizations investigating Vietnam atrocities, including the Citizens' Commission of Inquiry and Vietnam Veterans Against the War. You write a book, *Conversations with Americans,* citing war crimes testimony from returning servicemen. But the CCI decides you are "arrogant and sensationalistic," and that your book included "shoddy reporting." It refuses to deal with you any longer. The VVAW also separates from you, after the *Saturday Review* and *The New York Times Book Review* slam your book as irresponsible, even while conceding the validity of most of your arguments. The VVAW allows that your planning and legal assistance have been invaluable, and your sincerity and devotion were beyond doubt, but decides that merely associating with you would be counterproductive to their work. You've been wrong about a number of things, but you're stigmatized more for your manner than the accuracy of your assertions.

You accuse CIA agents of infiltrating the People's Temple, under the direction of Jim Jones. You're present at Jonestown when the mass suicides occur, and your reputation suffers from guilt by association. The issue of CIA involvement evanesces, but later revelations largely support your accusations.

In 1991, 26 years after *Rush to Judgment* spent 17 weeks on the best-seller list, you author *Plausible Denial*, again attacking the government's version of the JFK assassination. It does well. In 2010, at age 83, you're still alive and kicking, thanks to a thick skin and belief in yourself. Because a conspiracy theorist has a right to be wrong, and because a theory must entail the risk of error to be scientific, you may call yourself a good conspiracy theorist.

Now imagine you're William Randolph Hearst. You take over the *San Francisco Examiner* from your father at the age of 24 in 1887. Eight years later you move east and acquire the *New York Journal*, by which time you've built a reputation as a muckraking populist, railing against crooked business tycoons who conspire to monopolize markets. Your favorite targets are railroad barons. You aren't a conspiracy theorist; you're the public's favorite editorial foe of the rich and powerful.

Now that you're in New York, the geographic center of business and media, you shift your focus to politics. But you enter through the back door. You turn a rumored sexual assault on an obscure Cuban girl into an international incident involving the Spanish government. You bring the girl to New York, put her up in a fancy hotel and call her the Cuban Joan of Arc. You enlist the most prominent women in the country in your crusade: Julia Ward Howe, Clara Barton, Varina Davis (Mrs. Jefferson Davis), Ida McKinley (Mrs. William McKinley), even President McKinley's mother. You hold a rally for the beautiful señorita at Madison Square Garden. You're quoted as saying to a photographer colleague, "You provide the pictures. I'll provide the war."

A few months later, the battleship Maine explodes in Havana harbor. Your big chance has arrived. Along with rival newspaper mogul Joseph Pulitzer you convert this possible accident or random act of violence into a clarion call for war against Spain. President McKinley hesitates, but does declare war. For the rest of your life you claim credit for having started the Spanish–American War, and you thumb your nose at historians who don't accept your statement.

Now you're a big name. You run successfully for Congress from New York in 1902 and are reelected two years later. You seek the Democratic nomination for president in 1904, hoping to run against incumbent President Theodore Roosevelt, who wouldn't have become president to begin with except for the Spanish–American War, which you promoted. You finish second in the convention balloting, however. You remain politically active, battling New York's Tammany Hall in the 1920s. In the 1930s you involve yourself in European politics but are accused of being too close to the Third Reich. The criticism doesn't penetrate your thick skin; you just remind people that you're a fierce anti-Communist. That works. You pay for Bruno Richard Hauptmann's lawyer in 1935; you're criticized for this, too, but in return you know your papers have gotten every ounce of trial gossip out of the deal. The attorney does a poor job for Hauptmann, failing to pursue conspiracy angles that later become fuel for speculation. You once saw business moguls as conspirators against the commonweal; now you've provided ammunition for conspiracy theories in the Lindbergh kidnapping. You've become a lightning rod for criticism, but that's a familiar role. You've never backed down from a battle.

Orson Welles makes a caricature out of you in his 1941 film, "Citizen Kane." He mocks your empire and opulent lifestyle, which includes a megamansion at San Simeon and a resident mistress, Marion Davies, a former movie star. You threaten Welles and organize a public-relations campaign against the film. When Welles' name is mentioned at the Academy Award presentations that year, it's greeted with boos and catcalls, evidence of your abiding influence. The movie becomes a classic on its merits, but you shrug it off, just as Charles Foster Kane (Welles as Hearst) shrugged off his critics on the celluloid screen.

You're wrong about a lot of things, as good conspiracy theorists must be for their theories to be scientific. You lose money in real estate. You underestimate the danger from Hitler. You predict World War II will never happen. The Hearst Corporation goes through hard times in the 1930s. You never regain the personal heights, but when you die in 1951 the firm has recovered its bearings. It goes on to become a media giant. You've been a survivor, and your thick skin is a big reason.

Finally, pretend that you're Cynthia McKinney. But first make sure you have a thick skin, because you're going to be saying a lot of provocative things about some very powerful people, and their friends aren't going to like you a whole lot as a result.

You were the first African-American woman elected to the House of Representatives from Georgia, in 1992, and you served two districts for ten years before being defeated in the 2002 Democratic primary. In Georgia, Republicans are allowed to vote in a Democratic primary, and many voted for your opponent in 2002 because you'd had the nerve to suggest that

President George W. Bush knew in advance about the 9/11 terrorist attacks. That made you a conspiracy theorist whether you liked it or not. In the 21ˢᵗ century Georgia's a bad place to test any conspiracy theory involving a Republican administration.

Your primary defeat didn't deter you. In 2004 you signed the 9/11 Truth movement statement, which called for a new investigation. By that time, apparently, public opinion about 9/11 had shifted just enough that you were reelected to Congress after Denise Majette, who had defeated you in the 2002 primary, decided to run for the Senate. You continued to press the Bush administration over 9/11 and introduced articles of impeachment against President Bush, Vice President Cheney, and Secretary of State Condoleezza Rice.

You also called for opening up files on the assassination of Martin Luther King Jr. This shouldn't have been especially controversial, given that members of Dr. King's family had said openly that they didn't think James Earl Ray had acted alone. In adjudicating the family's civil suit in the case, a court had agreed with the family's contention that agencies of the US government had been involved. But given your reputation as a dissident, the King matter still made it easier for your critics to call you a conspiracy theorist.

You have a bad temper. When a Capitol Hill policeman whose responsibilities included checking credentials didn't recognize you as a member of Congress, you took offense and a physical confrontation resulted. Bad publicity followed, and you lost the 2006 primary election. You quit the Democratic Party the next year. In 2008 you ran for president on the Green Party ticket, earning only 12 votes out of every 1,000 cast. It was oddly fitting that you should have represented the Greens, because they were one of two parties (the other was the Libertarians) that had filed official challenges to the 2004 presidential results in Ohio after Democrat John Kerry conceded the election. In a sense, you were where you had belonged all along.

Integrity: Robert F. Kennedy Jr. has known tragedy. His father and his uncle were both assassinated, and like every publicly aware American, RFK Jr. heard all the conspiracy theories surrounding both assassinations, back in the day when the media still talked about conspiracies. He knows that Sirhan Bishara Sirhan remains in prison for his father's murder in 1968, and that after Sirhan's arrest the official investigation ended, albeit Sirhan's pistol could only fire eight rounds while the forensic evidence indicates at least

12 shots were fired. RFK Jr. could be forgiven if he were a card-carrying conspiracy theorist. But he has never spoken out publicly.

RFK Jr. knows all about the Warren Commission, and that a majority of Americans has never believed its conclusion that Lee Harvey Oswald, acting alone, killed his uncle Jack. He knows that his father was a dedicated foe of organized crime, that as Attorney General he had deported New Orleans Mafia don Carlos Marcello, and that Marcello later boasted of killing JFK in retaliation. RFK Jr. knows that his uncle had been sleeping with the mistress of Sam Giancana, that J. Edgar Hoover was concerned about it, and that Jack Ruby was connected to Giancana and the Chicago mob. He knows that RFK Sr. felt personally responsible for the events of November 22, 1963, but also realizes that if Oswald had really been a lone assassin, his father would have had nothing to feel guilty about. It had to have been bigger than that. Still RFK Jr. has never spoken out publicly.

RFK Jr. knew that his uncle's 1960 election had been tainted by Democratic hanky-panky in Chicago and that JFK had foolishly joked about it in an after-dinner speech following the election. RFK Jr. understood that election fraud had been a bipartisan non-issue for many years, and that the public was somewhat cynical about it. But when he looked at the 2004 presidential election, RFK Jr. felt honor bound to say something. He saw a mathematically impossible disparity between exit poll results that decisively favored John Kerry, and tallied results that reelected George W. Bush. He studied the situation in Ohio, where over 350,000 eligible minority voters, more than enough to have swung the state to Kerry, were illegally removed from registration rolls. He recognized that with only a handful of exceptions, every election irregularity had gone in Bush's favor. He knew about the unfair allocation of voting machines in battleground states where Republicans had administrative control.

So RFK Jr. wrote an editorial piece in *Rolling Stone* magazine in June 2006. He took on *The Washington Post* and *New York Times*, which had dismissed claims of election fraud as mere conspiracy theories. In his lengthy article RFK Jr. focused on the exit poll/tallied vote disparity, and discounted the argument, as advanced by GOP partisans, that it was the exit polls that were flawed, not the vote itself.

According to the Republican rejoinder, Bush voters had been less willing to speak to exit pollsters than Kerry voters, thus the exit polls were skewed in Kerry's favor. But RFK Jr. quoted respected pollster John Zogby as saying the theory was "preposterous." He cited further research by scholars, including Steven F. Freeman of the University of Pennsylvania, that showed the opposite was true. In Republican districts, 56% of those approached completed the exit poll survey, while in Democratic strongholds 53% were willing to do so.

RFK Jr. returned to private life after making his contribution to election integrity. He eschewed calls to run for office. The cause had been advanced, and that was enough.

Rev. Dr. David Ray Griffin achieved the impossible. He managed to convince a major newspaper and a television network that skepticism toward the official version of 9/11 was worthy of being taken seriously. In doing so he might have surprised even himself, because in an address at the University of Wisconsin–Madison in 2005, Griffin noted that the mainstream media had been ignoring his books and lectures since 2003.

Griffin's personal manner and background place him far afield from the normal stereotype of a conspiracy theorist. He's soft-spoken, scholarly, and not a political partisan. Throughout his adult life Griffin had been a theologian and professor of philosophy, involved with the abstruse concept of process theology, as advanced by Alfred North Whitehead and Charles Hartshorne. Griffin first decided to become a philosophical theologian after hearing a lecture series conducted by the renowned Paul Tillich at the Graduate Theological Union in Berkeley, California.

As a theologian, David Ray Griffin understood that in conflicts between faith and reason, conservative Christians resolve them in favor of faith. In political terms, given that the Bush administration had relied heavily on its fundamental and evangelical Christian base in "winning" the 2000 presidential election, Griffin realized it would have been impossible for the same Americans who elected Bush as God's chosen representative on Earth (that's not an exaggeration) to ever accept the notion that his administration could have been behind 9/11. The evidence wouldn't matter, because it would collide with faith, and for those voters, faith trumps reason.

Until 2003 Griffin himself disbelieved the rumors he had heard suggesting government involvement. Then he looked at the facts. Faith and intellect can coexist, even within conflict. Influenced by books authored by Paul Thompson and Nafeez Ahmed, Griffin concluded that at the very least, people in government had acquiesced to the terrorist attacks. His own first book, *The New Pearl Harbor: Disturbing Questions About the Bush Administra-*

tion and 9/11, appeared in print in 2004. In 2005 he authored *The 9/11 Commission Report: Omissions and Distortions,* and in 2006 produced *Christian Faith and the Truth Behind 9/11.* Since then he has brought out *Debunking 9/11 Debunking* (2007), and *9/11 Contradictions: An Open Letter to Congress and the Press* (2008).

Griffin's obvious sincerity helped him pierce the mainstream media's veil of silence in re 9/11. That makes him a true exception among skeptics. His Madison speech was nationally televised by C-SPAN, and even more significantly, an article about his work appeared in *The Washington Post* in 2006.

It's notable that even those who don't necessarily agree with Griffin appreciate him. Writing in *The Nation,* a left-leaning magazine that nonetheless eschews 9/11 conspiracy theories, the former CIA agent Robert Baer wrote that Griffin's writings amounted to conspiracy theories. But Baer conceded that Bush administration secrecy had led to the widespread skepticism to begin with, and Baer later added, "Until we get a complete, honest, transparent investigation...we will never know what happened on 9/11. David Griffin will never let this go until we get the truth." The Presbyterian Publishing Corporation, which brought *Christian Faith and the Truth Behind 9/11* out, did so out of respect for Griffin as a theologian, even while it concluded that "the conspiracy theory [sic] is spurious and based on questionable research." From this we may conclude that Baer and the Presbyterian Publishing Corporation are honest debunkers, and David Ray Griffin is an honest conspiracy theorist.

The label "conspiracy theorist" is often accompanied by accusations that the skeptic is hungry for publicity. Joan Brunwasser is a skeptic who defies that characterization.

Brunwasser is co-founder and director of Citizens for Election Reform (CER), and also serves as Election Integrity Editor for the on-line journal, OpEdNews. Joan is a self-effacing activist in behalf of progressive causes; she seeks no credit for her own work, instead serves as a conduit for the efforts of others. She and I have been Internet acquaintances since the aftermath of the 2004 presidential election. Joan told me the election had made her into an activist for the first time.

She recalled Election Night 2004 for the author. "I thought something was off immediately," Joan began. "Later, I read Steve Freeman's e-mail about his observations, and Jonathan Simon captured state projections... which later, miraculously changed, all in one direction...toward Bush." She continued, "I started...writing letters...calling for an investigation and meaningful election reform." After viewing the film "Invisible Ballots," which told of the dangers inherent in electronic voting technology, Joan amassed copies of its DVD and started a lending library. She distributed copies to attendees at the 2005 Take Back America conference in Washington.

In December 2008 Joan interviewed filmmaker Patty Sharaf, whose movie "Murder, Spies & Voting Lies: The Clint Curtis Story" (see Chapter 3) was chosen best documentary at the New Jersey Film Festival. A year later her interview subject was Bev Harris of BlackBox Voting, whose tireless work in the area of electronic voting technology has elevated objections to the 2000 and 2004 presidential elections from the stratum of conspiracy theorizing to overdue demands for electoral transparency. Joan recognizes that honest elections are a right of citizenship first recognized by the founding fathers, now sacrificed on the altar of laissez-faire capitalism...because voting machine companies and politicians form incestuous alliances.

Joan Brunwasser has interviewed a number of whistleblowers, and plans to continue. Her interview subjects have included Daniel Ellsberg of Pentagon Papers fame, Steve Heller, who exposed election fraud on the part of Diebold in California, and author Mark Crispin Miller, whose book *Fooled Again* introduced millions to the 2004 election disaster. Joan's work on the Don Siegelman case in Alabama, in which the former governor has alleged partisan prosecution under the direction of former Bush administration operative Karl Rove, is ongoing as this is written.

Joan describes whistleblowers as "American heroes." That could be because they embody the same integrity she does, though Joan would never put it that way.

CHAPTER 27. WHAT ARE THE MAINSTREAM MEDIA AFRAID OF?

This book has posited that America's major newspapers and TV networks have purposefully avoided touchy subjects like 9/11 and the 2004 presidential election out of a fear of offending stockholders and advertisers. This is an easy claim to make, because for the corporate media to deny it would open the subject for a debate they won't engage in.

The Washington Post is loath to explain why it was willing to investigate Watergate and bring down a president in 1974, yet dismissed claims of election fraud in 2004 as mere conspiracy theories. *The New York Times* doesn't want people asking why it published the Pentagon Papers in 1971, or that it knew before the 2004 election that the Bush administration had been spying illegally on US citizens (and lying about it), yet didn't bring this public until the end of 2005. *The Times* doesn't want to have to justify ignoring election fraud in Ohio in 2004, meanwhile using banner headlines to describe the same in the Ukraine two weeks later. No newspaper or TV network wants to rationalize having ignored the 9/11Truth movement, because merely to broach the subject would be a tacit admission that it had failed as a watchdog over governmental deceit.

This isn't rocket science. Media conglomeration has reduced competition for news to a handful of giant companies, all waist-deep in the corporate culture (see Chapter 2). An investigative journalist is now as familiar as a stegosaurus. But on a practical level, what specifically are these media giants afraid of, that they won't even broach unpleasant topics? What else has changed since the 1970s?

For one thing, America's economic/financial infrastructure has changed, and the potential for a financial train wreck from outside developments has increased exponentially. An economic calamity has implications extending far beyond the rights and responsibilities of a free press.

When the present author began his career as an account executive (broker) with Merrill Lynch in 1973, he was licensed to trade stocks, bonds, and commodities, as well as options (puts and calls). This required four separate registrations. It didn't seem important back then, but the Commodity Futures Trading Commission (CFTC) governed commodity trading, the New York Stock Exchange (NYSE) and the National Association of Securities Dealers (NASD) oversaw stocks and bonds, and the Chicago Board Options Exchange (CBOE) handled puts and calls on stocks (and later, options on stock indexes). A new broker had to be separately registered with all four. The Federal Reserve Bank determined stock margins (the amount an investor must fork over up front to buy shares on credit), and the CFTC controlled commodity margins.

The markets operated independently of one another, and each had its own regulator. Everything ran smoothly. That is to say, if a problem arose in a given market, it could be handled without compromising other markets.

Then, in 1982, without so much as a public announcement, the US financial universe developed a new galaxy. Stocks became commodities overnight by the introduction of something called index futures, which had first appeared in Japan several years earlier. The effect was that huge leverage was added to the equity markets, yet only major players on Wall Street and commodity specialists realized it.

The introduction of most new products into the economy is typically accompanied by promotional hyperbole. Index futures came in on cats' feet, so quietly and mysteriously that even retail stockbrokers (those who deal with individual investors as opposed to institutions) weren't aware of them at first.

What are commodity futures, after all? They are simply contracts for future delivery of a given product on a specified date in the future. Futures contracts came into being in the mid-19th century in Chicago as an aid to farmers, who harvested crops such as corn, wheat, and soybeans at a specific time of the year. Farmers knew that if they brought their entire harvest to market at one time, the price per bushel would plunge because excess supply would meet a static demand (Economics 101). Futures contracts spread out the supply over a period of months (while the cash crops were held in a grain elevator), meanwhile speculators who sought to gamble on price fluctuations met agribusiness interests who were content to lock in a known profit in advance. In order to make futures contracts attractive to speculators, the CFTC required a relatively small margin payment for them...perhaps 10% of the value of the contract.

The system worked well internally, because it provided a year-round marketplace for farmers whose crops were harvested at one time. Farmers could lock in profits and escape the vagaries of seasonality and weather. Chicago became a separate financial capital from New York.

Then greed took over in the marketplace. If people were willing to gamble on price fluctuations in wheat, corn, and soybeans, market honchos reasoned, why not create a futures market for non-farm commodities like gold and silver? Why not live cattle and pigs (called pork bellies in Chicago)? Long before 1982 all of these and more had been trading on commodity markets in Chicago and New York...eggs, orange juice, broiling chickens, platinum, lumber, plywood, sugar, as well as the traditional farm products. Seasonality no longer mattered. If a producer (not necessarily a farmer) would commit to deliver his product at a future date in a quantity mandated by the futures contract, and a speculator was willing to take the other side of the trade, a deal could be struck. Commodity markets became casinos.

Since Japan had already broken the ice, it was inevitable that an American technocrat would decide to put a group of stocks together into something like the Standard and Poor's 100 Stock Index (made up of blue-chips like IBM, Exxon and General Electric) and introduce it for trading on a commodity market. Large institutions owning these stocks might wish to hedge their positions by selling contracts that represented the same stocks for future delivery, and bullish speculators would come forth to buy these same contracts, *and now could do so using far greater leverage than was available to them on the corresponding stock exchange.*

The Federal Reserve Bank had always governed stock margins. In 1982 a trader who bought 100 shares of IBM, for example, had to give his broker 50% of the purchase price. The margin requirement had been only 10% in 1929, but ten-to-one leverage had made a bad situation worse when the market crashed, so the "Fed" had been conservative with margins ever since.

Now, suddenly it had effectively forfeited control of stock margins, because a commodity speculator could buy IBM and other blue chips through an index futures contract for a margin deposit comparable to 1929's stock requirements.

Because these were technically commodity transactions, trading in index futures fell under the jurisdiction of the CFTC, not the Fed, NYSE, or NASD. Wall Street had now reverted to 1929 conditions, and the Fed no longer controlled margins. The risk profile of the stock market increased at least threefold in a heartbeat, because margin deposits on index futures contracts were approximately one-third of the 50% requirement under Regulation T of the Federal Reserve System.

It was all a deep dark secret to the investing public, though, because brokerage houses never bothered to educate the majority of their account executives on the changeover. Only those representatives who handled large commodity accounts were aware of what had happened; retail brokers were made out as ignorant fools if a client asked, "What are these index futures I've been reading about?"

Because stocks had begun a bull market in 1982, and because of anti-regulatory bias in Washington combined with public ignorance about derivative products in general, everything was copasetic at first. The markets rode a tide of prosperity, and the leverage from index futures contracts gave them an extra boost.

Then, on October 19, 1987, the market went into a free fall. It was explained away by the financial media with vague references to "computerized trading," and even more bizarrely, to "triple-witching day." The allusion to hobgoblins meant that index futures contracts and stock and index options, all trading on different exchanges and under separate regulatory authorities, happened to expire on the same day four times a year (the third Friday of the month). Frenetic trading in commodities and options just before expiration had always spelled volatility, and to make things worse, in 1987 many institutional investors had been seduced into believing in a theoretical concept called "portfolio insurance," whereby a given stock portfolio could be safely hedged by computerized trades, programmed in advance, in whatever futures market corresponded to said portfolio. As with most technological concepts, this strategy worked until it didn't, at which point it became like a failed conspiracy theory. The outcome was no idle theory; instead it became the largest one-day drop in the history of the Dow Jones

Industrial average. To this day very few people in the media have any idea what happened that day, and even many brokers are clueless.

Since 1987 there have been a number of similar electronic trading melt-downs, notably during the Russian currency crisis and the collapse of Long-Term Capital Management, a giant hedge fund, in 1998. As this book was being written, the market swung from a 1000-point intra-day drop in the Dow Jones average to an immediate 700-point rally. Nobody on Wall Street has been able to explain it away, but we know that preprogrammed electronic trading of index futures contracts lay at the heart of the problem. One theory is that a trader meant to sell so many *millions* of shares, but typed in *billions* on his order ticket instead. A billion is a thousand million. With 10:1 leverage added to the mix, it surely means some folks went bust, and others got disgustingly rich, all in the space of less than an hour, on account of a trader's "careless mistake."

If this sounds like stuff and nonsense, it's undeniable that the public has come to expect the worst from the financial district in recent years. Ever since Japan invented index futures and Wall Street copied them, we've seen the introduction of other recondite derivative products like collateralized mortgage obligations and credit default swaps, which in the last few years turned what might have been a garden-variety real estate recession into a Wall Street crisis and taxpayer bailout of several Fortune 500 companies.

Leverage is a two-way street, and in an era of lightning-fast communications a rumor alone can create market swings unknown before 1982.

What would happen in the financial markets, then, if a new investigation revealed that rogue elements within our CIA and Israel's Mossad, in cooperation with neoconservatives in the Bush administration, had orchestrated 9/11? If history is any guide, the stock market would go into free fall at first, then partially recover, with electronic trading and high leverage multiplying the effect in both directions. But volatility alone wouldn't cause people to stop reading the *Wall Street Journal* or stop watching CNN. Long-term investors wouldn't abandon stocks. On the contrary, readers and viewers would be desperate for guidance.

The media might be more afraid of having to detail the consequences of a 9/11 scandal for years. That would include the prosecution of high-ranking officials in government, making the Nuremberg trials look like an episode of Judge Judy. Whoever was president at the time would be faced with the same decision Gerald Ford encountered after Watergate, i.e., "Should I pardon [whomever] in order to put all this behind us?" But Nixon's crimes were a pittance compared to 9/11. Pardoning a mass murderer and traitor would be unthinkable. And New York City, the epicenter of finance and media, would suffer the most from daily revelations about treachery in high places.

Electronic trading and the conversion of stocks into commodities aren't the only financial market changes since the 1970s. An increase in foreign currency trading has accompanied (and enabled) economic globalization. There's no question that a "weak dollar" (one that declines in value relative to foreign currencies like the euro and Chinese yuan) would be an immediate consequence of any shocking revelation about 9/11. American prestige would be shattered. While a weak dollar would benefit multinational companies in the short run (foreign interests could buy American products more cheaply in their home currencies), in the long run it could lead to runaway inflation. Imported goods would go up in price in the United States proportionate to the dollar's loss of purchasing power, meaning American competitors would be able to increase prices commensurately without losing market share. Runaway inflation would lead to higher interest rates (money is a commodity, so its cost would increase), thus crippling the real estate market and small business.

All things considered, *The New York Times* wouldn't have too many advertisers left if they were to investigate 9/11 and discover the awful truth. If you're Bill Keller, you might well decide to play ostrich and bury your editorial head in the sand.

What about the 2004 presidential election? Why, in the face of overwhelming evidence to the contrary and in the wake of the 2000 debacle, did *Time, The Washington Post*, and every TV network decide stolen elections only happen in the Ukraine? We can't know for sure, so we'll have to play the role we were assigned following the election itself...conspiracy theorists. Choose one or more reasons from the following:

1. A prolonged investigation could have caused a Constitutional crisis, producing a ripple effect in the economy and financial markets, regardless of the outcome.

2. Republicans would have blamed the "liberal media" for interfering with the "expressed" will of the American people, regardless of the outcome.

3. If Bush had survived the investigation and continued in office, his administration would have denied access to newspapers it considered responsible for the furor.

4. Bill Keller and his counterparts in editorial offices could have lost their jobs if enough major stockholders had protested to the corporate boards of directors, regardless of the outcome.

5. In the case of *The New York Times*, it had already decided to withhold proof that the Bush administration had been spying on US citizens until after the election. Thus, for the paper to lend credence to claims of election fraud would have defeated its own purpose.

6. Major newspapers and TV networks abhor the Internet, which lacks their editorial filter. The Internet had become the public's information source for election irregularities; so by avoiding the election issue, the media avoided competing with the lowbrow Internet.

7. Kerry conceded the election, and Democrats (except for Barbara Boxer) capitulated. Investigating alleged fraud even after Kerry's concession would have aligned the mainstream media with fringe elements within the political system, i.e., the Greens and Libertarians, who took the battle on. That's very "un-corporate." In the modern era, the mainstream media must remain in the mainstream, meaning they must be allied with the Democrat/Republican party.

This might be an incomplete list. It's enough to remember that we entered a new era about 30 years ago where public information is concerned. The corporate media focus on profit, not truth. A Pulitzer Prize for journalism no longer compensates for a plunge in a media company's stock, and if the bad news that drove it down first derived from an investigation by the media outlet itself, heads must roll. It's now clear that Richard Nixon was born 30 years too soon for the sake of his political legacy, and that politicians of the succeeding generation well understand that Watergate was a watershed event.

CHAPTER 28. THE INVISIBLE SMOKING GUN

It is de rigueur for authors of non-fiction books to document their postulates by sourcing other books on the same subject. Mainstream publishers, book reviewers, and a discriminating readership expect no less, the better to distinguish works of scholarship from opinion pieces or streams of literary consciousness. In the case of university presses, a peer review process poses an added burden for potential authors, whose submissions must conform to strict academic guidelines. Facts must be divorced from opinion, and objective analysis must supersede polemics.

Documentation is a difficult standard to meet, however, when the subject is conspiracies. Where government operatives are suspected of wrongdoing, as with 9/11 and the elections of 2000 and 2004, source material is scarce, even though library shelves and bookstores are well stocked with works chronicling the Bush administration's sins of commission and omission.

A searcher will find critical analyses of the war on terrorism and the invasions of Iraq and Afghanistan, of illegal spying and the "surveillance–industrial complex," of torture, and of the Patriot Act and its implications for civil liberties. But these books, even while presuming that 9/11 had been the lodestar for a Pandora's box of evils that followed, nonetheless take it for granted that the conventional wisdom is correct: that 19 Muslims, under the guidance of a bearded Svengali in a cave or hospital bed halfway around the world, managed to breach security at four different airport locations on the same morning, flew huge jetliners expertly while having little or no experience as pilots, and crashed those planes while the nation's air defenses failed to respond. Absent from all these works is even the vaguest allowance that the terrorist attacks might have been arranged or at least been allowed to happen, constituting a "new Pearl Harbor" that played to the needs of eminences grises operating within a shadow government.

In treating the suspicions of conspiracy-minded authors with benign neglect, the book publishing industry largely mirrors the mainstream media. As outlined in Chapter 2, non-enforcement of antitrust laws has led to "merger mania" among media companies in the last quarter century, with all the negative implications that fact carries for message control within a corporate culture. This is scarcely less true in book publishing. Harper & Row morphed into HarperCollins, and then became part of Rupert Murdoch's News Corporation. The German publisher Bertelsmann bought Doubleday (which owned Delacorte and Dell), then merged it with Bantam. Later Bertelsmann bought Random House. Harcourt, Inc. (once Harcourt Brace Jovanovich) bought Holt, Rinehart & Winston from CBS. Another German outfit, Holtzbrinck, acquired St. Martin's Press and Henry Holt & Co. Multimedia giant Viacom acquired Simon & Schuster, Prentice Hall, Scribner, and Macmillan (which had earlier been owned by an English firm), then sold out to the Pearson Group in England, which already owned Allyn & Bacon, Appleton & Lange, Penguin Putnam, and Silver Burdett Ginn. Time Warner acquired Little, Brown & Co., Warner Books, Time Life Books, and the Book of the Month Club. You can't tell the imprints without a program.

Unlike newspaper editors and TV network executives, book publishers don't have advertisers to keep happy, thus "forbidden" topics like treason in high places might seem a safer proposition for a Bertelsmann or a Harcourt than for a New York Times Company or a General Electric (parent of NBC). But wherever evidence of treason has been marked "classified," it's unavailable to an author; that in turn weakens the author's standing with a publisher seeking documentation of facts. Where evidence remains under the control of the same people who could be implicated, or is held by a succeeding administration that hopes to avoid the appearance of partisanship and just "move on," books hinting at treachery by government operatives must rely heavily on supposition and conjecture in framing arguments. This necessity not only collides with a publisher's need for documentation, it adds an element of legal risk wherever an author or editor lets an error of fact slip under the radar screen.

The path of least resistance for many book publishers is to avoid subjects like 9/11 and election fraud altogether. That said, it does raise eyebrows when the same publisher who won't touch conspiracy theories willingly provides a platform for a Karl Rove to provide his own self-serving version of past events, and even pays Rove a handsome advance for his propaganda. It's assumed that Rove's proximity to George W. Bush for the better part of eight years gives him credibility over matters presidential, even if that closeness was of no identifiable value to any living person other than Rove and Bush.

Luckily, once in a while an author searching the bookshelves will come across a source that provides unwitting help. James Bamford wrote *The Shadow Factory* to explain how 9/11 has given rise to an unprecedented increase in government spying, indeed has inspired a growth industry in surveillance. Bamford's copiously researched book has a decided point of view about government spying (it's mostly bad), but it's clear that in providing details about the terrorist attacks, the author had no intention of giving aid and comfort to conspiracy theorists.

But Bamford did so, by accident. In setting the stage for his dissertation on secrecy, Bamford referenced Theodore Olson's September 14 interviews on Fox Network and Larry King Live about the events of 9/11. In so doing Bamford left a smoking gun behind, possibly without realizing it.

Who was Theodore Olson? A lawyer and conservative Republican, he had pleaded the case of Bush v. Gore before the Supreme Court and was rewarded with an appointment as Solicitor General. He thus became the second-highest ranking government lawyer, behind only Attorney General John Ashcroft. On 9/11 Olson's wife Barbara, herself a high-profile figure, a lawyer, and a political gadfly who might have been to the right of even her husband politically, boarded Flight 77 at Dulles Airport, bound for Los Angeles. When the first reports came in of a plane striking the North Tower at the World Trade Center, Olson, from his office at the Justice Department, feared that it might have been Barbara's plane. He quickly reasoned that Flight 77 could not have reached New York that quickly from Virginia; as described by Bamford, though, Olson's relief had been short lived.

In the TV interviews Olson said his secretary next entered his office, saying, "Barbara is on the phone." When Olson picked up, according to his account, Barbara blurted out, "Our plane has been hijacked," after which the connection was broken. She called back shortly afterward, so Olson said, assuring him that the hijackers were unaware that she was on the phone, and in a soft voice describing how these men had hijacked the plane using box cutters and knives and had forced the passengers to the rear of the aircraft. She added that the pilot had announced the hijacking to the passengers shortly after takeoff; now, almost an hour later, Barbara supposedly asked her husband, "What shall I tell the pilot? What can I tell the pilot to do?" Neither the Fox hosts nor Larry King seemed to sense the absurdity of all this, of how a pilot whose throat had presumably been slashed an hour earlier would be in a position to hear or do anything.

Olson said he asked Barbara if she could tell where the plane was. She replied, so he said, that she could see houses, that a fellow passenger thought they were heading in a northeasterly direction, and that Barbara and the other passenger had reassured each other that things were going to be OK. But Olson told Larry King that he knew better. "I, by this time, had made the calculation that these were suicide persons, bent on destroying as much of America as they could," Olson said to a national TV audience, adding that the phone connection with Barbara had gone dead a second time at that point.

This is a compelling and heart-rending anecdote. A man in a high government position bears witness to a life-changing event for his country and suffers an immeasurable personal loss at the same time. We can assume Larry King and most of his audience had grapefruit-sized lumps in their throats as Olson bravely recounted the events of a tragic morning three days prior. What viewer could imagine going on TV and describing a spouse's horrific demise merely three days after it happened? Does arguing a case before the Supreme Court, as Olson had done, give a man the sang-froid to separate his professional life from his personal with such seeming insouciance?

There are just two things wrong with Olson's account of these conversations with his wife. Not one particle of his story is true. And it had to have been told for a malign purpose.

It's well to understand that the King interview wasn't the first Olson had given since his wife's death, though it probably attracted the largest audience. It was Olson's third interview. He'd been debriefed by the FBI on 9/11, and earlier on 9/14 with Fox Network, whose reporters Brit Hume, Alan Colmes, and Sean Hannity knew Barbara Olson well from her many appearances in behalf of conservative causes. Olson's description of events to the FBI, Fox, and Larry King was consistent in every particular. He wasn't confused. He never mixed up his facts. But how and why a man grieving for his wife could have seemed so eager to spread what turned out to be a false story is left to the reader and the judgment of history.

Suspicion fell on Theodore Olson's account almost immediately, though out of regard for his personal misfortune, none of the skepticism found its way into the mainstream media (it probably wouldn't have gotten there, regardless). Internet bloggers argued, "Cell phones don't operate at high altitudes." Debunkers responded, "Yes, they sometimes do. And how do you know what altitude the plane was at, or even if it was a cell phone Barbara had used to call her husband? Maybe it was the onboard (seat back) phone." The debate raged for years, but on the Internet only.

Initially, Olson had said Barbara called him on her cell phone, which he knew she always carried with her. That might have been only an incorrect assumption on his part. Later, Olson tried to clarify things by saying Barbara had used the onboard phone, not her cell phone. OK. But that raised new doubts...Barbara was dead, so how did Olson suddenly discover what phone she in fact had used? Who told him? According to one later account, the Boeing 757 in question had no onboard telephones. This issue remains in doubt; American Airlines could clear it up, but hasn't seen fit to do so. In the final analysis it's a moot issue. We now know the supposed conversations never happened.

All the early debate on the Internet about the conversations between Olson and his wife was focused on secondary issues. Why had the pilot announced the hijacking shortly after takeoff, yet almost an hour later Barbara Olson had supposedly asked her husband what she should tell the pilot to do? Where exactly was the pilot at the moment? Had his throat been slashed? If not, was he still at the controls in the cockpit, or in the back of the plane with the passengers? How did Barbara know the hijackers had used box cutters and knives, if her only awareness of the hijacking had come from an announcement by the pilot? Had the pilot mentioned box cutters? According to Olson, Barbara wanted him to tell her what to say to the pilot, but if the pilot's throat had already been slashed with a box cutter, what good would that have done? Had the knives and box cutters been wielded in a threatening way only, with the pilot still in control of the plane? If that were the case, how would Barbara have been able to transmit advice to the pilot from the back of the aircraft? The debate raged. Nobody knew yet that Barbara had never spoken to her husband that morning, or that the whole story had been invented out of whole cloth.

Olson continued to use 9/11 and his wife's death as source material for an outpouring of political rhetoric against the terrorists, all of which was greeted warmly in the immediate aftermath of the attacks. Anyone who dared ask, "How can this man be on a political soapbox so soon after losing his wife?" or "Will he be taking time off from media appearances to attend his wife's funeral?" was speaking off the record, or to the nearest brick wall.

On September 16, Olson delivered a speech to the National Lawyers Convention. He prefaced his words by announcing that the Federalist Society (a right-wing organization of which Barbara was a member) envisioned that what followed would become the first annual "Barbara K. Olson Memorial Lecture."

Olson began the body of his talk by reciting "facts." He said, "...(Barbara) somehow managed (I think she was the only one on the flight to do so) to use a telephone in the airplane to call, not only for help from the outside, but for guidance for herself and the flight crew in the battle that she was already undertaking in her mind. She learned during those two telephone conversations that two passenger jumbo jets had already that morning been turned into instruments of mass murder at the World Trade Center [Editor's note: she couldn't have known this without Olson's having told her]. So she knew the unspeakable horror that she was facing—and I know without the slightest doubt that she died fighting—with her body, her brain and her heart, and not for a moment entertaining the notion that she would not prevail. Barbara died therefore not only because she was an American, but as one more American who refused to surrender to the monstrous evil into whose eyes she and her fellow countrymen stared during those last hideous moments." The audience sat transfixed.

Olson continued his talk with references to Israel and the Holocaust, and to persecution of Christians, Jews, Hindus, Buddhists, and women. Olson became Patrick Henry, Salman Rushdie, and Nelson Mandela rolled into one. He said passionately, "...(terrorists) must hate America because America stands for tolerance and freedom and respect for all races, all religions, and all peoples, regardless of their sex, color, national origin or accent. They are despots who will not permit children to go to school. So they must hate the nation that commits vast resources to the education of its children, and whose Supreme Court has said that free public education cannot even be withheld from those who are in this country illegally. These terrorists can enslave the people they wish to subjugate only be keeping them poor and destitute, so they must undermine and discredit the one place in all the world that stands the most for the rule of law and individual liberty and that allows its people—and the people who flock here daily by the thousands—the opportunity to rise above all those conditions."

Olson was in mourning, but he might have been running for office or addressing the United Nations. He spent the rest of his speech eulogizing his wife, concluding with the stirring words, "I know, and [Barbara] knows, that her government and the people of America will win this war, however long it takes, whatever we have to do. We will never, ever forget or flinch. We will prevail for Barbara and all the other Americans we lost on September 11 and for the American spirit for which they stood and their lives embodied. And, most of all, we will defeat those terrorists because Barbara and those other American casualties of September 11, and our forbears, and our children, would never forgive us if we did not."

It was a remarkable speech. It did seem overtly political coming from a man in his situation, but that possibly could be excused by Olson's emotional state. After all, he and Barbara were intensely political animals, and now she had died at the hands of people they both had viewed as natural enemies of their beloved country. One can imagine there wasn't a dry eye in the house.

What, in the year 2010, must those who heard Olson speak that day, those who shed tears of compassion and patriotic fervor in his behalf, be thinking now, knowing that every word Olson uttered nine years ago was based on a lie? Are they even aware of this, or are they honorary soldiers in Dick Cheney's war on the Muslim Caliphate, the one that extends from Spain to Indonesia?

The truth didn't come out until the trial of Zacarias Moussaoui in 2006, as the culmination of a bizarre sequence of legal maneuvers. A research project conducted at the University of Missouri–Kansas City provided a timeline of Moussaoui's activities leading up to the trial. He was 43 years old on 9/11, a French-born Muslim with a Masters degree in international business. In 1995 Moussaoui had first attended a training camp run by Osama bin Laden in Afghanistan. He attended a second camp in 1998, by which time he had been added to an extremist watch list in France. Bin Laden, who in 1996 had rejected a plan similar to the 9/11 attacks, changed his mind in 1999, and told his ally, Sheikh Mohammed, that such a plan "now has al Qaeda's full support." Bin Laden suggested that it target the Pentagon, the Capitol and the White House.

Later that year Sheikh Mohammed shifted gears. A new plan imagined five planes being flown into East Coast targets, and another five exploding in midair over the Pacific Ocean at the same instant. In conjunction with the revised plot, Sheikh Mohammed sent Moussaoui to Malaysia for flight training. But in the spring of 2000 Osama bin Laden decided it would be too difficult to execute the new plan. He canceled the part involving the five to be exploded in the Pacific, but let the rest of the plot stand.

September 2000 found Moussaoui in Kuala Lumpur, Malaysia (other potential hijackers had been sent to the United States for training). Moussaoui apparently wanted to join his comrades, so he contacted a flight school in Oklahoma. In October he returned to London, still seeking American flight schools, and in December he went to Pakistan.

During February 2001 Moussaoui was on the move. He returned to London from Pakistan, obtained a new French passport, and next flew to Oklahoma City via Chicago. In June 2001 he made inquiries about crop dusting (!) and purchased flight-deck videos for Boeing aircraft. In July he enrolled in a commercial flight-training course, ironically conducted by Pan Am International Flight Academy. In August he bought two leatherman knives in Oklahoma City, then flew to Minnesota and paid Pan Am International Flight Academy $6,300 in cash for his tuition.

One of his flight instructors regarded Moussaoui as suspicious and contacted the Minneapolis FBI office; this led to Moussaoui's arrest on immigration charges. The FBI in Minneapolis determined that Moussaoui was connected to terrorism plots, but for reasons that have never been explained FBI headquarters in Washington refused to allow them to search Moussaoui's computer records. In September, after France had described Moussaoui to the FBI as an Islamic extremist, an FBI agent in Minneapolis, Harry Samit, wrote a memorandum to the effect that Moussaoui might have planned to fly a plane into the World Trade Center. On September 10, Samit's plan to deport Moussaoui to France was approved, with the proviso that French authorities would search his belongings. Next came 9/11.

Three days afterward, as Theodore Olson was describing phone conversations with his wife to Fox Network interviewers and Larry King, Zacarias

Moussaoui was transferred to New York and held as a material witness in the hijacking. In December 2001 Moussaoui was indicted and moved to Alexandria, Virginia, for trial. His request for release on bail was denied.

In January 2002 Moussaoui refused to enter a plea to six charges in re 9/11. Judge Leonie Brinkema entered a "not guilty" plea in his behalf. In April Moussaoui dismissed his court-appointed lawyers and asked the judge to let him defend himself. Judge Brinkema ordered Moussaoui to undergo a mental evaluation, after which she did allow him to defend himself, with his former court-appointed lawyers on standby. Finally, in February 2003, Moussaoui asked to enter a guilty plea, but the judge refused to accept it, unsure that Moussaoui understood what he was doing. Finally, after Judge Brinkema had approved Moussaoui's request to depose Ramzi Bin-al-shibh (an al Qaeda operative) as a witness over the government's objections, the judge postponed Moussaoui's trial indefinitely.

More legal wrangling followed. Moussaoui wanted to question al Qaeda leaders, was denied that request by the court, and the Supreme Court refused to hear Moussaoui's appeal of the denial. In April 2005 Judge Brinkema finally decided Moussaoui was mentally competent and accepted his plea of guilty. A trial was set to determine Moussaoui's punishment. It began in March 2006, with the only remaining question seemingly being, "Will he get the death penalty, or a life sentence?" No party to the legal goings-on could have imagined what would come next.

At the trial, which resulted in a life sentence, the FBI submitted evidence (Exhibit number P200055). It had no bearing on the trial or on Moussaoui's fate, but it did reveal that only one *unconnected* phone call had been made from Flight 77 to the Department of Justice (Olson's office) on the morning of 9/11. *The call had lasted zero seconds.* The failed call might or might not have originated from Barbara Olson's cell phone, but it hardly matters. Unless the FBI submitted a fraudulent or erroneous exhibit (it was accepted by the court, and no one has contradicted it since 2006), the unpleasant truth is that no conversation between Theodore Olson and his wife ever took place.

Thus, Olson had invented a detailed story about two separate conversations with his (supposedly doomed) wife by telephone, had repeated the story to the FBI and to two television networks on 9/14, and on 9/16 had embellished it with bombastic political rhetoric in a speech to a room full of lawyers, in the midst of something he pompously identified as the first annual Barbara K. Olson Memorial Lecture. This all occurred within five days after his wife had supposedly perished in a horrific terrorist attack. If all this was too bizarre for the mainstream media to deal with, even five years after the fact, it's almost understandable.

The FBI's evidence was irrelevant to the court's decision about whether Zacarias Moussaoui should be executed or sent to prison. The exhibit showing one non-connected phone call was presented as a legal formality in court, but its historical significance will resonate long after Moussaoui has disappeared from the radar screen.

Olson lied, but why? Put aside the appearance that his conduct inevitably creates, of a man supposedly in mourning yet willing to sacrifice his wife's precious memory to a political cause. Focus instead on what might have motivated the US government, driven as it was by ideology and the need for some excuse to implement an aggressive foreign policy it had already decided upon, to have caused or even faked Barbara Olson's death.

Focus on the fact that all evidence of a plane crash somehow vanished from four sites on the same morning for the first time in aviation history, including human remains, airplane debris, and black boxes. Also, on the appearance of nanothermite, a deadly substance used only by the military and only for the biggest explosions, at Ground Zero. Focus on the similarity between the collapse of the Twin Towers and that of WTC 7, which wasn't struck by any plane. Having considered all that, consider whether Theodore Olson, in the five days following 9/11, behaved like a man in mourning for a beloved wife, or did he act like someone following a carefully prepared political script? Didn't the first Barbara K. Olson Memorial Lecture sound like a George W. Bush foreign-policy speech, with its maladroit references to terrorists who "hate America for our freedom," and with its reiteration of American ideals that people having been taking for granted since 1776? Finally, one must ask, "Aren't Theodore and Barbara Olson soul mates of the same zealots who designed the Project for a New American Century in 2000, and wouldn't PNAC have been sufficiently motivated to orchestrate 9/11 and manufacture a cover story for it?"

Once it is clear that Theodore Olson told a prearranged falsehood, and once it is accepted that sufficient motivation on the part of malevolent insiders is plausible, then questions about 9/11, and Flight 77 in particular, can be asked without stigma. It had always been the hardest of the four crashes to comprehend, for the following reasons:

1. The damage to the Pentagon wasn't consistent with its having been struck by a huge jetliner. The hole might have accommodated the fuselage alone, but not the wings. This much is clear from the photographic evidence.

2. If the wings had been sheared off just before the body of the plane hit the Pentagon, would that not have deflected the plane's flight path?

3. If the wings had been sheared off, where did they go? No debris was found, and even if we take at face value the improbable claim that the plane had been incinerated into dust by the crash, that can't have included wings that had been separated from the aircraft before it ever struck the Pentagon.

4. The intricate maneuvers that would have been required to circle the Pentagon and bring a Boeing 757 in at an extremely low altitude without crashing first might well have been beyond the capability of even an experienced pilot. But a rank amateur was at the controls.

5. Planes had already struck the Twin Towers when Flight 77 supposedly slammed into the Pentagon. If Theodore Olson's account of two phone conversations with his wife was true, then the pilot of Flight 77 had announced almost an hour earlier (just after takeoff) that it had been hijacked. Together with events in New York, this would have constituted an obvious mass terrorist attack on the United States, yet no response came from the air defense system, even though Andrews Air Force Base is just a few miles from the Pentagon.

6. The testimony of Transportation Secretary Norman Mineta demonstrates that certain standing orders had been in effect regarding Flight 77. Those orders were either to shoot down the plane, or to allow it to strike the Pentagon. There is no third possibility. Mineta's testimony also shows that Vice President Cheney was already at the command center in the White House basement when Flight 77 supposedly struck the Pentagon, yet the Secret Service logged Cheney at a later time. No explanation for the discrepancy has been offered.

This isn't an easy chapter to write. Intruding on a man's grief is unseemly, even in the interest of full disclosure. The deference extended to Theodore Olson three days after 9/11, by Fox Network and by Larry King, was certainly appropriate. Olson's interviews moved his audiences to tears and reflected public anger toward the terrorists. Whatever was going on in his mind, Olson exhibited remarkable self-possession and equanimity for a man who had been widowed a few days earlier under traumatic circumstances.

That was then; this is now. The FBI's deposition at the Moussaoui trial proves that Olson lied. He wasn't in error. He lied. His televised statements about what happened on 9/11 weren't momentary lapses brought on by grief and confusion; instead they were carefully framed falsehoods, prepared for delivery to two national audiences and a room full of lawyers. Olson's identical descriptions of non-existent telephone conversations with his wife were rehearsed, not spontaneous. Whatever his motivation, Theodore Olson is no longer entitled to the benefit of the doubt. He was serving as the second-highest ranking legal official in the United States; meanwhile he willfully misled the public about the worst terrorist attack in our history.

What was he up to? Did Barbara Olson's plane land safely somewhere in a remote spot, far from the nearest TV camera, in a live replay of the imagined Operation Northwoods scam in 1962? That was the plot that involved CIA agents posing as college students, landing at Eglin Air Force Base while a drone plane was being shot down over Cuba, followed by mock funerals for the so-called students. Are scattered reports that Barbara has been seen in Europe accurate, or were they contrived by conspiracy theorists?

If they're true, Olson's later remarriage adds a charge of bigamy to whatever crime he might have been committed by inventing two non-existent phone conversations (obstruction of justice?). If the reports are false, the question remains: Why would Olson have invented an account about hijackers with box cutters? Was this to take the heat off security personnel who had neglectfully allowed 19 Muslims to board four planes carrying guns, thus possibly forestalling lawsuits filed by negligence lawyers? Why would Olson have quoted Barbara to the effect that the pilot of Flight 77 had announced shortly after takeoff that it had been commandeered, then quoted her as having asked her husband what she should *tell the pilot to do* almost an hour later? Did Olson realize how absurd that would sound to a clear-thinking person, and how it cast doubt on his entire account? Was it the slip-up that doomed the cover-up to failure?

The author refers to Olson's lies as *The Invisible Smoking Gun* because they remain a mere footnote to 9/11 and are unknown to every citizen who relies on newspapers or television for information. Yet those lies, whether Fox Network and Larry King realize it, are incompatible with any benign explanation for what happened that day.

One can imagine that burning jet fuel first weakened and then brought down the Twin Towers, however unacceptable that theory is to most scientists. It's possible that the passenger manifests for four jetliners were redacted after the fact to conceal the identity of the hijackers, for some obscure reason relating to national security. The fact that terrorists chose the only day when NORAD was standing down because of anti-terrorist war games might possibly have resulted from a leak on the part of one disloyal insider. It's barely conceivable that amateur pilots could have maneuvered Boeing 757 airplanes with precision.

But it's infinitely more likely that Olson's invention of "box cutters" was meant to cloak a darker truth, i.e., the hijackers had smuggled guns onboard, had pointed them at the temples of the original pilots and had instructed them to fly according to their own chosen flight paths, and had shot the pilots dead once the planes were on due course to strike the towers. The talk of box cutters would have been designed to save the government from embarrassment over the failure of security personnel to prevent firearms from being carried on board, and might have limited the government's financial culpability for negligence.

Theodore and Barbara Olson were Republican Party loyalists, somewhere to the right of Louis XVI politically. From their track records, either would have been ready, willing, and able to carry any sword into any battle for the GOP.

Of course, nothing Olson said on television on 9/14, or in the first Barbara K. Olson Memorial Lecture on 9/16, could ever have explained away the existence of nanothermite at Ground Zero, which remains the *visible smoking gun* in re 9/11. But Olson spoke before the discovery was made and before any explanation was called for. Nothing in Olson's prepared remarks rationalized the implosion of WTC 7 or a BBC newscaster's foreknowledge of its demise. That could have been a random act on the part of owner Silverstein, one the Bush administration hadn't expected and didn't understand. Olson's comments included no explanation for the total absence of airplane debris or human remains from three separate crash sites (except for an undisturbed passport belonging to one of the alleged hijackers that magically appeared in the rubble at Ground Zero), quite obviously because no satisfactory explanation had been given to him. That was an issue to be dealt with later, by other folks.

If Theodore Olson had never appeared on television and had never delivered a Barbara K. Olson Memorial Lecture, 9/11 would remain an unsolved mystery. All Olson accomplished by setting his own pants on fire was to *temporarily* convince Americans that hijackers had used crude weapons to commandeer four jetliners. But the mere fact that he lied with impunity suffices to indict the administration for fraud. Theodore Olson didn't act alone, and his immediate bosses knew he had lied through his teeth.

CHAPTER 29. A PRESIDENTIAL REPORT CARD

The author's life span coincides with the nuclear age and with the heightened emphasis on secrecy in government over the past 70 years. He closes this text with an admittedly subjective grading of presidents who served from 1941 to the present, with specific reference to their skill in balancing national security needs against the American ideal of an open society.

Franklin D. Roosevelt (B+). FDR served while the Manhattan Project developed the first atomic bomb, but died in office four months before Harry S Truman used it to devastating effect on Japan. His administration managed to keep the secret the whole while, even from Senator and Vice President Truman. This news blackout was a singular achievement, only possible because during World War II Americans voluntarily sacrificed the need to know to security exigencies. Roosevelt used his "fireside chats" on radio to communicate with the public, giving them confidence in the midst of economic crisis, but was less than candid about his own failing health in the final years of his presidency. FDR was in no shape to run for a fourth term; he had to have known it, but can be forgiven if he'd been motivated by a desire for continuity in wartime.

Harry S Truman (B). Truman created the CIA as a successor to the OSS. It was a logical administrative step in concept, but it led to excesses that Truman openly lamented ten years after leaving office, and which are worse today. Truman also created the National Security Agency, arguably a vital asset during the Cold War but now a huge and anonymous bureaucracy that has given rise to what author James Bamford, paraphrasing Dwight D. Eisenhower, has called the "surveillance–industrial complex." Truman was upbeat and sunny in public, often cranky and profane in private. His dismissal of the iconic general Douglas MacArthur safeguarded the principle of civilian control over the military. On balance Truman upheld the American ideal of open government while honoring the nation's security needs.

Dwight D. Eisenhower (A-). Ike promised, "I will go to Korea," and within six months of his first inauguration a truce had been signed. The outcome satisfied neither the antiwar left nor Cold War hawks, but it did forestall potential armed conflict between the United States and Communist China. Eisenhower said, "I won't get down in the gutter with that guy (meaning Joseph R. McCarthy)," but he worked quietly behind the scenes for McCarthy's eventual censure. The military–industrial complex grew during Ike's presidency, but he performed a valuable public service by warning Americans about its dangers in a valedictory address. Ike was a true moderate and an avuncular presence.

John F. Kennedy (B-). JFK sought to reverse the Cold War trend toward what Truman called "cloak and dagger operations" on the part of the CIA. But he mishandled the Bay of Pigs crisis, and his decision to fire Allen W. Dulles as CIA director, while valid on the merits, was clumsy as to timing. The anger that followed within the spy community may have cost JFK his life. Kennedy was magnetic and a brilliant communicator, but he did the cause of election integrity no favor by joking about his father's efforts to persuade Mayor Daley in Chicago to keep fraud to a minimum in 1960. Had Kennedy survived, we'd probably have avoided the mess in Vietnam, and the military–industrial complex that he and Eisenhower mistrusted would enjoy a fraction of its current influence on policy.

Lyndon B. Johnson (D). LBJ's entire career consisted of behind-the-scenes political wheeler-dealing, beginning with his highly suspect first election to the Senate in 1948. Johnson had a folksy manner and got things done in Congress, but his methods were always incompatible with transparency in government. His decision to escalate America's presence in Vietnam through the phony Gulf of Tonkin incident will always outweigh his domestic achievements, which were substantial. Johnson owed John F. Kennedy's memory more than a blatantly political Warren Commission; LBJ clearly considered his own reelection a higher priority than uncovering the truth about the assassination.

Richard M. Nixon (D-). No man who hated the press as passionately as Nixon did could ever pass a test on openness in government. He cynically used the Cold War to political advantage, though he did leverage his reputation as a Cold warrior into overdue recognition of China, something no liberal Democrat could ever have managed to do. Nixon adored secrecy and surrounded himself with aides who loved it equally; his insincerity about Vietnam will forever identify him as a dishonest leader. Watergate was his personal downfall, but Nixon's soul mates in government didn't forget its consequences. They've used Watergate as an excuse for instituting a system of news management (which together with corporate conglomeration on Wall Street has obliterated the watchdog role of media over government) and to pursue the cause of the "unitary executive" (executive branch hegemony). To that extent, Nixon might be said to have won his fight with the press posthumously.

Gerald R. Ford (C). Jerry Ford was a nice guy. Historians have given him a pass on his pardon of Nixon, agreeing that absent the pardon the ongoing furor would have hampered Ford's ability to deal with day-to-day governmental function. But Ford's openness and cordiality were always compromised by his confusion about things. He told us Poland wasn't an Iron Curtain nation and went to his death insisting that Lee Harvey Oswald was nothing more than a "nut." Ford wasn't secretive, and his next-door neighbor manner did come as a welcome relief from his predecessor's. Paradoxically, perhaps, his administration did give rise to the careers of Donald Rumsfeld and Dick Cheney, both of whom worship at the altar of government secrecy.

Jimmy Carter (C+). Carter told Americans, "I'll never lie to you." He probably kept to that pledge in his heart, but Carter was never able to translate honesty and genuineness into effective government. He wasn't to blame for the Iran hostage crisis, but the delayed release of the hostages until Reagan's inauguration showed Carter's ignorance of political gamesmanship. Runaway inflation became his Achilles heel, and the inability to account for it satisfactorily to the public cost him any chance at reelection.

Ronald Reagan (C-). The Great Communicator was a paradox, on the one hand a sunny optimist about the future, on the other an ideologue who subverted the law to assist so-called freedom fighters in Nicaragua. Even after Ferdinand Marcos had been exposed as a fraudulent tyrant who stole elections and ordered his political foes murdered, Reagan was hailing him as a loyal friend of the United States. Reagan's ideology bordered on naiveté, but he did inspire confidence even in people who disliked his politics. His signature achievement was convincing Americans that inflation was not an inevitable by-product of economic growth. Reagan received more credit for the collapse of the Soviet Union than he deserved (a bear market in oil was the main reason). His rigid adherence to inchoate economic theory and his disavowal of government as a possible instrument for good overshadow the warm memory of his bold plea, "Mr. Gorbachev, tear down that wall!"

George H.W. Bush (B-). Foreign policy was Bush 41's strong suit. He managed the Persian Gulf conflict with determination and skill, meanwhile prevailing upon Israel not to retaliate when Iraq lobbed scud missiles toward Jerusalem. Bush showed restraint in not carrying the battle to Baghdad afterward. But Bush 41 might have wanted to be president too much for his own good. People won't forget how he first called Reaganomics "voodoo," then accepted the vice presidential nomination on Reagan's ticket. They'll remember how he tripped himself up by claiming he was "out of the loop" on Iran–Contra.

Bill Clinton (C+). Bubba Clinton was like that kid we used to know in school who misbehaved but always talked his way out of trouble. Things started out badly for him, with the Branch Davidian debacle in Waco, the World Trade Center bombing, the failure to pass national health insurance, and the Oklahoma City bombing. He shouldn't have gotten involved in Somalia. But Clinton was careful to work with NATO in the former Yugoslavia, and more people liked him for taking the tough road on taxes and for converting a federal deficit into a surplus, than disliked him for lying about oral sex. He was generally candid about things that mattered most to the country, like welfare reform, which he dealt with successfully. The jury is still out on whether intelligence failures that might have led to 9/11 originated in Clinton's administration. If it turns out they did, a grade of C+ might be too high.

George W. Bush (F). Bush 43 undid all the good his father had accomplished in the Middle East. The United States was admired and respected around the world when Bush 41 left office, hated and feared when his son's term ended. Bush 43 was more inept than venal, seemingly a caricature of a Wild West cowboy who couldn't stay on his horse. Both his elections were marked by voter disenfranchisement and electronic fraud, and it isn't clear he ever understood what had gone on behind his back. He told the truth only by accident, and his verbal gaffes kept late-night TV comedians in business. Bush 43 seemed to finally comprehend what a disaster his administration had been near the end, but far too late to save his legacy. It remains to be determined if Bush, who yielded more power to his vice president than any president in history, knows what really happened on 9/11/01.

Barack Obama (D+). It might be too early to fairly analyze Obama's performance, but let's try. He sold himself as an instrument of change, but he's held to a status quo in Iraq and has upped the ante in Afghanistan. He apparently cares nothing about election fraud. He won't consider prosecuting Bush administration lawbreakers, and his Justice Department wants to treat whistleblowers even more harshly than Bush's did. He appointed Cass Sunstein to the Office of Information and Regulatory Affairs, a man who once recommended infiltrating places where conspiracy theories originate in order to discredit them.

In the aggregate this suggests that Obama favors secrecy over open government. He is bright and articulate, and he did inherit an ungodly mess from his predecessor, so he deserves to be cut a little slack. To use a sports metaphor, Obama spent his first year in office on grass, trying to find common ground with an opposing party playing on Astroturf. He doesn't seem to have caught on to the fact that his political opponents want him to fail so they can regain power. Obama has made some well-received speeches, but on balance things aren't going well for America's first African-American president as of this writing.

Postscript

This volume has consisted of over 80,000 words, but its guiding premise can be summarized in a few sentences. The author believes that toxic public controversies can only be examined objectively if skeptics and those who contradict them avoid the pitfalls of partisan political bias, ad hominem attacks, and the jingoistic colloquy common to debate in the 21st century. Further, that until the mainstream media are willing to risk offending stockholders and advertisers, they will not regain the confidence of the public and cannot reassume their historical role as watchdogs over government. To the extent the author has advanced those precepts in the reader's mind, he will consider the book a success.

The author relied on many books read over the course of almost 60 years, the most helpful of which are cited in the bibliography. At least equally important was information gathered through Internet sites and blogs since the late 1980s, some of which has been retrieved from his earlier books, *It Didn't Happen the Way You Think* and *The Lindbergh Syndrome: Heroes and Celebrities in a New Gilded Age* for use here. Websites such as Bradblog and Free Press (on election issues) and Raw Story and Huffington Post (on governmental deceit), in particular, have been valuable research sources.

The horror of 9/11/2001 is an ongoing story. Since this manuscript was completed, support has grown for a new investigation that could answer ongoing questions and bring closure. The Colorado Democratic party has called for a new study. Former Judge Andrew Napolitano, a Fox Network host, has said, "I'm a truther," in particular concerning the collapse of WTC 7. Former President George W. Bush, in his book *Decision Points*, concedes that he assumed all along that Flight 93 had been shot down in accordance with his order, even as he allowed the public to believe afterward that rebellious passengers had overcome the hijackers and brought down the plane near Shanksville, Pennsylvania. By the time this book appears in print, it's likely that others in public life will have said they disbelieve the official story of 9/11.

BIBLIOGRAPHY

Arnold, Samuel Bland, *Memoirs of a Lincoln Conspirator* (edited by Michael W. Kauffman). Heritage Books, 1995

Bamford, James, *The Shadow Factory*, Anchor Books, 2009

Behn, Noel, *Lindbergh: The Crime.* Penguin Group, 1994

Blumenthal, Sidney, *How Bush Rules: Chronicles of a Radical Regime*, Princeton University Press, 2006

Berg, Scott A., *Lindbergh.* G.P. Putnam & Sons, 1998

Clarke, Asia Booth, *John Wilkes Booth* (edited by Terry Alford). University Press of Mississippi, 1996

Cook, Monte, *The Skeptic's Guide to Conspiracies.* Adams Media, 2009

Dean, John W., *Worse than Watergate: The Secret Presidency of George W. Bush.* Little Brown & Co., 2004

Dowd, Maureen, *Bushworld.* G.P. Putnam's Sons, 2004

Eisenchiml, Otto, *Why Was Lincoln Murdered?* Little, Brown & Co., 1937

Friedman, David M., *The Immortalists.* HarperCollins, 2007

Hanchett, William, *The Lincoln Murder Conspiracies.* University of Illinois Press, 1983

Kauffman, Michael W., *American Brutus.* Random House, 2004

Lee, Dr. Henry and Labriola, Dr. Jerry, *Famous Crimes Revisited.* Strong Books, 2001

Leek, Sybil and Sugar, Bert R., *The Assassination Chain.* Corwin Books, 1976

Manber, Jeffrey and Dahlstrom, Neil, *Lincoln's Wrath.* Sourcebooks, Inc., 2005

Milton, Joyce, *Loss of Eden.* Harper Collins, 1993

Nasaw, David, *The Chief: The Life of William Randolph Hearst.* Houghton-Mifflin, 2000

Palast, Greg, *The Best Democracy Money Can Buy*, Plume, 2004

Palast, Greg, *Armed Madhouse.* Penguin Group, 2006

Roberts, Alasdair, *The Collapse of Fortress Bush: The Crisis of Authority in American Government*, New York University Press, 2008

Roscoe, Theodore, *The Web of Conspiracy.* Prentice-Hall, 1959

Schoenfeld, Gabriel, *Necessary Secrets.* W.W. Norton, 2010

Ventura, Jesse, with Russell, Dick, *American Conspiracies.* Skyhorse Publishing, 2010

Winik, Jay, *April 1865: The Month that Saved America.* HarperCollins, 2001

Wright, Theon, *In Search of the Lindbergh Baby.* Tower Books, 1981

INDEX

9/11 Contradictions: An Open Letter to Congress and the Press (book) 198

A

Abramoff, Jack, 115
Adams, John, 17, 27
Adams, John Quincy, 27
Adler, Alfred, 181
Ahlgren, Gregory, 158
Ahmadinejad, Mahmoud, 116
Ahmed, Nafeez, 197
Ailes, Roger, 161
Aldrin, Buzz (Edwin), 172
Allen, Fred, 18
Allen, William, 99
Allende, Salvador, 126
al Qaeda, 16, 91, 216-217
American Conspiracies (book), 1, 36, 171, 232
American–Turkish Council (ATC), 69
Amerithrax, 25
Anschluss, the, 55
Arbenz (Jacobo Arbenz Guzman), 3, 126
Armed Madhouse (book), 109, 232
Armstrong, Neil, 172
Army–McCarthy hearings, 18
Arnebeck, Cliff, 36
Arnold, Samuel, 119, 231
Arthur, Chester Alan, 78

Ashcroft, John, 211
Atta, Mohammed, 115
Atwater, Lee, 161

B

Bach, Bob, 65
Baer, Robert, 198
Bailey, F. Lee, 170
Baker, Duane (Duane Bacon), 100
Balfour, Arthur James, 87-88
Balfour Declaration, 87-88
Bamford, James, 41, 56, 211, 224, 231
Barbarians at the Gate (book), 21
Barruel, Augustin, 86
Barton, Clara, 50, 193
Bay of Pigs Invasion, 12, 63, 72, 112, 126, 133, 138, 156, 224
Behn, Noel, 158, 231
Benny, Jack, 102
Bernstein, Carl, 19, 190
Bin-al-Shibh, Ramzi, 217
bin Laden, Osama, 3, 41, 57, 66, 113, 116, 119-120, 146, 185-186, 215-216
Birthers, 117
Blackwell, Kenneth, 33, 36, 191
Blaine, James G., 29, 78
Boad Nelly (non-existent vessel), 98-99
Body of Secrets (book), 56
Boland, Edward P., 127
Boland Amendment, 3, 127

Boleyn, Anne (Queen of England), 163
Bond, James (fictitious character), 131-133, 182
Booth, John Wilkes, 45, 48, 89-90, 118, 136-137, 189, 231
Borden, Abby 165-168
Borden, Andrew 165-168
Borden, Emma 165, 167-168
Borden, Lizzie (Lisbeth), 165-170, 190
Boxer, Barbara, 30, 178, 207
Bradblog, 33-35, 191-192, 229
Bradlee, Ben, 190
Branch Davidian incident, 226
Brinkema, Leonie, 217
Brinkert, Ernest, 169
Brown, Dan, 87
Brown, John, 136-137
Brunner, Jennifer, 36, 192
Brunwasser, Joan, 33, 198-199
Brzezinski, Zbigniew , 86
Buchanan, Pat, 177
Bull, Gerald, 129
Burchard, Samuel, 29
Bureau of Investigation, 100, 105
Burr, Aaron, 27
Bush, George Herbert Walker, 3, 86, 129, 226
Bush, George Walker, 3, 23, 30-31, 36, 66, 76, 86, 120, 129, 146, 176-177, 195-196, 211, 218, 226, 230-231
Bush, Jeb (John Ellis Bush), 31, 34
Bush, Prescott, 86

C

Caesar, Julius (Roman Emperor), 90, 117, 173
Capone, Al, 104-105, 159
Carnegie, Andrew, 19
Carter, Jimmy (James Earl Carter), 175, 225
Case Closed (book), 25, 35, 61
Castro, Fidel, 8, 56-57, 68, 71, 126, 132, 138, 156
"Cemetery John", 98-100, 103-105, 159
Central Intelligence Agency (CIA), 2-4, 8, 12, 52, 56-57, 59, 63-64, 70, 72-73, 75, 79, 91, 107, 120, 125-129, 131, 133, 138, 141, 147, 156, 174-175, 182, 186, 192, 198, 205, 220, 223-224
Chancellor, Henry, 132
Cheney, Richard B., 9-10, 23-24, 32-33, 52, 58, 66, 74-75, 83, 112, 116, 121-122, 129, 146,

191, 195, 215, 219, 225
Cheney, Liz (Elizabeth, daughter), 146
Cheney, Lynne (wife), 75
Chiang kai-shek, 110
Chicago Board Options Exchange (CBOE), 202
Chiniquy, Charles, 89
Christian Faith and the Truth Behind 9/11 (book), 198
Churchill, Sir Winston Spencer , 86, 109-110, 132
Cisneros, Evangelina Cosio y (Cuban Joan of Arc), 50
Citizens' Commission of Inquiry (CCI), 192
Citizens for Election Reform (CER) , 198
Civil Rights Act of 1964, 18
Civil War (War Between the States), 19, 29, 47, 89, 111, 164
Clarke, Richard, 23
Clay, Henry, 27-28
Clayton Antitrust Act, 20
Cleveland, (Stephen) Grover, 29, 164
Clinton, Hillary Rodham, 23
Clinton, Bill (William Jefferson Clinton), 3, 52, 147, 176, 226
Clouseau, Inspector (fiction character) , 122
Cold War, 2, 18, 51, 127, 131, 223-225
Colmes, Alan, 212
Commodity Futures Trading Commission (CFTC), 202-204
Condit, Gary, 176
Condon, John F. (Jafsie), 97-101, 103-105
Conkling, Roscoe, 78
Connally, John B., 7
Connally, Nellie, 7, 14, 155
Connell, Heather, 36
Connell, Michael, 35-36
Connery, Sean, 133
Conover, Sanford, 119
Conversations with Americans (book), 192
Cool, Misty (imaginary character), 185-188
Cool, Trey (imaginary character), 81-84, 121-123, 185
Cosby, William, 17
Cossiga, Francesco, 59
Costner, Kevin, 152
Coughlin, Charles Edward (Father Coughlin), 18
Craft of Intelligence, The (book), 133
Credit Mobilier, 29
Crier, Catherine, 192

Crime of the Century (book), 105-106, 151, 158
Crook, William, 49
Crusades, the, 121
Curtis, Clint, 33, 35, 199
Czolgosz, Leon, 78, 136-137

D

Da Vinci Code, The (book), 87
Daley, Richard, 30
Daschle, Tom, 24
Davies, Marion, 194
Davis, Jefferson, 47, 89, 119, 164-165, 193
Davis, Varina, 193
Debunking 9/11 Debunking (book), 198
Deep Throat, 190
Defrauding America (book), 127
Delmont, Ronelle, 158
Dickerson, Melek Can, 69
DiMaggio, Joe, 79
Domino Theory, 112
Douglas, Helen Gahagan, 110
Douglas, Melvyn, 110
Dow Jones Industrial Average, 204-205
Downing Street Minutes, 112, 118
Dulles, Allen, 8, 133, 138, 156, 224
Dulles, John Foster, 133

E

Eberling, Richard, 170
Edmonds, Sibel Deniz, 68
Eichmann, Adolf, 128
Einstein, Albert, 181
Eisenhower, Dwight David, 174-175, 224
Eisenschiml, Otto, 164
Elders of Zion, 85-87
Electoral College, 27-31, 176-178
Election Protection Coalition, 32
Elizabeth I (Queen of England), 163
Ellerson, Charles Henry, 96, 100
Ellsberg, Daniel, 199
Emerson, Ralph Waldo, 2
Enabling Act, 55
Enron scandal, 4
Epstein, Edward Jay, 12
Estler, Gavin, 145
Exner, Judith Campbell, 63

F

Fair Play for Cuba Committee, 12, 71
Farmer, John, 147
Faulkner, J.J. (fictitious person), 100-101
Faulkner, Jane (daughter, Mrs. Carl Geissler), 100-101
Faulkner, Jane (mother), 100
Federal Bureau of Investigation (FBI), 8, 25, 63, 68-70, 74, 79, 100, 107, 155-156, 159, 212-213, 216-218, 220
Federal Communications Commission (FCC), 26
Federal Reserve Bank, 20, 202-203
Feeney, Tom, 33
Ferrie, David, 65
Fetzer, David, 1
Fifty Years in the Church of Rome (book), 89
Fillmore, Millard, 89
FISA law, 4
Fisch, Isidor, 101
Fleming, Ian, 131-133
Fleming, Lucy, 132
Fool, Dan (imaginary character), 81-84, 121-123, 185-186
Fool, Tipsy (imaginary character), 185-188
Fooled Again (book), 147, 199
Ford, Gerald Rudolph, 8, 19, 77, 175, 205, 225
Foster, Vince, 123
Franklin, Benjamin, 152
Freedom of Information Act, 84
Freeman, Steven F., 197
Freud, Sigmund, 181
Friedman, Brad, 33, 191
From Russia with Love (book, movie), 131

G

Garfield, James Abram, 77
Garrison, Jim, 62, 64, 152
Gates, Robert, 123, 142
Geissler, Carl, 100
George II (King of England), 17
George V (King of England), 87
George VI (King of England), 132
Giancana, Sam, 63, 196
Giuliani, Rudolph, 24, 178
Glenn, John, 107
Glorious Revolution, The, 107
Godfrey, John, 131

Goldberg, Rube, 21
Goldman, Emma, 78, 137
Gorbachev, Mikhail, 226
Gore, Albert, 31, 34, 176-177, 211
Goring, Hermann, 55
Gow, Betty (Bessie Mowatt Gow), 96
Grant, Ulysses Simpson (Hiram Ulysses Grant), 28, 45, 78, 118, 165
Greeley, Horace, 28
Greenspan, Alan, 20
Gresham's Law, 163-166, 169, 171-172
Gresham's Law of Conspiracy Theories (Gresham's Law Revisited), 163
Gresham, Sir Thomas, 163
Griffin, David Ray, 197-198
Guiteau, Charles J., 77
Gulf of Tonkin incident, 3, 224

H

Hacker, Ralph, 100
Half-Breeds, 78
Hamilton, Alexander, 27
Hamilton, Lee, 9, 24, 74
Hanna, Marcus (Mark), 51
Hannity, Sean, 212
Harding, Florence, 168
Harding, Warren Gamaliel, 168
Harris, Beverly, 33
Harris, Katherine, 31
Harrison, Benjamin, 19, 29
Harrit, Niels, 39
Hartshorne, Charles, 197
Harvey, Paul, 54
Hastert, Dennis, 69
Hauptmann, Bruno Richard, 64, 101, 158, 168-169, 194
Hayes, Lucy Webb, 29
Hayes, Rutherford Birchard, 28-29, 78
Hearst, William Randolph, 18, 35, 50-51, 103, 193, 231
Heller, Steve, 199
Henry, Patrick, 214
Henry VIII (King of England), 163
Herder, J.G., 85
Hidell, A. (Lee Harvey Oswald alias), 8
Highfields (Lindbergh family residence), 93-97, 100, 102-103, 159
Hiss, Alger, 18, 110
Hitler, Adolf, 55
Hobart, Garret, 51
Hochmuth, Amandus, 102

Hoffa, Jimmy, 63
Hoffman, Dustin, 19
Hoffman, Harold, 102
Holocaust, the, 129, 214
Holt, Rush, 25
Hoover, J. Edgar, 63, 100, 108, 138, 147, 196
House Un-American Activities Committee (HUAC), 109
Howe, Julia Ward, 50, 193
Hume, Brit, 212
Hunt, H. Howard, 147
Hunt, Howard St. John, 147
Hunter, Bill, 64
Hussein, Saddam, 3, 41, 112-113, 129-130, 176

I

Illuminati (Illuminati Order, Bavarian Illuminati, Perfectibilists), 85-86
In Search of the Lindbergh Baby (book), 159, 232
Industrial Revolution, 107
Iran–Contra scandal, 3, 176, 226
Israel, Lee, 65
Ivins, Bruce Edwards, 25

J

Jackson, Andrew, 17, 27, 77
Jackson, Michael, 77, 80, 157
James Bond: The Man and His World (book), 131-133, 182
James Zadroga 9/11 Health and Compensation Act of 2008, 40
Jefferson, Thomas, 27, 47, 89, 119, 164-165, 193
Johnson, Andrew, 47, 164
Johnson, Henrik "Red", 96
Johnson, James, 176-177
Johnson, Lady Bird (Claudia), 7
Johnson, Lyndon Baines, 3, 7, 11, 138, 156, 171, 175, 224
Johnston, Joseph, 118
Jones, Jim, 192
Jones, Paula, 176
Jones, Steven, 39
Judge Judy (abusive TV personality), 205

K

Kaczynski, Theodore (Unabomber), 128

Kagan, Robert, 57
Kean–Hamilton Commission (National Committee on Terrorist Attacks upon the United States), 15, 24, 122, 147
Kean, Thomas, 9, 24, 69, 116, 122
Keller, Bill, 206-207
Kelly, Grace (Princess Grace of Monaco), 77, 79
Kennedy, Jacqueline Bouvier, 7-8, 13
Kennedy, John Fitzgerald, 7, 11, 13, 30, 61, 66, 72-73, 76-77, 79, 88, 109, 131-133, 138, 146-147, 156, 171, 182, 190, 192, 224
Kennedy, Joseph P. (father), 30
Kennedy, Robert F. Sr. (brother) 2, 63, 138, 156, 171, 195-196
Kennedy, Robert F. Jr. (nephew), 195
Kent, Clark (fictional character), 74
Kent State Massacre, 18
Kerry, John, 36, 147, 178, 195-196
Kevorkian, Jack, 135
Khomeini, Ayatollah, 68, 175
Kilgallen (book), 64-65, 82, 154, 170, 190-191
Kilgallen, Dorothy, 64-65, 82, 154, 170, 190-191
Kilgallen, James, 64
King, Larry, 74, 211-213, 216, 219-220
King, Martin Luther Jr., 2, 195
Kitchener, Horatio Herbert (Lord Kitchener), 109
Koethe, Jim, 64
Korean Conflict, 111
Kreskin, the Amazing, 145
Kristol, Irving, 57
Kristol, William, 57
Kupcinet, Irv, 64
Kupcinet, Karyn, 64

L

Lane, Mark, 12, 192
Law of Unintended Consequences, The, 19
Lay, Kenneth, 4
Leahy, Patrick, 24
Lee, Robert E., 45, 47, 118
Lemme, Raymond, 34
Lemmon, Jack, 189
Levy, Chandra, 176
Lewinsky, Monica, 3, 176
Life of Ian Fleming, The (book), 131
Lincoln, Abraham, 17, 28, 45, 77, 88-89, 109, 136, 164

Lincoln, Mary Todd, 49
Lincoln, Victoria, 166
Lindbergh, Anne Morrow (wife) 93-96, 168-169
Lindbergh, Charles A., 18, 93-105, 158-160, 168-169, 190, 194, 229, 231-232
Lindbergh, Charles A. Jr. (son) 93-99, 101, 103-104, 158-159, 168-169
Lindbergh, Jon (son) 105
Lindbergh Kidnapping Hoax Forum, 158
Lindbergh, Reeve (daughter) 160
Lindbergh: The Crime (book) 158
Lloyd George, David, 88
Long-Term Capital Management (hedge fund), 205
Louis XVI (King of France), 173, 221

M

MacArthur, Douglas A., 111, 224
Mackay, Neil, 58
Macleod, Henry Dunning, 163
Madison, James, 17
Mafia, 12, 63, 65, 70, 80, 100, 138, 153-154, 156, 175, 196
Majette, Denise, 195
Mandela, Nelson, 214
Manhattan Project, 132, 174, 223
Marcello, Carlos, 63, 65, 138, 196
Marcos, Ferdinand, 147, 225
Marie Antoinette (Queen of France), 173
McCain, John, 52
McCarthy, Joseph R., 18, 108, 111, 224
McCormick, Donald, 131
McGovern, George, 88
McKinley, Ida, 50, 193
McKinley, William, 18, 77-78, 136, 193
McKinney, Cynthia, 194
McLean, Evalyn Walsh, 168
McQuillan, Dara, 148
McVeigh, Timothy, 128
Means, Gaston B., 168
Mencken, H.L., 18
Mengele, Josef, 129
Merrill Lynch, 202
Miller, Ernest, 169
Miller, Mark Crispin, 147, 199
Mineta, Norman Y., 74
Mohammed, Khalid Sheikh, 118-120, 146
Monier, Stephen, 158
Monkey Trial, 18

Monroe, Marilyn, 77, 79
Moriscos, 121-122
Morris, Dick, 161
Morrow, Dwight Spencer, 93
Morrow, Elizabeth Cutter (wife), 94, 168
Morse, John Vinnicum, 167
Mossad, 59, 91, 128-130, 205
Mossadegh (Iranian leader), 2, 63, 175
Moussaoui, Zacharias, 215-218, 220
Mudd, Samuel, 119
Muhammad (Muslim Prophet), 121
Murrow, Edward R., 18, 24, 111
Muslim Caliphate Theory, 113

N

Napolitano, Andrew, 229
Nation, Carrie, 136-137
National Association of Securities Dealers (NASD), 202, 204
National Fire Protection Association, 40-41
National Security Act, 125
National Security Council, 3, 127, 175
Newton's Laws of Motion, 190
Nee, Henry, 34
Nero (Roman Emperor), 53-54
New Pearl Harbor, The: Disturbing Questions About the Bush Administration and 9/11 (book), 197-198
New York Stock Exchange (NYSE), 202, 204
New York Times, The, 5, 19, 22, 24, 32-33, 166, 192, 196, 201, 206-207, 210
Next Day Hill (Morrow family residence), 96
Nicholas II (Czar of Russia), 173
Nixon, Richard Milhous, 3, 18-19, 26, 30, 51, 108, 110-111, 127, 147, 175, 190, 206-207, 225
No, Dr. (fictional character), 182
North American Air Defense System (NORAD), 10, 26, 66, 116, 122, 142, 221
North, Oliver, 175
Norton, Teresa, 64
Nostradamus, 145
Nuremberg Trials, 205

O

Obama, Barack Hussein, 1, 30, 37, 41-42, 52, 86, 116-118, 137, 146, 178, 187, 227
Occam's Razor, 11, 13-16, 82
O'Dell, Walden (Wally), 33, 191

O'Donnell, Rosie, 83, 123
O'Laughlen, Michael, 119
Office of Information and Regulatory Affairs, 1, 37, 117, 227
Office of Strategic Services (OSS), 125, 223
Ohio Corrupt Practices Act, 36
Olson, Barbara, 211-214, 217-218, 220-221
Olson, Harold, 159
Olson, Theodore, 73, 115, 211, 213, 216-222
O'Neill, Paul, 23
Op-Ed News 33, 198
Operation Gladio, 59
Operation Northwoods, 56-57, 68, 71-72, 76, 138, 141, 156, 220
Operation Ruthless, 132
Ortega, Daniel, 175
Orwell, George, 161
O'Sullivan, Maureen, 172
Oswald, Lee Harvey, 2, 8, 12-14, 61-66, 70-73, 79, 81-82, 133, 147, 151-156, 171, 182-183, 190, 192, 196, 225
Oswald, Marina, 71
Ottoman Empire, 122

P

Pahlavi, Reza (Shah of Iran), 175
Paine, Lewis (Lewis Thornton Powell), 46
Palast, Greg, 109, 231-232
Palin, Sarah, 25
Palmer, A. Mitchell, 108
Parker, Ellis, 103
Parker, John F., 45, 48
Patriot Act, 41, 45, 209
Paul (Apostle), 53
Pentagon Papers, 19, 199, 201
People's Temple, The, 192
Persian Gulf Conflict, 226
Peter (Disciple), 53, 78
Phillip III (King of Spain) 122
Pinochet, Augusto, 127
Pius IX (Pope), 89
Plame, Valerie (Valerie Plame Wilson), 4, 160
Plausible Denial (book), 63, 182, 193
Popper, Sir Karl, 181, 183, 189
Posner, Gerald, 61
Presley, Elvis, 80
Priory of Zion, 87
Project for a New American Century (PNAC), 57-59, 138-139, 218
Project FUBELT, 127

Private Disgrace, A: Lizzie Borden by Daylight (book), 166
Protocols of the Elders of Zion, The, 85-87
Pulitzer, Joseph, 50, 193

Q

Quay, Matthew, 29

R

Rainier III (Prince of Monaco), 79-80
Ray, James Earl, 2, 171, 195
Reagan, Ronald Wilson, 3-4, 19-20, 26, 51, 77, 127-128, 175-176, 225-226
Reconstruction, 28-29, 136, 165
Redford, Robert, 19
Reich, Al, 97
Reichstag Decree, 55
Reilly, Edward J., 103
Rice, Condoleezza, 49, 195
Richards, A.M., 46
Richards, Ann, 4
Richardson, Bruce G., 155
Roberts, Paul Craig, 26
Robison, John, 86
Rockefeller, David, 86
Rockefeller, John D., 20
Rockefeller IV, John D. ("Jay"), 88
Rockefeller, Nelson A., 88
Rogers, Will, 18
Romney, Mitt, 116
Roosevelt, Eleanor, 88
Roosevelt, John 88
Roosevelt, Franklin Delano, 18, 49, 77, 88, 109-110, 223
Roosevelt, Theodore, 20, 26, 50, 77, 193
Rosenberg, Ethel, 34
Rosenberg, Julius, 34
Rothschild Dynasty, 85-88
Rothschild, Lord Nathan, 88
Rothschild, Mayer Amschel, 87
Rothschild, Second Baron, 87
Rove, Karl, 23, 30, 32, 36, 161, 199, 211
Ruby, Jack, 8, 13, 62, 64, 66, 151, 153-154, 190, 196
Rumsfeld, Donald, 112, 145, 225
Runyon, Damon, 102
Rush to Judgment (book), 166, 192-193
Rushdie, Salman, 214

Russell, Dick, 36, 232
Russian currency crisis (1998), 205

S

Saacher, Dennis, 69
Safire, William, 26
Samit, Harry, 216
Sandinistas, 127-128
Scalia, Antonin, 177
Schieffer, Bob, 146
Schoenfeld, Dudley, 105
Schoenfeld, Gabriel, 41, 49, 232
Schwarzenegger, Arnold, 88
Schwarzkopf Jr., H. Norman, 94-95, 176
Schwarzkopf Sr., H. Norman, 94
Sedition Act, 17
Scopes, John, 18
Selgin, George, 163
Seward, William H., 46
Sha-Toe (speakeasy), 100
Sharaf, Patty, 199
Sharpe, Violet, 96, 168
Shaw, Clay, 152
Sheen, Charlie, 83
Sheppard, Marilyn (wife), 169-170
Sheppard, Samuel, 170
Sheppard, Samuel Reese (son), 170
Sherman Antitrust Act, 19-20
Sherman, John, 19
Sherman, William Tecumseh, 19, 118
Shriver, Maria, 88
Shriver, Sargent, 88
Siegelman, Don, 199
Silverstein, Larry, 148
Simon, Jonathan, 198
Simpson, O.J., 31
Single bullet theory (Magic bullet theory), 154
Sirhan, Sirhan Bishara, 2, 171-172, 195
Smith, Florence, 65-66, 154
Snatch Racket, the, 94
Spangler, Edman, 119
Spanish–American War, 51, 54, 193
Spanish Inquisition, 121
Spears, Britney, 157
Specter, Arlen, 14
Speed, James, 118
Spirit of St. Louis (airplane, movie), 93
Spoonamore, Stephen, 36
Stalin, Josef, 32, 108-109, 147

Stalwarts, 78
Standard and Poor's 100-stock Index, 203
Stanton, Edwin M., 118-119, 164-165
Starr, Ken, 123
Stephanie (Princess of Monaco), 80
Stewart, Martha, 74
Stich, Rodney, 127
Stock Index, 203-204
Stone, Oliver, 63, 151-152, 182
Sullivan, Bridget, 167
Sullivan, John, 168
Sunstein, Cass, 1-2, 37, 117, 227
Surratt, John Harrison, 89, 119
Surratt, Mary, 89-90, 119

T

Theory of Relativity, 181, 190
Thompson, Paul, 197
Thoreau, Henry David, 2
Tilden, Samuel J., 28-29
Tillich, Paul, 197
Tippit, J.D., 8, 12, 65
Toto, fictional dog, 86
Trafficante, Santos, 63, 156
Trickey, Henry, 165
Truman, Harry S, 77, 125, 127-128, 131, 136, 223
Turrou, Leon, 104

U

U-2 Incident, 112
Underhill, Gary, 64

V

Valachi, Joe, 104
Valachi Papers, the, 63
Vanderbilt, Cornelius, 19
Vanoff, Nick, 65
Ventura, Jesse, 1, 36, 171, 232
Victoria (Queen of England), 88
Vietnam Conflict, 3, 5, 112, 175
Vietnam Veterans Against the War (VVAW), 192

von Goethe, J.W., 85
Von Hindenburg, Paul 55

W

Walker, Edwin, 71
War Between the States, 17, 46, 90
War of 1812, 17
War Powers Resolution, 51
Warren, Earl, 8
Warren Commission, 2, 8, 11-14, 62-65, 73, 133, 147, 151, 155-156, 171, 175, 183, 192, 196, 224
Washington Post, The, 19, 22, 24, 33, 175, 190, 196, 198, 201, 206
Watergate scandal, 22, 175
Weill, Sanford I., 21
Weisburg, Harold, 12
Weishaupt, Adam, 85
Weissman, Bernard, 65
Welch, Joseph, 111
Welles, Orson, 194
Whateley, Elsie, 96
Whateley, Aloysius (Ollie), 96
Whited, Millard, 102
Whitehead, Alfred North, 197
Whitman, Christine Todd, 105
Why Was Lincoln Murdered? (book), 45, 118, 136, 164-165, 231
Wilentz, David, 105
Wilhelm II (German Kaiser), 88
William of Ockham, 11-12
Winchell, Walter, 18, 169
Woods, Tiger, 157
Woodward, Robert, 19, 190
World War I, 108-109
World War II, 49, 55, 111, 125, 131, 174, 181, 194, 223
Wray, Fay, 172
Wright, Theon, 159, 232

Z

Zangretti, Jack, 64
Zapruder, Abraham, 12
Zapruder film, 12-14, 70, 82, 151-152
Zeller, Jr., Tom, 32
Zenger, John Peter, 17, 22
Zogby, John, 196